DAWG BUTLER
CHARACTERS
ACTOR

DAWS BUTLER CHARACTER ACTOR

BY
Ben Ohmart
AND
Joe Bevilacqua

FOREWORD BY
Nancy Cartwright

BearManor Media
2005

Daws Butler Characters Actor
© 2005 by Ben Ohmart and Joe Bevilaqua
All rights reserved.

All Hanna-Barbera characters © Warner Bros. Pictures. All rights reserved.

Beany, Cecil and Time for Beany images & scripts © Bob Clampett Productions, LLC. All rights reserved.

For information, address:

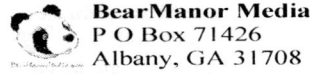

BearManor Media
P O Box 71426
Albany, GA 31708

bearmanormedia.com

Cover design & chapter illustrations by Lorie Kellogg and Joe Bevilaqua

Typesetting and layout by John Teehan

Published in the USA by BearManor Media

Library of Congress Cataloging-in-Publication Data

Ohmart, Ben.
Daws Butler, characters actor / by Ben Ohmart and Joe Bevilaqua.
p. cm.
Includes index.
ISBN 1-59393-015-1

1. Butler, Daws. 2. Voice actors and actresses--United States--Biography. 3. Animated films--United States--History and criticism. I. Bevilaqua, Joe. II. Title.

PN2287.B894O38 2005
791.4302'8'092--dc22
2004026021

ISBN—1-59393-015-1

Table of Contents

Foreword i
    by Nancy Cartwright

Introduction 1

One Short Wave 3

The Voice of Radio 29

"Gentlemen," Einstein said, "it's *Time for Beany*" 47

Time After *Beany* 75

Hanna, Barbera & Yogi 97

Unknown Superstar 137

The Workshop 153

Mentor Remembered 201

The Great Comeback 215

Credits 259

Index 285

Foreword

It is so wonderful that Ben Ohmart and Joe Bevilacqua have written a book about the late great, and rare human being, Daws Butler. Daws entertained millions of people with his unique sounds and voices: Huckleberry Hound, Yogi Bear, Quick Draw McGraw, Elroy Jetson and dozens of others.

I originally met Daws on a telephone call in June of 1977, and we immediately bonded as student and mentor, which developed into a lasting friendship; and though the father of four sons, I felt like the daughter he and his wife never had—I was very lucky!

Daws was the most incredibly generous teacher a "kid from Ohio" could ever dream of having in her life. I would catch a bus at UCLA and ride the twenty minutes into Beverly Hills for my hour lesson, which always lasted no less than four! We would watch films, listen to radio shows and commercials and work side-by-side in his in-home studio. Daws cared for me the way a gardener cares for his flowers—pulling weeds, trimming unnecessary "dead wood," and cultivating the earth to help me grow into a strong and capable artist. He was always careful about not giving me too much guidance, always making sure I had plenty of freedom to create on my own, and completely aware that I needed to clear my own path to success, and he made sure I did just that. I will forever be grateful, as no man or woman succeeds alone.

Like most artists, Daws needed a good team around him. I would be remiss not to include his lovely wife of many years, Myrtis, in the mix. Likewise, his sons, David, Don, Paul and Chas all remain close to each other and were such fun to be with.

In my heart, it was Daws who inspired me to go for my dreams. And to you, good reader, I encourage the same.

– Nancy Cartwright

Introduction

If Mel Blanc was the famous one, and Paul Frees was the mysterious one, then Daws Butler has to be the universally loved voice man. Dramatically, he did not have a sensational life; no ego, affairs, great tragedies, his was not an incredible rags-to-riches story. He was simply a great man with a great talent who rose to a height few people in television have ever achieved. This short, shy man could walk into a room and be easily overlooked, but all he had to do was open his mouth for a single sentence, and he could command that room and every subject in it for hours. Within this altruistic actor, there was a dignity, a caring soul and a superpower that shined greater than all the Brandos and Bogarts of entertainment history. He knew his mind, his characters and every piece of syllable he uttered.

Speaking with the current cream of the crop of voice actors who continually obtain movie, TV and radio work today, two things emerged. One: no one who knew Daws—NO ONE—had one unkind thing to say about the man. That's quite a feat in Hollywood. That he was giving, and caring about his craft, and that he gave back to a new and upcoming stream of professionals, without regard for his own bank account or self, is without doubt. Two: most of the pros working today are heavily influenced by this "gentleman of the voice world" or at the very least took his infamous workshop, which sought less to make a financial killing (as do many conferences and workshops where one learns from top teachers today) than to pass on very specialized and important knowledge to a group of dedicated up-and-comers.

He also proved that the voice was an often neglected tool for a good actor to cloak himself in his part. Daws never did voices. He physically became a character. He cast his spell with the wave of a lip, the raise of an eyebrow, the shrug of a shoulder, the jutting of the lower jaw, the intertwining of fingers. His body transformed, his brilliant mind cranked into gear, Daws became any amount of bears, innocent kids, or quick-drawing horses imaginable.

We might even to go as far as to coin a new phrase: Dawsian, *for how else to describe the discernible stylistic influence he had on the work of Stan Freberg, Messers Hanna and Barbera, even Bob Clampett*—Dawsians, *all.*

Daws Butler was a master, a mentor, a father and a husband whose life has thankfully been chronicled by many interviews, articles, personal letters and phone conversations, not to mention the reminisces of collegues, friends and family. We have sought to collect up everything available and give something back to a man who has given us countless hours, days and years of mirth and wonder.

To that end, we owe the deepest respect and admiration to the many people who have made this hopeless biographical attempt at pinning down a genius possible. Myrtis Butler and her children Charles, Don, David and Paul were kind enough to let us capture their thoughts and memories on the beloved man who still haunts their houses.

Special thanks go to Arnold Kunert for letting us quote from his priceless Daws Butler, Voice Magician documentary; Milt Gray for letting us quote from his impressive printed interview; and to Keith Scott for always having the answer, the credit list and the time.

And zealous thanks must also go to the following people, without whom there would be no thickness to the book: ASIFA-Holloywood, AOL-Time-Warner, Joe Barbera, Bob Bergen, Lucille Bliss, Greg Burson, Corey Burton, Bob Clampett, Jr., Nancy Cartwright, Eric Owen Costello, Craig Crumpton, Brian Cummings, Dr. Demento, Walker Edmiston, Mark Evanier, Gary L. Flynn, Stan Freberg, June Foray, Craig Fuqua, David Garland, Matt Giarrizzo, Marty Halpern, Bill Hamlin, the late William Hanna, Ted K. Hering, Doug Higley, Don Hunt, Charles Hutchinson, Paul Kattelman, Jackson King, Brian Kistler, Freddie Steady Krc, Earl Kress, Andrew Leal, Betty Lougaris, the late Jan Meredith, the late Don Messick, Vernon Morris, Henry J. Quinn, the late Tony Pope, Ed Ryba, Toni Silveri, Laura Wagner, Whimsical Will, Lee Withers, Sean Wright, Steve Worth, James M. Wylie II., and Doug Young.

– Ben Ohmart & Joe Bevilacqua

Chapter 1
One Short Wave

It was 1916. The Great War raged. The *Saturday Evening Post* published its first cover containing a Norman Rockwell painting. President Woodrow Wilson signed a bill incorporating the Boys Scouts of America. And a comic genius was born.

Six-foot-tall Charles Allan Butler met and married five-foot Ruth White in Toledo, Ohio, and on November 16, 1916, they became the proud parents of Charles Dawson Butler who, unfortunately and fortunately, took after his mother on the size front and only made it to 5' 2". Daws, for "short," takes up the story:

Left: *Daws, age 2;* right: *Daws, age 5.*

"I was an only child—shy and with the mark of the 'loner' on me. I was drawn early to books and those of my peers who had something to say. I was inhibited and withdrawn in school and feared oral expression in class. I was more secure with a pen. At recess, in the playground, I found that I was a budding comic with the guys. I found the girls unapproachable. But in the classroom I was a mumbling muddle of ineptitude.

"Looking back, there is no question but that a certain Aunt and Uncle played a fundamental part in my development. My Uncle, Bill Butler, read Shakespeare and the classics. He was witty and metaphoric. He did crossword puzzles with a pen (his hand never stopped moving)! He was a 'closet' intellectual who was content with that. He was satisfied with a 'job' job—and lived within. There were probably those who thought him a 'loser.'

"He recognized early on my wit and quickness of thought. He sensed and encouraged my feeling for expression, and he quoted my latest mots and referred to me as 'Dawsy Butler—the boy-wonder!' He was my first fan and supporter. He laughed at my cartoons.

"Then there was my Aunt Cecil Perry, my mother's sister—a marvelously articulate woman. She gave stature to verbosity. She was a bright, Auntie Mame type of a woman who accepted me as an equal.

"Of the two, she was the most articulate. Bill was wittier, funnier, but

Daws would often enclose cartoons with his early letters.

Charles Dawson Butler

she would enthrall me with her descriptions of everything and anything. I never delved as deeply into things as she did; she always knew much more than I felt myself capable of understanding, but I was always aware of her vibrations. She taught me to explore, to respect technique, to be aware of structure, and dedication. Whatever subject interested her, she would research completely. From her, I learned that, in today's vernacular, 'You can't luck out!' If you want it, you go after it. She encouraged me in my early ambitions and respected me as a 'Nephew-Person.' With my handful of barely presentable impersonating ability I started to hit the nightclubs with my act—and she was the one who kept a scrapbook which I still have and treasure.

"They were the catalysts I needed and they were there. They gave of themselves. They were the mentors who shaped me and suggested a direction, confident that my then fragmentary artistic psyche would eventually 'puddle' like separate drops of mercury at last coming together and I would see things whole. I learned the first stirrings of articulation and the shaping and shading—the love—of words from Uncle Bill and Aunt Cecil. I realize that now—long after they are gone."

Early on, the Butler family moved to Oak Park, Illinois (the birthplace of Ernest Hemingway). His parents were also and always supportive in Daws' choices. At first, he wanted to be a cartoonist and writer, having a clever, quick mind that was constantly creative, with a proficiency for comedy in the absurd or non sequitur vein.

Daws attended Oak Park High School where he drew cartoons for *The Trapeze* and wrote for his high school yearbook, *The Tabula* ("a word of Greek origin, meaning a tablet bearing a record of events"). In December of 1933, students could read one of his earliest published writings, a subtle, slightly ridiculous work:

> The Burlitzer Prize
> Dawson Butler
>
> Considering the fact that I've written hundreds of novels, it seems peculiar that, out of all of them, one which I deemed mediocre received special attention and the "Burlitzer Prize."
>
> I once admitted, when a certain critic referred to my work as "lousy," that he was right. I didn't exactly admit it voluntarily but rather as an apology that I was forced to give at a very unwelcome assault and battery trial in which this critic and I were unfortunately involved. I let bygones be bygones, however, and forgot about the whole thing. Except, of course, the ten-grand that I gave the critic for damages.
>
> Of course you aren't interested in my troubles and I won't bother you with them anymore.
>
> A very complimentary editorial, which appeared in the Lamar, MO *Democrat* was pointed out to me the other day by a very intimate friend. He said, "Joe, if you wanna find any praise in the newspaper about your novel, you'll have as much chance finding it in the Lamar, MO *Democrat* as anywhere."
>
> So I rushed down to Tony's (he sells out of town papers) and panted, "Gimme a copy of the Lamar *Democrat.*" He searched through his stock and finally found the

desired paper. I grabbed it, ran all the way home, and searched the contents madly for any mention of my novel. Reading carefully and sifting every article, I finally reached the editorial. It didn't exactly mention my story and, while there was no direct reference to my novel, it was very evident that the editor had me and my literary work in mind. The editorial is well worth your attention and, for that reason, I reproduce it here:

LET'S GET TOGETHER, FELLOWS.

"Tom Perkins went to the barn dance Saturday night and got in a fight with Lem Smithers. Both boys got pretty banged up. Now, if our boys can't go to barn dances without fist-a-cuffs, I think they better not go. You'd think we was living in a roughneck city like Chicago, judging from the way we been cutting up. We'll show Lamar we can behave!"

I was mighty proud when I read that editorial, and I showed it to several of my friends.

For the benefit of the few people who haven't been fortunate enough to read my novel, I am going to print a few excerpts which I consider outstanding. There is one, in particular, that I think you will enjoy. And this, I'm afraid, is it:

"Wesley had a peculiar feeling that he was being followed. He was, therefore, filled with an unmistakable sense of impending danger, which overwhelmed him as he pressed his fingers to his temples and screamed in a shrill soprano voice. Recovering from his old fright to clear his throat for the next scream, he momentarily glanced behind him and witnessed a sight that made his blood run cold. His hair stood on end and his teeth chattered incessantly as he shrieked:

"Montgomery! You cur! How dare you follow me? Is it not bad enough that I have to contend with you, thwart you, match wits with you, without your following me all over London, which, if I remember correctly, is the largest city in the world, and grinning like a madman? Oh, Montgomery. I can't bear it! I can't! I can't!"

No doubt after reading the above paragraph you were immediately impressed by my inimitable style of writing. You probably marveled at the way I make my characters, or my puppets, as I call them, live.

A very fine tribute was paid me the other day by a very dear friend. He said: "Sometimes I read your stories." I appreciate things like that and if any of you would like to send me a few lines of appreciation, or even a gift, I would be thankful. One lady sent me her autograph. Unfortunately her signature was preceded by the words, "Please pay the rent!"

Getting back to the paragraph quoted from my novel, I wish to make clear just what it was all about. You see, Wesley's dog, Montgomery, had followed him with Wesley's best hat hanging from his mouth. Wesley, seeing this, went into hysterics. Now I'm sure you understand that plot. Therefore, I'll brighten your lives with another episode which is taken from my soul-stirring novel, *Heart Throbs*:

"Pausing at the doorway, Genevieve heard her aged uncle gruffly remark: 'Daddy, can I go out and play football with Grandpa?' His dad gave his approval, so Uncle went to find Grandpa, who was spinning his top in the alley. Genevieve passed through the hall and stopped by the fireplace. 'Could it be true,' she asked herself, 'that the Senators lost the World Series? Yes,' she said, 'that might be so because, if I remember correctly, most Senators are pretty fat and probably wouldn't be such good ball players.' And with that, she flung herself on the floor and completed her uncle's jigsaw puzzle."

(Ed's Note: This work may be purchased at any up-to-date fruit store.)

Daws also composed the words and music of many novelty songs. "It is a hobby which he hopes to turn into a life work," said one March 4, 1937 newspaper. He also saw his poetry printed in *The Tabula*, such as this "epic" from December of 1934:

OH, LOVE, LOVE, LOVE (An Epic)
Oh, what unhappy
Earth are suffer.
People eat nothing
And starve on it mostness.
We who are perhaps,
Retard slowly!

LULLABY
Radio so nice,
Radio tune on,
Radio croon softingly.
Oh, radio stop swiftingly.

The Tabula printed at least one more poem in May 1935.

When Dawson's mother was away from home in 1934 or 1935, he composed the following poem:

Motherless Soliloquy

I leer at the dishes – they're piled to the ceiling
My mind's in a daze – I feel myself reeling
I grab for a chair – I miss and fall flat
I feel something beneath me – I look – and it's "Pat."

I rise to my feet – a job is before me
The dog wants a walk – he kneels to implore me
I turn a deaf ear on his whining forlorn
And turn to the dishes; with "Oh why was I born?"

I turn on the water – it gurgles and splashes
I'm listening to Winchell – he's citing some flashes.
A truck thunders past – I hear something fall
I know it's the dishes and hysterically bawl.

I look at the mess that lies on the floor
And smiling, I murmur "No dishes: no more!"

Daws spent at least as much time drawing as working with words. "I was a fair cartoonist—good enough to amuse my family and the kids at school, but it was the weakest of my talents. Writing came first and even in elementary school I felt the inclination to parody the type of essay we were assigned to do. To fabricate—to stretch the truth—to fictionalize. And to be funny. I dreaded having to stand up and read my latest opus to the class but the few scattered laughs my stuff would get made the whole thing tolerable.

"The only club I belonged to in High School was a writing club, The Scribblers. I was a bit of a snob and liked to be with those with whom I was comfortable. The shyness had persisted so I signed up for a public speaking class. I didn't realize it, but I was in the process of becoming my own shrink. I was frightened at first, but I had the ability to 'write' on my feet, which is what improvisation is all about. Good improvisers are writers whether they know it or not. Soon I was parodying what others who had spoken before had said."

Oddly, the man who would build such a fan base with his range of vocal skills found it difficult to speak in public as an Illinois schoolboy. He was so shy he passed up oral credits in school, claiming he didn't know the answers when teachers called upon him. Speaking before classmates tied his stomach in such knots he finally had to buckle down and force himself to take a speech class to focus himself and, his favorite pastime throughout life, learn. "That course," he later said, "not only forced me to stand up and speak before an audience, it gave me an addiction to applause." His youthful shyness was almost completely cured when one of his friends gave a serious talk on the vulgar impropriety of putting one's hands in one's pockets; Daws countered with an ad-libbed discussion of the advantages of giving speeches in pocket-less suits, and though the teacher didn't find it amusing, a star was born.

In high school Daws began flaunting his gift as a way of combating his enveloping lack of self-confidence. His first two voices were impressions of then President Franklin D. Roosevelt, and a sputtering Ford automobile starting out on a chilly morning.

"One of the assignments we had was How to Give a Talk. The first boy up made the point that one shouldn't put one's hands in his pockets. The following few, with little imagination, said more or less the same thing, so it took very little thought on my part to make the shortest talk of all and my advice was to have a suit made with no pockets. My instructor was quite academic and conventional and found me not all that amusing. In fact, he admonished me for frivolity and not taking the class seriously…but my peers (zits and all) were laughing it up! And that was my redemption! It felt good to get laughs, and I felt my inhibitions diminishing.

"My former early-recognized talents of drawing cartoons for the school newspaper and writing articles for same were lessened in my mind and my newly-discovered talent of amusing others was the breakthrough and the beginning of what would someday be my major career."

A March 15th newspaper reported a joint meeting of the two writing clubs of Oak Park High School. At the Story-Scribblers meeting, apart from reading his poem, "The Cartoonist," Dawson also entertained the members during their refreshments. "He did some very fine imitations, which were the 'hit' of the meeting. Butler imitated many movie and radio stars, among whom were Joe E. Brown, Lionel Barrymore, and Joe Penner. He also gave his impression of a 'flivver' trying to start on a cold day. An imitation of an intoxicated man was also done in fine style. After Butler had returned to his cake and melting ice cream, President Van Vliet adjourned the meeting."

Daws later admitted, "Maybe it was because I was so short, but I was extremely, almost fatally introverted. I was always the kid in the back of the crowd, never at the center, and because I was short, I couldn't see or be seen. So I started to make some noise, doing voices, doing impressions of movie stars and our teachers. The kids loved it—especially the girls—and I suddenly had status and stature."

The move toward performing also had to do with his stature. Daws was often picked on by towering bullies because of his diminutive size. Rather than fight fire with fists, the up-and-coming actor decided to use his talents toward making his enemies laugh at him and alter their threats to chuckles.

It was this combination of battling shyness and the thrill of making others laugh that soon led Daws to drop out of high school a mere two months before he would have graduated. He talked it over with his supportive parents and they agreed to let him have a stab at becoming a professional entertainer.

His son Don Butler recalled, "He was supremely self-confident. He knew his skill, he exactly knew how to handle it. And that self-confidence was self-taught. His stories of himself in high school remind me a lot of myself in high school. I was very shy, very withdrawn. But unlike me, my father did something about it while he was still in high school. He forced himself to take public speaking classes, and he forced himself to get up in front of groups, until he learned how to be relaxed and to be himself."

"As a single," said Daws, "and while still going to school—my Senior year—I won an amateur contest in a big nightclub in Chicago. The prize was a week's engagement, which called for me to participate in four shows each night—the last one being at three o'clock in the morning!

"This was the happenstance which led to my not finishing High School. I was always pretty good with hunches so here's what happened. After that last show and by the time I had gotten home and grabbed an hour's sleep or two, I was so sleepy when I dragged myself into my 'homeroom' that some sort of decision had to be made. I explained the reason for my sleepiness to the concerned homeroom monitor because he had noticed (as had the rest of the room) that I was snoring with my head on my desk. He advised me to do one of two things: either I should finish High School and get my diploma, or go into show business actively. But he made it plain that I couldn't have it both ways.

"So I made my decision. The next day I didn't show up at school. I was a dropout, but it was the only decision I could make. Luckily, everything turned out well and I did okay. But I just followed a gut-level hunch. With the raw talent I was blessed with—and for which I can take little credit—I had discovered that as a mimic I had eyes and ears that saw and heard all, and I was about to retool it for my own artistic expression.

"I'm grateful to my parents for understanding this abrupt move on my part and not contesting my decision. Looking back, I realize that they determined that this poor student who was blessed with raw talent for writing and acting had finally found something he 'could do!' So God speed and hope for the best, they probably said, and while I wouldn't advise my action for others, it did work for me.

"The gut-level realization that I had an ability to entertain was not academic. I never appeared in any theatrical activities in school, and I had yet to do my own thing. I learned by observing and sifting the information so obtained until I found the essence of what I wanted. And later, when I had entered the nightclub circuit, I learned much from the kindness of professionals who took the time to tell me where my timing was off and how I could improve my performance. They shared their knowledge with me. People will help you…if they find you deserving of their help. They must sense your talent and your potential and then instead of being jealous or threatened, they will help you to nurture and advance it. I have been helped all along the way.

"Back to writing for a moment and my love affair with words. I was only a fair student and I felt a sense of inadequacy with my academic peers, and it was only when I was introduced to the world of words did I come alive. One particular English teacher turned me onto writers like Bob Benchley, Stephen Leacock (who was actually the forerunner of Benchley), Ring Lardner, Corey Ford, Frank Sullivan and Donald Ogden Stewart—very funny guys! Also some of the heavier authors—such as Charles Dickens and Sinclair Lewis and Ernest Hemingway who took the embroidery out of writing and exposed the bare patterns of life as it really is. Thomas Wolfe came later and James Thurber. Herman Melville reads aloud like butter! Words, words!

"I learned, early on, to respect and love and try to imitate their vibrations; these literary giants!"

It was that combination of writer and actor that gave Daws a more complete understanding of how to get into character; even more so that his surrounding competitors.

"Amateur contests were quite the thing at that time and I, to bolster my newfound ability to communicate, found the courage to try out my few meager impersonations to compete for the public's approval.

"I had practiced duplicating the facial expressions of the few stars I could impersonate in front of my mother's vanity mirror: one big central mirror with two wing-types on the sides. This gave me a head-on view and two profiles. I was determined to do my impersonations all the way—the face, the body movements—the voice.

"My instinctive theory about impersonations, and which was to apply later to original characterizations, was that if you could assume the proper facial expression, the proper voice would ensue. And it proved out. Later, I was to discover in doing dialects and characterizations that many vocal characteristics could be obtained by the position of the tongue, the flexibility of the jaw, the lips and so forth. I call it 'working through a conflict.' The conflict is the articulating around the obstacle (numb lips, tight jaw, tongue held high on the palate) and the ensuing speech pattern will sound nothing like your own. Withal, you must be understood, you must enunciate; the prerequisite of the actor is to be heard.

"I learned much about timing by studying famous movie and radio stars. Everyone has his or her own music or speech pattern, individual accents and inflection differences.

"I discovered the use of syncopation—one of the most difficult things to teach. Jack Lemmon and James Stewart and George C. Scott have a beautiful sense of syncopation—what they say sounds completely 'thought-produced.' (Dick Van Dyke is no slouch, either!)

"Attitudinal changes are vital and the literacy and intelligence of the person to be portrayed must be known.

"It is the writer's responsibility to make heavy suggestions. It is the actor's responsibility to interpret and to let the character mature.

"So I was in show business even though it was only amateur contests. I was learning my craft. Within a year I met two other competing impersonators, and, as we would take turns wining, we decided to join forces and become an act.

"That's the way it all started. I was blessed by serendipity! My first two talents were cartooning and writing, and so I had gone off on two paths and discovered a third.

"We must have been good for each other because within a year we were playing all the night-spots in Chicago."

In a later letter to Keith Scott, Daws wrote, "Well, these were the late days of the Great Depression and there were many amateur contests in various nightclubs, etc. This way they could get entertainment (such as it was) for a few dollars prize money. I went around to the places which sponsored this sort of event, which were several, and lo! and behold! (as Mr. Grimm and Mr. H.C. Anderson would have it) I started winning! Usually top prize was three to five dollars, but in those days a nice plum. During this little adventure, or series of adventures, I began to regain my cool. Before I would be announced by the M.C., my whole insides would churn. I would have given anything not to go out in front of people. But once in front of those same people, my fears faded, and I took delight in one or the two of the laughs I would get. I never really lost my shyness— I don't like big parties—I still get butterflies at a new audition—but I can control it and I enjoy my work."

Whether he won contests given at spots like the State Lake Theatre or Edgewater Beach or the Blackstone Hotels, it was the applause that made him feel like a winner. It was during the Depression and sometimes the only person who got paid in a talent competition was the winner, so Daws was not above getting the performers together to "throw" the show if there was a particular performer who desperately needed the money.

In 1935 Daws won a contest on Quin Ryan's amateur show on WGN, then other similar Illinois-area contests: the Walkathon in Maywood in the spring, at the Sherman in the late summer, and at Harry's New York Cabaret which led to a two-week engagement. He got a café booking, then was featured for two weeks at the Edgewater Beach Hotel. A booking agent saw him perform at the College Inn at one of bandleader George Olsen's amateur nights, and he was engaged as one of the stars to open Pierre's Continental Casino, "attended by Chicago's most glittering socialites." Numerous vaudeville bookings followed.

On November 16, 1935, Daws signed up for a solo one-week engagement to play the State Lake Theatre in Chicago, to commence on December 14, 1935. Others on the bill included tenor Bob Smith, Frank Payne, an impersonator of radio personalities, and blues singer Jane Littlejohn. Rehearsals were set to start at 8:30 a.m. It was an exclusive contact for 32 shows for $35 net. Bob Hawk, famous for his *Red Hot and Low Down* show over station WCFL, emceed. The theatre also played movies – that week, the Perry Mason movie, *The Case of the Lucky Legs*, was showing.

As the number of auditions and amateur nights began to congeal, more and more Daws found himself standing in the wings with the same two young men. Jack Lavin, Willard Ovitz and Daws became such good friends they decided to team up on the assumption that variety in variety shows was the key. Three might work better than one.

"I met two fellows," Daws explained in a 1970 letter to Keith Scott, "who were trying to get into show business, via the amateur contest route, and we formed a team. To me it was still a lark, a way to overcome my shyness, a sort of self-inflicted therapy. But they were dead serious, and when we began to get professional bookings, for real money, they wanted to costume the act, have music written and all the things necessary for a professional debut. I said that I'd go along for a while, but I really was determined to go to art school. They kept trying to talk me into staying with the act. Finally, I was in so deep and was enjoying show business so much that I surrendered. We worked together for a couple years in theaters (you've heard of vaudeville? We delivered the last rites), nightclubs, etc."

Thus was born The Three Short Waves: Daws Butler, Jack Lavin and Willard Ovitz.

Three Short Waves.

"I called it the Three Short Waves. We were all short and it was the radio period and anyway, it wasn't all that hokey a name. I wrote the material we used; in fact, my first move when we went to another city for an engagement was to rent a typewriter—I was still a little in awe of the chorus girls. I was eighteen."

They enjoyed regional success, with Daws leading the troupe with his impressions of famous people of the day. Not only through voice, but through an impressive array of costumes and an eye for character detail, Daws physically *became* Jimmy Durante, W. C. Fields, Adolph Hitler, Franklin D. Roosevelt, Rudy Vallee, George Arliss, Jack Oakie, Ned Sparks, Joe E. Brown, Charles Laughton, Lionel Barrymore, Stepin Fetchit, Fred Allen, Walter Winchell, Bob Burns, Ben Bernie, Kate Smith, Boake Carter, Bing Crosby, Morton Downey, Charles Butterworth, and that old standby: a Model T. Ford "starting out on a chilly morning." Jack Lavin always served as master of ceremonies.

"The strange thing is," Daws later wrote, "that while I've made my living behind the microphone and camera—I made my initial mark by doing the facial and physical impressions of those I impersonated, learning the art of timing by studying honored and established players. They were my 'workshop.' I also studied the work of other professionals with whom we played."

As early as December 7, 1935 they were being touted as "America's finest mimics." In their confident strides, Eton jackets, ascots and striped trousers, they appeared at the Trianon Ballroom in the first week of December. One of their first performances occurred at the Blackhawk Café's celebrity jamboree, entitled Midnight Flyers. Daws had appeared on the Flyers' radio program by himself on November 11. One Chicago newspaper reported that "the Midnight Flyers program has become national in scope. Each Monday scores of telegrams and phone calls are received at the Blackhawk, expressing best wishes to Joe Sanders and his orchestra and asking the maestro to play favorite songs of the callers." The crowded Blackhawk Café also boasted that "countless thousands throughout the country are enjoying the program via the loudspeaker." Actually it was broadcast over Chicago's famous WGN radio station every Monday night. The Flyers would begin at midnight, and typically lasted past 3:00 a.m. One paper quickly proclaimed Daws and company "a trio of youngsters whose impersonations of radio, screen and stage stars will soon become the sensation of the show world."

When the Waves appeared on Midnight Flyers for the first time that fateful Monday evening, they stopped the show when they were recalled to the microphone four times. After a second hit show, they were signed to appear on the Blackhawk floor show. Daws later recalled, "While the other two guys were chasing the girls, I would stand in the wings and watch comics who were on the bill and see how they got their laughs. I learned a lot from the wiser-heads who told me why I *didn't* get the laugh. I found a great kindness in them. They were *willing* to advise. Those few years in nightclubs and theatres was like going to Harvard.

"At this time it wasn't all that easy to come up with voices—it took much work. We were constantly trying to impersonate famous radio and movie personalities, and as we mastered each new one, our repertoire grew. But I was building a technique, a way of analyzing not other people's voices, but their characters, which is more important. I would find voices while riding on the bus, in shops—I listened and stored up characters. Now when I'm called on to give vocal life to a cartoon character, I dip back into this file and come up with several variations, one of which I hope will please the director."

Apart from learning his craft, Daws was also assembling a teacher's mind-set. These analytical exercises became so ingrained in his acting and comedic self that Daws would often dictate explanations later on the art of vocal character development.

Daws: "Finding myself in the new environment of a nightclub with scantily-clad chorus girls and worldly-wise variety performers, I was a bit fearful of what I felt to be my short-comings as a budding entertainer. My material wasn't all that polished and I was rather overwhelmed at being in a 'real' night-spot. The compassionate M.C. took me aside before he introduced me and said, 'Kid, you got a great little Irish mug—so just get out there and give'm the teeth.' That's the line! 'Give'm the teeth!' Of course, he meant 'smile.' 'Let'm like you, kid—if they take a likin' to ya, they'll be on your side—they'll want that funny-faced little kid to make it!'

"Good advice, huh? It came at a time when I really needed it. I was (fearless youth!) coasting on raw talent but it sufficed. I was the writer—learning—but we were getting more laughs and I was getting exciting, emotional reactions to the serious, dramatic impersonations I did.

"We were only together for a few years, but in that time, I learned how to play an audience, how to change the timing to fit a particular situation; an inattentive nightclub audience, for instance, where the business deals being consummated or propositions or whatever, were more important than watching a trio of kids trying to get through to them. When the audience wasn't with it, you fell into the cosmetic performance—it looked just about the same, but there was no heart in it. When the audience was hot, we'd run over the ad-libs and the joy of pleasing people.

"We played everything there was to play in Chicago and then hit other states in the mid-West, and headed south and east.

"These were the latter days of the Great Depression (what was so great about it?) and we did our share of laying off, but we made enough to pay our way."

The three young men appeared at the Trianon Ballroom in mid-December 1935 for the annual "Attaches' Party," along with the orchestras of Jan Garber and Anson Weeks. 60 cents admission for ladies; 90 cents for gentlemen. "Hours and hours of swell dance music—entertainment—laughs—and thrills" prevailed. Positive mentions in the *Chicago Times, Chicago Daily News*, and the *Chicago Evening American* were only the beginning.

That same month they were also heard again over WGN with Harold Stokes and the WGN Orchestra on the *Mardi Gras* variety show, at 9:30 p.m.

On January 4, 1936, they appeared along with legend Victor Moore and soon-to-be-legend Vivian Vance (both hot off the heels of Cole Porter's *Anything Goes*) at *The Chicago Tribune*'s annual banquet at the Drake hotel. For a whopping $25 between them the Three Short Waves also performed for a January 26th Dodge Brothers Program over station WBBM in Chicago.

Toledo, Ohio's bitter cold on January 31, 1936 didn't keep 3,000 people away from President Roosevelt's birthday anniversary ball at the Civic auditorium where many acts entertained both Democrats and Republicans in the audience. *The Toledo Blade* reported that Daws "won plenty of applause with his clever mimicking" of his usual repertoire. The President did not attend, but all collected funds went to fight infantile paralysis.

In Clark Rodenbach's *Cafe Table Topics* March 18th column from the *Chicago Daily News,* Daws was singled out from the other two Waves for a moment: "The 'Three Short Waves' (particularly the little one with the funny face) give highly credible impersonations of radio and movie greats." Just the day before in the *Chicago American,* Charlie Dawn wrote that they "clicked heavily." However, in all ads of the day, a rival team, the Three Variety Boys, continued to headline.

With your $2 dinner of broiled sea bass, or jumbo frog legs sauté, or broiled filet mignon, or grilled sirloin steak, complete with vegetables, sherbet, American fried potatoes, pineapple cake and coffee, you would also receive a generous helping of Faith Bacon (ex-Ziegfeld Follies beauty and "originator of the fan dance"), Don Enrico, tenor of the Chicago Civic Opera Company, Irish comedian Bobby Danders, and The Three Short Waves, among other acts. Four times nightly (8:30, 11:30, 1:30 and 3:30), Mike Potson presented twelve acts for "Chicago's Oldest Cafe," *Colosimo's,* on South Wabash Avenue. The time: April of 1936.

Again, the lads could do no wrong. One of their staunchest supporters, *Chicago American* writer Charlie Dawn, gave the night at *Colosimo's* another thumbs up in the April 3, 1936 edition of the newspaper. "The Three Short Waves are giving Mike Potson's musical revue at *Colosimo's* a real touch of quality comedy—and are a grand contrast to the abundant exotic and semi-nude dances night-lifers find on the program. The addition of The Three Short Waves rounds out a bill of fine entertainment which makes lull moments nil! And they know their stars." Praise again for the impersonations of Fred Allen, George Arliss, Durante, and Schlepperman from Jack Benny's radio program.

Rave after rave followed. "The Three Short Waves are three lads who actually do some remarkable things with their impersonations," said an April 11, 1936 magazine, and a May 1st paper called them "among the highlights of the current revue." The *Chicago Daily Times* on May 12, 1936 wrote that they came "near stealing the show. The impression of George Arliss is one of the best ever offered on a local cafe floor." It took guts for a teen to impersonate a 60+ year old. Daws later explained the

Daws as W.C. Fields.

creation of his favorite early impression: "Arliss had a sort of angular face; mine was round. By putting my tongue in my lower lip, I could look like him—by hooking my eyebrows, slumping my shoulders a little bit, by getting a laxity in my hands I made them old."

Daws appeared by himself, doing his characters for the 5th birthday of the Oak Park (Illinois) Kiwanis Club, and was obviously popular enough to have his picture in the paper announcing the event.

On May 19, 1936, the Three Short Waves appeared at the Veteran's Hospital in Hines, Illinois for a special 2:15 p.m. program sponsored by the American Legion's Marshall Field Post #11. They were on a bill with a blues singer, a vocalist, a "harmonica king" and an "eccentric dance team."

The June 5, 1936 edition of *This Week in Detroit* magazine contained a back ad highlighting the Three Short Waves, Frank Gagen and his Club Commodores and The Commodore Dancing Darlings at the Commodore Nite Club at 72 Peterboro.

When the lads appeared at The Capitol Theater in Binghampton, NY in the 1937 edition of *The Kit Kat Klub Revue* at the end of October 1936, *The Binghampton Sun* reported on the 28th that the Three Short Waves were "a grand laugh riot. Their impersonations of Vallee, Charles Laughton, Morton Downey and others were excellent. The satire debate between Hitler, Mussolini and Haile Selassie is a classic of high comedy, absolutely original and brought bursts of laughter."

At the Strand Theatre in Shenandoah, PA the local newspaper called them the standout attraction of the Revue. "These three young men do more than entertain audiences; they startle them, and then make them laugh. They offer scenes from shows in which the ones they are aping have appeared – logical sequences correctly presented."

Still, Daws began to tire of the constant shows and touring. In a letter from his Hotel Churchill in Canton, Illinois, Daws wrote, "Dear Aunt Cec: I'm a *rat*, ain't I? I don't know, honest to Gosh, what's gotten into me. I put off writing so much more than I used to. Getting home has been on my mind so steadily, I haven't thought of much else. See, pal? The reason we're staying longer is—I just *couldn't* come home with nothing to show for all the time I've been away – subsequently, the delay. I don't suppose my folks can easily understand that, so I'm telling you frankly just why. You see, I know that to them I'm still a little boy – and that the door is still open to me, and all that – that they don't care what I've gained – just that they want me home with them. Boy! that suits me fine – the thought of being home. But I've come to the point where I have to use my own mind and not depend entirely on them. In other words, to stand on my own feet. I may not have much when I do get home, but at least it will be something. And after all this time being away, a few more weeks won't matter.

"I've learned so much since I've been gone. The act is more polished, but above all, we've learned to shift for ourselves. That, to me, was the reason for coming. I don't think so much of this business, tho – maybe I'll get over it. Hope so. The thing that hurts me is that I have no desire to draw – no moods – no nothing. I have written a little, and become quite interested in writing lyrics for songs. If I could find some guy who knows something about music, who could compose, I think I'd really enjoy songwriting. I'm working on a couple now and have completed about five since I've been gone, which isn't a bad average.

Drawn October, 1937.

"One of the main reasons I look forward to home so much is to recover that lost peace of mind, to get back in the swing of things I love. To get away from Josh [emcee Jack Lavin] for a while. I'm getting to hate his guts (if you'll pardon my bluntness). Willie's O.K. – I'll always consider him a friend. We seem to see things in the same light – and at least he's sincere, and that's what counts. This business seems so shallow, so cheap, I almost hate to be considered a part of it. It's not the acting part, that's still fun, but it's the life you lead. I value security so highly – and this is a base opposition of the word itself.

"I bet you think I'm an ole pessimist, doncha? I don't think I am. It's just that I find the atmosphere repulsive – and undesirable. Through it all, tho, I've stayed clean and level headed, and what mistakes I have made haven't been serious.

"Well, it's getting kinda late – 12:15 to be exact, so I guess we'll close. Love, Daws."

It was particularly difficult around his birthday, November 16th, but luckily he was not forgotten by his aunt and uncle who sent the 20-year-old Daws cupcakes and encouraging letters. Daws spent most of his off time reading from a thesaurus they sent him and going to more shows, always learning, always eager to find new stars to imitate. On the road, in a letter from Hazleton, PA, he told of one such personality he found in *Three Men on a Horse*. "There's a fella in it named Sam Levene. He's awfully funny and I can imitate him. I'll show you, when I get home. Yeah, *when*."

Another complaint Daws had about his rigorous touring schedule was the almost constant change of routes. On December 12, 1936, the line-up had been altered to shows in

    Clearfield, PA   Dec. 18-19
    Bellefonte, PA   Dec. 21
    Lancaster, PA   Dec. 22-24
    Allentown, PA   Dec. 25-26
    Jonesville, OH   Dec. 31 – Jan. 2
    Chonton, OH   Jan. 5-6
    Wheeling, WV   Jan. 7-9

While in Lewistown, PA, Daws was able to take advantage of the theatre's "added attraction"—a photographer up on the mezzanine floor who was taking pictures of the patrons. "Regular little four for a dime photos," Daws wrote in another letter to Aunt Cecil and Uncle Russ, "only these are free, Gratis, you don't have to pay nothin'! Neat, huh? He took a liking to us and took three sets of pictures of each of us. They aren't so good, tho, are they? I had some taken in character. Joe Brown's pretty good, but that's about all."

The end of January 1937 saw the Three Short Waves in *The KKK Revue* in Lincoln, Nebraska at the Orpheum Theater, where *Billboard* reported on January 22 that "the impression boys make off with plenty of applause" and later that "the one kid who does Joe E. Brown and Jack Oakie is a honey."

After a rigorous touring schedule with his two buddies, 20-year-old Dawson had to come back to 423 Wisconsin Avenue for a rest on March 4, 1937. Paul Cholot's *Kit Kat Review* had played five months through the cities and towns of New York, Pennsylvania, West Virginia, Maryland, Ohio, Oklahoma, Kansas, Missouri, Iowa and Illinois. Daws was tuckered.

For a few weeks in March 1937 the Three Short Waves appeared at The Mayflower Casino, "the smart new supper club on the South Shore" of Chicago, joined by the Ritz Brothers-like Three Variety Boys, Lou Sale and his orchestra and other variety acts. The Three Short Waves ended their act with "a big Lionel Barrymore 'thank you' for the close." As always, the papers reported them as "clever" and they continued to draw much applause.

On April 12, 1937, they got a feature spot in Harry's New York Cabaret on 400 N. Wabash Ave. ("The Town's Gay Spot"), calling them "mimics of the stage and screen." Dinner and drinks were served along with at least one other act—Marion Morgan, "the daring darling of dance. Not to mention 8 Parisian Beauties.

Charlie Dawn's review in the *Chicago American* newspaper on April 14, 1937 said less about Miss Morgan's scantily clad charms and more about the "young Chicagoans who have established themselves well with night-lifers downtown, on the South Side and the North Side, too. Their radio impressions embrace those of many stars…of many types. The Charles Laughton bit, in a scene from *Mutiny on the Bounty* and Oswald ["Oswald" was a regular comic character on Ken Murray's radio show, played by Tony Labriola] were the standouts last night."

Billboard reported on April 24, 1937 that the "THREE SHORT WAVES added to Harry's New York Cabaret Show."

The State-Lake Theatre in Chicago had them for a week starting June 17 where they shared the stage with "screen sensations" Betty Burgess and Sonny Lamont, and vaudeville acts Vox and Walters, the Foran Sisters & Tom, and others.

For the week of August 28, 1937 they had an engagement in the Continental Room of the Stevens Hotel in Chicago, performing on the same bill as Carlos Molina and his orchestra, Violet Love ("song delineator") and Alice Kavan ("tops in taps"). And as of November 11, 1937 the team had appeared at Chicago's leading nightspots: Blackhawk restaurant, the College Inn, Colosimo's, the Commodore club, the State-Lake Theatre and the Stevens Hotel.

In December of 1937, *The Kit Kat Klub Revue* was still wowing 'em. A 35-cent ticket to the Ritz Theatre on the 18th and 19th was a grand deal for a grand 10 feature attractions. As a poster for the event (sharing the house with Charles Ruggles and Alice Brady in *Mind Your Own Business* on the movie screen) proclaimed, "We proudly present a group of personalities that our Churches, Schools, Homes, etc. need not refrain from sending and recommending to children, or to anyone who enjoys good, clean amusing caliber entertainment."

On January 3rd, the Three Short Waves filed their two-week notice with the company. Though they wanted to break out earlier, in a letter written from the Zane Hotel in Zanesville, Ohio, Daws explained, "It was the only thing to do, as we had to think of the rest of the kids. It would have meant the canceling of the next two dates, and would have left a bad taste in our mouths – so we did the only right thing."

In November of 1938, Daws played with a variety road show called *Boys Town*, made up of youngsters who did just about everything: songs, dancing, acrobatics. During their two-day stop at the Coronado stage, Daws was once again singled out by the *Rockford Morning Star* on November 29, calling him "exceptionally talented" and praising, above all else, his Charlie McCarthy (Edgar Bergen's wooden dummy) impression. After a week of exams, the show would move onto a full week's engagement at the Palace Theatre in Chicago. Then, onto the eastern states.

Though several newspapers claimed that every one of the 71 performers – ages 6 to 16 – were from Flanagan's Boys' Town in Omaha, Nebraska, 22-year-old Daws was not. But in city after city, his talent obtruded and the favorable reviews continued. In the Mural Room of Dallas, Texas' Baker Hotel, his several-times-daily act was called "great." In the Fox Tower in Kansas City, MO "his impressions of screen and radio stars stand out in the performance." In April of 1939, he "kept the laughs a-rollin'" at the Capitol Theater in Atlanta, GA.

The Boys Town show always began with more than 50 voices singing the official song of the haven for homeless boys. The a cappella choir was directed by Edward Paul and was typically a highlight. The "fast tap and challenge dancing by Jim and Joe, a pair of Negroes; a Wild West scene with roping specialties; exceptional violin playing by Hyman Shulman," and Daws Butler followed.

The Aurora Daily Beacon News July 20, 1939 paper announced a surprise number from Daws when he appeared on stage at a sports convention in the Phillipps Park Amphitheatre. "Dawson Butler, impersonator, came on with The Four Bees and their 'Honey,' an instrumental and vocal quintet, brought the house down with his mimics of cinema and radio favorites. The Geneva youth was perfect in his impersonations" of Charles Laughton, Tizzie Lish (radio's old maid jitterbug) and others. Reports stated that he was regularly featured with the Four Bees.

The following letters from Daws give a good sampling of his thoughts on the road.

One Short Wave 27

From Hazleton, PA, Thursday 1:15pm

Dear Cec:

Received your card and letter—and today the cupcakes. Gee, you're swell. It isn't so bad being away on your birthday when everyone remembers you. Thanks loads—(I like you). Are these cakes neat! They taste like Brownies. They're almost all gone, too.

I've been studying my Thesaurus about every day. It sure is swell—I'm not altogether sure of it, yet, but I'll get to understand it better as I go along.

Did you see *Three Men on a Horse*? Don't miss it, under any cost. Try and get Russ to see it, too. He'd like it—I know.

Well, thanks for everything—and I got a pretty swell Aunt and Uncle.

Love,
Daws

From the Hotel Marquette in Binghampton, NY

Dear Aunt Minnie—er, Cecil.

I got your card, so to show you I appreciated the thought, I take my pen in hand and dash off a loving note to one who little realizes my true feeling or its sincere depth—Oh, Auntie Cecil if you only knew! But, alas! (They only use that in stories—Quote: *Grimm's Fairy Tales*—"Snow White—(or Cecil)—and the dwarfs," who have recently been signed up by Ringling's Bros.—Snow White, incidentally, is now a waitress in a restaurant, down by the waterfront, being known now, as "Snow White and the Wharfs." My feelings must always be veiled by that barrier that stands between us, like an omen of foreboding evil—that barrier being your husband. Hi Russ! Been fishing thru the ice lately?

I'm enclosing a clipping (an ecstatic review) that my

mother has probably shown you by this time, but this one is for you, and you alone. Isn't it neat? When I first saw it, I turned seven back flips in my unsurpassed joy, so have been given an acrobatic bit in the show—aw, shucks—I don't get paid extra, either.

Well, so long. I don't know what you're gonna do—but I'm going to bed. The time—2:00 A.M. Friday morning—and very early.

        Love,
        Charles Dawson Butler
        Oh shucks—just let it go at Daws

The Three Short Waves had toured the country, from Chicago to Atlanta, from St. Louis to Memphis, for four years. But with war clouds looming, the team finally broke up in 1941, when Daws enlisted in the navy.

Daws as Hitler.

Chapter 2
The Voice of Radio

Daws had joined the Naval Reserve (Naval Intelligence), but he didn't see much action. Friend, and later radio co-worker, Bill Hamlin recalled, "When he was finally allowed in the Navy, after a couple people told him he was too short to join, Daws wanted to get on a battleship or aircraft carrier, but he ended up as a typist."

It was there, in Washington, D.C., at a party he didn't want to go to in the first place, that Daws met the love of his life.

Myrtis Martin was the oldest of five children, born in the small town of Albemarle, North Carolina (about 40 miles from Charlotte) on January 31, 1917. Her father, Ernest M. Martin, was a veterinarian, whose partner, Dr. Howard, unknowingly was to help change the face of cartoon voicedom. Howard was also the Martins' neighbor, a friendly sort who would often find himself sittin' on his front porch when Daws was on leave to visit Myrtis. As he knew Daws quite well, Howard would call out, "Howdy, Daws. Why don'tcha set yo'self down a spell so's we can tawlk?" Howard's voice was that sweet, laid-back southern style that rang like music in Daws' ears. It was from Howard that came the spark of the Wolf's sound in his Tex Avery/Droopy Dog cartoons and later, Reddy and, finally, Huckleberry Hound.

"I love the southern dialect," Daws often said. "People may ask for a Georgia or South Carolina accent, but I am rather generic in my treatments. I try to play the things I do with love, a non-chauvinistic approach. Don't hurt. Be nice. That doesn't mean your character has to be nice."

"I went to school in Albemarle," said Myrtis, "and after high school I took a year secretarial's course in Charlotte, NC. I worked for the Stanley

Daws and Myrtis' wedding photos.

County Health Department for 4 or 5 years. When the war started I went to Washington, D.C. and worked at the Pentagon in their temporary buildings, in Special Services (the part I liked best was proofreading and transcribing booklets for soldiers to have when entering a different country . . . the 'do's and do nots' of being there). They were concerned with the morale of the soldiers in the Army and the Navy and so on. And that's where I met Daws.

"Very few men were working in the division I was in. A friend of mine who was working there, who lived with her family on the outskirts of Washington, asked her date if he knew of any young men who would like to go to a party, so he asked Daws who reluctantly said okay. We all met at a bus stop, and went out on the bus together. So when people ask, how did you meet your husband? I say I met him at a bus stop.

"At first I thought his name was Butler Dawson. But we straightened that out. At that point he was a Yeoman First Class in the Navy, and was not on active duty. I believe that Daws joined the Navy because it was easier to reach height requirements…he told me he was told to come back early in the morning and to practice hanging from something to make the height needed."

Daws was shy, and self-conscious about his height. Myrtis was only 5'4", but Daws was two inches shorter. Myrtis said, "Whenever I see photos of Winston Churchill and his wife, they remind me of Daws and I! His voices were a main ingredient of his personality even back then."

Yet she quickly discovered that, for all his talent, Daws wasn't the show-off kind who would put on his increasing storehouse of voices just for attention. She found him to be self-effacing with the talent of a star and the ego of an unlit candle. It was while in character, while in voice, that Daws reached his full potential of confidence, knowing exactly what he could do and who he was.

The young wartime couple began a courtship that evolved quickly. They began dating in August of 1941 and were married on March 2nd the following year in Washington, D.C. Daws remained married to Myrtis for 45+ years. He said it was "like a vaccination that really took. I'm only 5' 2" and my shortest of four sons is 5'11" and the others are six-foot or over, so I don't know what happened."

"After some time in Intelligence (I have no remembrance of what he did)," stated Myrtis, "Daws was sent to boot camp. He was in boot camp when David, our first-born, arrived [on January 9, 1944 in a Washington D.C. Naval hospital]. He was then stationed on Staten Island and assigned to a repair ship (of all things!). David and I joined him there, we had an apartment and stayed for just about a year. I know he illustrated some technical booklets for one of the officers. He was due to go out to sea, and I had gone home with David to my mother in North Carolina, when the war ended. Daws never saw duty afloat."

His two Short Wave cohorts had gone in other military directions: Jack died during the first few months of the war, killed in Borneo while there with a USO troupe. Willard had toured war areas as a member of an acting group, and after his discharge went into banking as an officer in a Denver, Colorado bank. In 1976 Daws recalled, "Willard never really had the desire to make show business a career. He and his wife occasionally appear in amateur theater productions. That satisfies him. He keeps in touch. I stayed in the business, although some of my old reticence had returned and I wasn't at all sure of where I was going."

With the war's end, Daws decided to try his luck at radio, so the new family and his parents piled into the Packard and drove from Geneva,

Illinois to Los Angeles. With no promise of steady employment or even friendly contacts, it was a radical departure, and frightening. Daws' parents were still very supportive with his outlook, and not just emotionally. When they rented their Geneva, Illinois house, Mom and Dad (now living just a few doors down from Daws and Myrtis) had their tenant send his monthly checks directly to Daws. Because radio was a tough nut to crack.

"At that time I had no burning ambition to be an actor," wrote Daws. "I had never done any 'acting'—I was an impersonator. Unknown to myself, I had stored up all the ingredients which were to spell my success in my subsequent career. But being at sixes and sevens, I harkened back to my old penchant for cartooning and tried to sign up for one of the fabulous art schools in Los Angeles, but they were full up. So my dad suggested my taking a course at a radio school, which meant entering a medium I knew very little about. Radio had a few years to go before its comedy and dramatic demise and I got in just before the last rites."

Myrtis recalled that Daws "went to a couple of radio conductor schools to get his foot in the door. One of the first things he worked on was with Jean Hersholt [the *Dr. Christian* program]; it was a story based on the Canadian Dionne Quintuplets. Of course, in those early days you had to have so many radio appearances before you could join the American Federation of Radio Artists (AFRA). It seems like it took *forever* before he got enough to apply."

Daws had wanted to enroll in art school on the G.I. Bill (as voice actor Paul Frees would do), "but the good ones were filled." So, at his father's suggestion, he enrolled in a radio school on the corner of Fairfax Avenue and Wilshire Boulevard and "in no time at all I became quite adept at mike technique, and with the able assistance of a few sensitive instructors, I found that I could now leave my impersonations behind, because I was 'cold reading' scripts I had never seen before. And I was coming up with original characterizations which I instinctively tailored to the demands of the script. I just happened to be a natural at giving 'non-cosmetic' interpretations. Before the term was up, I started going out on auditions for the big programs of the day. I finally landed one and I was signed up with the American Federation of Radio Actors; I had my card and I was ready to make my move.

"I still consider radio the most imaginative of all of the media—a theatre of the mind—and we have allowed it to disintegrate. It was a

Daws Butler, impressionist.

precious time for me, but I am not nostalgic about it. The old radio shows sound hokey to me now, with some exceptions, of course. One show which has stood the test of time, and of which you've probably never heard, was *Vic and Sade*, a daily satire on small town life in Illinois. The writer was Paul Rhymer, one of the writers who has been a tremendous influence on my writing. His dialogue and characterizations were as close to perfection as could possibly be. *Vic and Sade* was a daily fifteen-minute program and the humor was completely unique. I have nothing to compare it with. He was my favorite comedy writer!

"Robert Benchley was another strong influence of mine. Aside from being a complete original in his particular brand of humor and whimsy and social comment, he was a master of concise 'no fat' short pieces which have since become classics, and most of his stuff holds up today.

"Fred Allen was another. He, too, was terse, lyrical and utilized great comedy rhythms which I loved and studied and which molded my own sense of musical dialogue. Records of his shows hold up very well today.

"So I got into radio by the skin of my larynx—because it was terminal as I mentioned above."

Merely a week into school, Daws read for a radio part for the advertising company McCann-Erickson. Neil Reagan, brother of later President Ronald Reagan, gave him the part, which meant everything to him. It was also his first professional radio credit, the aforementioned *Dr. Christian*.

"I think there was more love in radio than any other media. You loved your partner, because between the two of you, you were going to be good. There were no retakes, you just *did* it. It was a living thing. For *that* show you were going to make it the greatest thing you ever did.

"You would get a call, and no matter how small the part was, that would be a credit. That credit would help you get more credits." Unfortunately, Daws wasn't as pushy as he should have been, and consequently didn't gain as much work as he might have had. But working on classic radio shows like *The Whistler* and *Suspense* was quite an ego boost.

One role required a Hispanic voice, which the native Midwesterner could not second guess. Before the show, he drove out to the barrio in LA and spent the whole day listening to voices. Though he mastered the dialect in a short time, when it came to saying the character's name, Pedro, Daws slipped and introduced himself as "Pee-dro," which "blew the whole thing."

Yet for all his hard work, Daws still found it arduous to break into the big programs. "It was difficult at that time to play comedy for Jack Benny or Eddie Cantor or any of the other shows because they wouldn't trust a new comedian. Jack Benny and people like that were scared to death of anybody new! That you might step on laughs. They had to be assured of a great feeling of continuity and discipline in their show."

He wanted to play comedies, but kept finding himself in heavy, dramatic parts. He credited radio as giving him versatility as an actor, and, even more than his stage years, it certainly gave him the stature of Actor, not merely mimic.

Daws began making the rounds to audition for the various radio directors, where his versatile talent was quickly picked up and put to use in that economical genre where an actor wasn't paid by the role or the page. To get an edge over the competition, it helped to have a breadth of characters in your throat. Only those who could consistently play a plethora of parts were called back time and again; unless the voice was distinctive (like Andy Devine) enough to be "worth it" to pay for a single role.

Al Pearce and His Gang was his first national radio show, broadcast on September 13, 1946. "Dawes Butler" puffed up his cheeks for an Edward G. Robinson sound, wanting to take over for the departing sound effects man. "Of course I'm tough. People expect me to be tough. I'm the kind of a guy who gets blamed for everything. Even as a baby they tried to pin things on me!" "Dawes" had a good workout on that show, returning as Fred Allen, Charlie McCarthy, Archie from *Duffy's Tavern*, and Jimmy Durante.

It was while socializing during radio work that Daws met and bonded with a group of friends who would last him a lifetime. While working on *Dr. Christian* and *Dragnet*, he met a young Doug Young. They also did a syndicated Bible story show at the end of the 1940s called *The Hour of St. Francis*.

"We shared the same agent in radio, Miles Auer," said Doug. "In those days producers loved you if you could do double and triple roles, saved hiring other actors. You wouldn't get hired otherwise. Of course, Daws was much more versatile than I. Great impressionist, too. In fact, one of the ways our characters came about was remembering the great character actors from movies. Say, Daws would take W. C. Fields, and not only take his voice, but his attitude, his manner and come about creating a character based on that.

"In CBS studios there was a place where we would hang out in the lobby a lot. There was a phone for the answering service, and a lot of actors would hang out there between going around to different agencies. And we would swap tips and who was looking for what. People would help each other if they could. But when you got into TV and film, it was a hard-nosed situation. I don't know why that was."

To make a good salary in radio, an actor had to take on a lot of work. *Lux Radio Theatre* may have paid $100 for a single episode, but to charac-

ter actors like Doug Young, "It was a fortune! The average show was about $35 or $40 per show."

It was also the day before unions, when directors preferred to take on actors who could walk in and do any dialect, any character, especially for supporting roles. His work as a Wave would pay off for the rest of his life.

Daws: "I then became aware of the theatrical cartoon and as I had a lot of funny and provocative vocal characterizations, I decided to take a crack at that field.

"I dropped in to see a fellow named Johnny Burton who did the casting for Warner Brothers cartoons. I auditioned (ad-libbing all the types of characters I did—writing on my feet, if you will) and he seemed to be favorably impressed, but his approval was dampened when he told me that Mel Blanc did all of their voice work at Warners. Mel was and is a giant in the field, and his product is now classical.

"Johnny Burton suggested that I go to see a fellow named Tex Avery at MGM cartoon studio. On my behalf, he called Tex and put in a good word for me. This is another example of those catalytic people you meet along the way, who, recognizing talent, allow you to take a giant step.

"I called Tex—a cartoon director with exquisite comedy timing—and set up a meeting. I auditioned for him as I had done with Johnny. I entered a little studio theater. It was like a storeroom, with stuff piled all over. He sat in the theater, and I got on mike, bending his ear for a half-hour, sliding from characters to dialects to regionalisms to age variances." Scotch, Irish, cockney, Russian, Polish, Southern, old men, little kids: Daws ad-libbed his larynx off. And Tex was suitably impressed. "He dug me. He booked me for a cartoon voice—a very proper English-type—coming out of an animal, of course.

"This assignment got me my card in the Screen Actors Guild. I was really rolling now and the calls for radio shows were coming in. I did the job for Tex, not even being aware that he was one of the true animation geniuses. (Nothing like starting at the top!)

"I worked for Tex for several years, getting to do all sorts of funny stuff with delicious dialogue. At MGM I also met Bill Hanna and Joe Barbera who were producing the now-classical Tom and Jerry cartoons. They were mute so no voices were called for usually, but they started to call me for incidental speaking characters who appeared occasionally in the Tom and Jerry cartoons. This meeting was providential because I did quite a bit of work at MGM and in 1958 when the studio closed its doors and Bill and Joe formed their own Hanna-Barbera Productions, I was the one they called to head up their new cartoons."

Avery had directed cartoons at Leon Schlesinger Productions (for release by Warner Bros.) from 1935-41, then he moved to MGM, still keeping in touch with his old friends.

Daws' premiere cartoon work had been for Screen Gems' studio in 1946, released in 1948 as *Short Snorts on Sports*. But his first major cartoon role was as the City Wolf in Avery's *Little Rural Riding Hood*, released in 1949. (There was a long gap from initial dialogue recording to the cartoon's final release; Daws had recorded this track in 1947.) For the sophisticated character, Daws used his low-key, close mic-ed impression of British actor George Sanders. The voice of Goofy, Pinto Colvig, was the Country Wolf while Colleen Collins portrayed the title role. Red was featured in a number of Avery's MGM shorts, including *The Shooting of Dan McGoo, Red Hot Riding Hood, Swingshift Cinderella,* and *Uncle Tom's Cabana.* She was pure sexual excitement, driving the wolf into an eye-popping, tongue-unraveling frenzy at her mere appearance. In the 1988 film, *Who Framed Roger Rabbit*, the character of Jessica Rabbit was based on Red.

Possibly Avery's favorite vocal candy he extracted from the veteran radio actor was Daws' Southern voice. He tried for a year to come up with a suitable character to complement that drawling sound, but no permanent character emerged until he used the voice for the dog Reddy for Hanna-Barbera beginning in 1957. The voice eventually lent itself to one of Daws' most successful and enduring characters—-Huckleberry Hound.

"Tex was a marvelous guy to learn the business with," Daws told interviewer Milt Gray. "He was the first brilliant director I ever worked for, and he's such a fussy man. It was so beautiful the way it used to be. Like, Tex would call me out, and he'd say, 'This is the character,' then you'd go over and do it. You didn't have 30 people to audition with to get the part." At a time when everyone was afraid of wasting film and tape, Tex would rehearse and rehearse and Rehearse and REHEARSE the parts until Daws found himself virtually voiceless. The trouble was, Tex Avery loved yells. And to do these over and over *and* over required the stamina of an opera singer.

"A yell is a yell, and I do pretty good yells, but he would have me do about eight of these, then he would say, 'Gee, that's close.' Then he'd say, 'Well, let's lay one down,' then we'd do it on the film. Then he would always throw in a couple himself, just for protection."

The Wolf usually menaced poor, flat-faced Droopy, a deadpan character originally vocally-created by Bill Thompson (who had originated the character as Wallace Whimple on the *Fibber McGee and Molly* radio program). When Thompson was out of town or otherwise unavailable, the little dog had to be recast. Tex asked Daws if he'd like to give it a try. Puffing up his cheeks, he could approximate the sound, but Daws was never completely happy with the imitation. Instead, he suggested a better substitute. Don Messick.

Years later, Daws recalled that the most important thing he learned from Tex Avery was that you laugh at the timing of the gag, not necessarily the gag itself. It was a trick that kept Blake Edwards popular for years. "You can see the gag coming," said Daws, "but it's the anticipation of it, the set up, that really makes it hilarious. Tex was a master at that." He worked for Avery for three or four years on 15 to 20 cartoons.

Then in 1947, Daws began working for Armed Forces Radio. Marty Halperin, one of three people brought in to set up AFR's own first recording room, remembered those days. "We were sort of running in the dark and learning it as we went. A lot of the recording was done at other places like Radio Recorders, Western Recorders, United, and Universal Recorders. They did all the assembly. We had to delete all the commercials on all the programs that went out from AFR, because the government cannot endorse a product. Any mention of a date had to come out. This was before tape, so we were using discs to do editing. By the time everything was edited out of the show, it took 6 weeks between the time the show went on the air and the time it went overseas. Therefore, holiday programs were delayed for one year.

"One of the shows we worked on was *Let's Pretend*. By the time we took out the Cream of Wheat commercials and things like that, it was down to 25 minutes roughly. So we had to do something for the other 5 minutes. We would put out the 25-minute version, but for the AFR radio stations overseas, they had to fill in with another 5 minutes. So we came out with a lot of 5-minute programs. One was tagged onto the end of *Let's Pretend*, voiced by Daws and Marian Richman, another wonderful voice person. It was written by a producer at AFR and they would do all the parts."

Halperin agreed with Daws' assessment of radio workers. "Radio people are just so wonderful because it was like a family. If the actors were too busy, they call a friend and say, look, I can't do this role, why don't you go try for it? That doesn't happen in television."

Though the Golden Age of radio basically died out at the end of the 1940s when television was cutting deeply into sponsors' interest, radio was to remain Daws' favorite medium, and he would never give it up.

1947 was also the year he met longtime vocal collaborator Don Messick, who recalled the meeting to interviewer Craig Fuqua.

"When I got discharged at Fort XXXX Lewis, I returned to Southern California and made contact with some other Army buddies, and I just started making the rounds. Sometimes doing the ventriloquist act, eventually getting into a workshop for ex-G.I.s who were professional radio people — acting, writing, announcers and so forth, and that's where I first met Daws Butler. He had done some theatrical cartoons, particularly for

Tex Avery at MGM. We became the best of friends from that time on, from early 1947 on. We eventually worked together on one thing and another, long before we ever did any cartoon work together.

"Daws and I produced a little play, *Night Must Fall*, for my local church in West Hollywood. First, he was directing it and then I had a change of cast. I fired the the lady who was doing Mrs. Branson—she was disturbing the cast by being totally amused by her husband, who was also performing. So I let them both go, not that it made any difference because they weren't getting paid anything. We were debating, 'What are we going to do now? Who's going to play Mrs. Branson?' And a mutual friend of ours, an actress, a lady that was a good friend of Daws', she was in the cast and she says, 'Daws, why don't you do it?' We were out having a drink after that particular evening, and wondering what to do about the cast. And he said, 'Well, maybe I could.' So, we got a lady's gray-haired wig

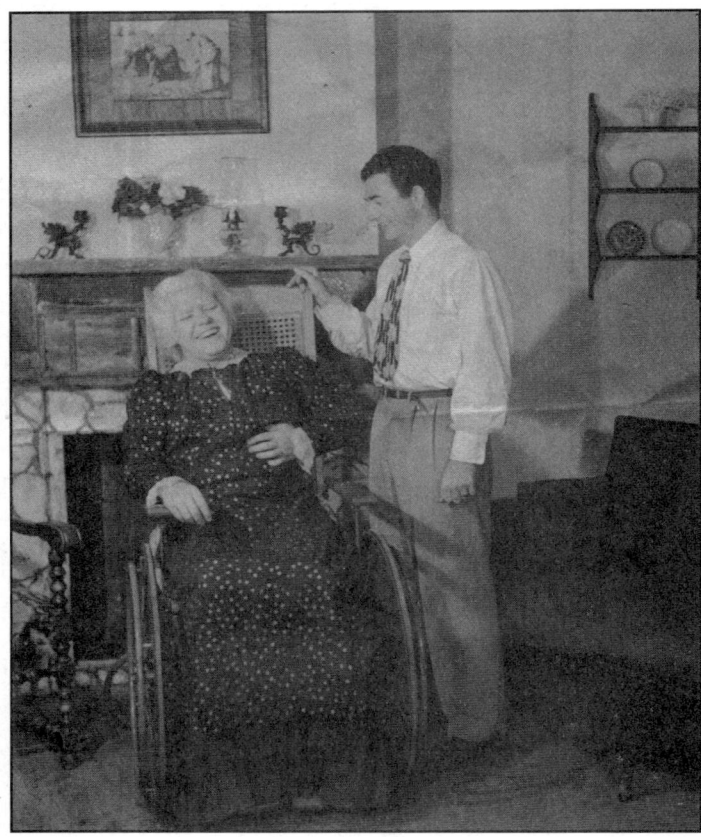

Daws (in drag) and Don Messick.

from Max Factor. He got an old-fashioned dress. This was in the sort of Dame May Whitty mode, because she had done it in the film, and I think also on the stage. Until the curtain call, nobody knew that it was a man playing Mrs. Branson.

"It's actually due to Daws that I got my Screen Actors Guild card because he recommended me to MGM and Tex Avery. They were looking for somebody to do the Droopy character voice and Daws knew I did that kind of voice. Apparently, Bill Thompson was unavailable at that time, but he was still living. So anyway, I did Droopy on a couple of theatricals at MGM and that was the first thing that entitled me to become a full-fledged member of Screen Actors Guild. All due to Daws' recommendation. From then on, we continued to be the closest of friends."

As Daws stated, through Avery, Daws met Bill Hanna and Joe Barbera around 1946 at MGM. The Oscar-winning cartoon team used Daws for a few incidental voices on Tom and Jerry cartoons. They would use him on the odd Tom and Jerry cartoon that needed the voice of "legs" for a man (just as Lillian Randolph of *The Great Gildersleeve* fame would appear as the maid with "big feet"). "'Now, Tom, I want you to take care of the house while I'm gone...' – little things like that, they used to do. But they became aware of me," Daws said. He also worked on a *Spike and Tyke* cartoon, another Hanna-Barbera creation for MGM.

In the late 1940s, Daws worked on Paramount's *Speaking of Animals* shorts, in which live animals talked through the magic of animated mouths. One of the entries Daws can be heard in is *Going Hollywood*. It was during this time that he met lifelong friend and co-worker, voice actress June Foray. Although Tex Avery created *Speaking of Animals* in 1941, Daws did not meet him at that time. Avery was working at Warner Brothers in 1941 when producer Leon Schlesinger insisted on changing the ending of Avery's 1941 Bugs Bunny cartoon *Heckling Hare*. Tex left Warners in protest and developed the *Speaking of Animals* series at Paramount, in collaboration Jerry Fairbanks and Bob Carlysle, before moving to MGM in 1942, where for the next twelve years he would turn out his greatest work. Satirist Stan Freberg also worked on the series in the late 40s, by then solely produced by Fairbanks, but Stan and Daws would not team up to make history until several years later.

June, Daws, Mel Blanc and Stan also separately worked for Capitol Records, voicing children's records. It was June's work on these that caught Walt Disney's eye, securing her a lengthy contract for his studio. Daws, with few exceptions, was never able to find much work in Disney's corner of animation. Lucky for Hanna-Barbera.

Daws' kiddie recordings were sometimes lavish, sometimes simple productions that taught morals through an aura of innocence. In "Peppy Possum," over music, Daws facilely narrates, "In the forests of the South lives a quiet, friendly little animal with a sharp nose and a long tail called a possum." He sings "I'm a little possum who won't play possum" which concerns his poor Pappy. He's caught by the dog Major, but pretends to fall asleep so Major has to fetch water to wake him up. Peppy escapes and sings his little song, realizing that "a possum's gotta do what a possum's gotta do."

On "Hiawatha," Daws begins by singing, "I'm a little Indian, ugh, that's me," in a non-Elroy kid's voice. Narrated by Jack Benny's announcer, Don Wilson, it was a cute, straightforward musical morality piece about being kind to animals. The flip side contained "Bongo the Bear," also narrated by Don Wilson. Daws sings in a smaller voice as the performing bear at the circus. "I stand on my head, you heard what I said, I'm Bongo the Circus Bear." Bongo runs away into the woods to try to be a "regular" bear and finds and fights for a girlfriend. It also ends on a song.

Recorded for the Teletalkie (an audio Viewmaster-type toy), "Tomcat" gave Daws an older character for a change, as Grandpa Tomcat, narrating a tale of why kittens shouldn't be curious, to his grandson, much in the style of Daws' own later Uncle Dunkle writings. He also sings "Curiosity" at the start and end. "Tomcat" was also released as a record, and retitled "Casper the Curious Kitten."

The adorable but simple orchestral arrangements of his songs as "Inky" put Daws at his sweetest, in a voice near Beany. "Lucky Pin" and the rather adult-humored "I'd Rather Be Anything Than You" were both pleasant pop songs.

Once Daws began to establish himself as a top voice man for cartoons and albums, offers trickled in. One interesting sideline that came to pass was the "talking comic book" that pulp fiction writer Robert Leslie Bellem wanted to get going. The 46-year-old author from Pasadena needed a change from the lagging sales of his prolific blood an' guts novels and jumped on the passing bandwagon of increasing comic book sales. Bellem wrote and edited the tales, but in order to combat the growing competition in the marketplace, he came up with the talking comic book. "Then the kids can listen to the story and learn to read at the same time," the author said in an interview.

He lined up a small staff, including composer/director Frank Hubbell, cartoonist Mel Millar and other artists, and voice actors Daws Butler and Marian Richman (who was great at hyena laughs). The idea was a hit, winning praises from *Parents* magazine and parent-teacher groups which requested records for use in classrooms. *The Los Angeles Times* ran several articles on the hit notion. Daws helped with the scripts while Bellem's partner and owner of a record pressing company in Pasadena, Larry Mead, handled the impressive distribution of 200,000 records a month. They boasted countrywide distribution and that "they're selling like hotcakes." Mead's plant had seven presses running, employing about a dozen people.

Daws did at least three of these records: "Chripy Cricket" (story by Frank Bonham, adapted and produced by Bob Bellem, told by Daws Butler and Tip Corning, with music by Frank Hubbell & his Orchestra), "Flying Turtle" (told by the Authors, Daws Butler and Marian Richman. Adapted and produced by Bob Bellem, music by Robert Mitchell, "screamingly funny sound effects" by Ray Erlenborn), and "Sleepy Santa" (story, songs and production by Bob Bellem, told by Daws Butler and Marian Richman, music by Robert Mitchell, and sound effects by Ray Erlenborn). The 10-inch "Flex-O Disc" records came in bright four-color envelopes, with simplified piano arrangements and a full-sized KOMIC BOOK in four brilliant or "glowing colors." Price, 98 cents, postage-paid.

"Sleepy Santa" was possibly the last work that Daws did for Talking Komics. The Christmas record contained some fun musical numbers, such as "Lonesome Octopus," about the octopus who lived in a lake rather than the sea, "Grumpy Shark," "Happy Grasshopper," and "Chirpy Cricket" (the latter full of square dance music).

In 1948 Daws was a part of the audition show of *The Hawthorne Thing* for ABC. "The Mutual Network prevents *The Hawthorne Thing*, so ABC, the American Broadcasting Company presents ...!" (Trumpeted music!) "Me, for half an hour," states Jim Hawthorne modestly. Recorded before a live audience, with Ike Carpenter's orchestra, comic Mickey Katz and singer Lee Leslie, the show had an irreverent absurdity to it that was reminiscent of *The Goon Show*'s jokey, punchy, rule-breaking comedy. Sometimes the set-ups for jokes had nothing to do with the punch lines, which, in absurdity, made it funny. When Hawthorne held his stringed Hogantwanger up to the microphone to show the audience and related his actions in his Jack Benny-style delivery, Lee laughed and asked, "What's

that got to do with being a mother?" Wild, eclectic comedy may have eventually turned *The Goon Show* into a national British institution, but the plot-less *Hawthorne Thing* was obviously too far out for American audiences and was never picked up as a series during radio's final years.

Daws also took part in the audition show of a very popular, breezy crime drama starring Dick Powell. The first *Yours Truly, Johnny Dollar* episode was entitled, "The Milford Brooks, III Matter" and was broadcast on December 6, 1948. The fast-talkin', wise-quippin' insurance investigator Johnny Dollar (Dick Powell) was an adventurous, cleverly written hard-boiled detective series. Daws Butler, Joseph Kearns, and Betty Lou Gerson as "Butter" supported the tough Dick on his quest through a case that racked up a mean expense account. Milford Brooks the 3rd wanted to commit suicide so his special $2 million life insurance policy would pay off to the beneficiary: a certain notorious gangster to whom Milford owed money. But the title character was the real baddy, trying to frame him for his own death. Johnny figured it out all right, spewing priceless lines in the process like "Don't pop your corn" and "Ah, that kid's liquor sure can hold him."

As radio and cartoon work continued, and gained pace, it was only inevitable that Daws should find himself with a series, on that new *other* box: television. Yes, it was *Time for Beany*.

Chapter 3
"Gentlemen," Einstein said, "it's *Time for Beany*"

Master cartoonist Bob Clampett began his illustrious career in the Warner Brother cartoon department in the 1930s, led by top directors Hugh Harman and Rudolf Ising. As he gained more power as a respected artist and gag man, he would become a top animator just a few years later; highly motivated, as many were, by Tex Avery's manic brand of comedy. Clampett's almost surreal style made his animated antics easy to spot, such as *Porky in Wackyland* (1938) and Daffy Duck's dream-induced Dick Tracy spoof, *The Great Piggy Bank Robbery* (1946). Clampett and Avery developed the intense, loony Daffy together, while Clampett alone is credited for Tweety Bird's creation. In May 1945, Clampett stepped away from Warners (although his final cartoons were completed and released into '46) to develop his own ideas, the most famous of which involved a seasick sea serpent.

"After seeing the silent movie *The Lost World*," recalled Bob Clampett on the commentary from the *Time for Beany* DVD, "I did up sketches of the serpent, which led to my aunt helping to make a puppet of the character. After seeing the advent of television in 1935, two years later I started my own studio, but Warners, to whom I was still under contract, had first refusal on anything I did. It was in this little garage studio that I first began developing the Beany and Cecil idea. When I'd completed the package, Leon [Schlesinger] thought it was clever but had no interest in doing anything besides cartoons, so I had to go out and find buyers. There was very little money in TV at the time, but in 1948 I got an offer from the newly-opened Channel 9 [in Los Angeles] to do a show for a year. The next year, I sold *Beany* to Paramount television. They wanted a show for kids.

"I saw a little Jewish boy wearing a skull cap and I began to sketch him. For some reason, I put the propeller on top. I don't remember if there was such a thing as a beanie before that or not. I had difficulty in interesting people in puppets, and the beanie cap. They thought the cap was a little too radical."

Clampett was careful to design the puppets so that they wouldn't be frightening to kids. He wanted Beany to transcend the origin of Punch and Judy shows, into something modern children – and their parents, hopefully – could embrace in the new medium of TV. At the time, the creator stated, "It breaks down the barriers of the puppet stage, yet it has all the scope of the movie."

He had wanted his wife, Sody, to create the original Cecil puppet, but as Clampett stated in an interview, since she "would take a little while to get the final Cecil puppet finished, Daws mentioned that his wife could make a simple sock puppet to use for rehearsals. She did a great job, it looked good enough to use on the air." And it was.

Myrtis explained that she made the first Cecil puppet "from a stretch-type toweling patterned from the foot of Dr. Denton's sleep wear the boys were wearing, that I had purchased on Staten Island, at one of the first 'yard sales' I ever attended… it just happened to be flexible enough for use. Our sons, David and Donald, were wearing Dr. Denton's sleeping garments with enclosed feet. I used that as a model for it. The nostrils were suction cups we had to hold a line for hanging items to dry… the eyelids were felt cut as eyelashes. It was made just to use until something else could be devised, but when Stan manipulated it… nothing else was needed."

Bob Clampett, Jr.: "Dad, while he was pitching the show, was basically writing the first script, and would get feedback from the performers and work that in. Then a few months later Charlie Shows came in. My understanding is that the show got picked up so quickly, they were writing scripts from that core group right from the get go."

"For the CBS audition," said Clampett, "I had a little show prepared with three sets. First, the Explorer's Club with Beany and Uncle Captain, setting up the adventure to the Lost Land. Second was Huffenpuff's ship on an ocean scene, then a jungle set with a professional guy in a gorilla suit. But then I decided that rather than do too much, I'd do one bit really well—a very dramatic ocean scene, with my best gags. The network executives came to my garage theater. After the five-minute bit, Klaus Landesberg from Paramount wanted me to go on the following Monday."

Satirist Stan Freberg recalled the origin of his award-winning work in interviews with Joe Bevilacqua and also his *Beany* DVD commentary:

"Daws Butler and I met through Bob Clampett who had an idea for a children's puppet show about a little boy who sailed around the world with his uncle, Captain Huffenpuff. But he didn't know where they'd go or how he wanted to do it, except that he wanted to do it with puppets. Quite frankly, he wanted to do a West coast version of *Kukla, Fran and Ollie*, and even went so far as to have a woman singing like Fran Allison did, at a piano. It was Daws and I who talked Clampett into making it into an adventure with moving sets. That show became *Time for Beany*."

In his 1988 autobiography, *It Only Hurts When I Laugh*, Freberg wrote, "I was born on August 7 between the NBC chimes and a Rinso commercial, which makes me a Leo, with Lever Brothers as my rising sign." Actually, Stan Freberg was born of Swedish descent on August 7, 1926 in Blaine, Washington. He won scholarships to Redlands University and Stanford because of his speech championships, and quickly got into Warner Broth-

Daws, Stan Freberg and Daws' agent Miles Auer.

ers cartoons where he met Bob Clampett, Chuck Jones and Friz Freleng after auditioning with funny voices and impressions of FDR, Jimmy Durante, among others. At Warners, he worked with Mel Blanc a lot, but as Mel was the only one ever to receive screen credit, it's difficult to say just what roles he took on (though he was one of the two polite Goofy Gophers in several cartoons, as well as the Lenny-type character in *Cat-Tails for Two* [1953], and others).

Stan's first radio show was *Coffee Time at Harmony Homestead* where Merle Travis and Tennessee Ernie Ford (also announcer) appeared in the band. Other radio shows included Jack Benny, *The Henry Morgan Show*, and *CBS Radio Workshop*. Stan's radio heroes were Fred Allen and Vic and Sade, so he and Daws shared a sense of humor. Perhaps it was the odd, acquired taste of Vic and Sade's dialogue which indicated an early like-mindedness between the two veteran voice actors.

"So Daws and I were brought in basically as voice people and after the first couple days of doing the voices and looking at the puppets we said to Clampett, 'Where are the puppeteers?' And Clampett said, 'You're the puppeteers.' This came as news to Daws and I who had never worked puppets in our lives but we shrugged and I said to Daws, 'It's called on the job training.' Next thing we knew we were holding up these puppets and doing the voices and the writing. So Clampett managed to pull us together and it was the start of a long and terrific association."

Daws explained the series thusly: "I fell into a TV children's show which ran for five years, done 'live,' of course. It was syndicated, via kinescope (an early television technique of photographing the TV image on film) and made available for nationwide distribution. The visual quality was poor and the show was really a West-coast triumph: very popular. Stan Freberg and I did all the characters. We won three Emmys [for Best Children's Program, 1949, 1950, 1952; also a Peabody award and other honors; the American Junior Red Cross even awarded *Beany* a patch for distinguished service], and the very sharp, adult-type dialogue was written by Charles Shows and Lloyd Turner. It was directed to kids but was so sophisticated that we had a large adult following as well.

"Stan and I ad-libbed our heads off and with the creamy material we had to work with, it was an exciting show to do, side by side, for five years, five shows a week, fifteen minutes each. We became each other's comedy university—we did every schtick in the book! Stan's humor had more of a bite to it; mine was rather subtle and fey (as the Irish put it), and we

Daws and the Emmy.

rubbed off on each other and learned from each other; it was a fulfilling collaboration."

"At first we thought it was the worst kind of casting," said Freberg, "to cast a six-foot man, myself, next to a five-foot man, Daws Butler, who would have to hold their puppets up into the scene. It was murder! But it turned out to be one of the most *brilliant* jobs of casting in the history of television. Daws and I were like a well-oiled machine once the show got going. Daws at one point was pulling tendons in his arms from reaching up into the scene, and I developed a slumped back. To this day people are telling me, 'Stand up, Stan.' Through the earphones I kept hearing the people in the booth yell, 'Keep your head down, we can see your head!'"

Once Klaus suggested digging a trench that Stan could walk in, which Daws thought a good idea, but Stan did not, so Daws came up with the idea of buying a pair of paratrooper boots, then went to a shoemaker and had him build up the shoes into something that looked like the ones Elton John wore in *Tommy*. Finally Daws was looking into Stan's face! Daws had to wear what he called those "Frankenstein shoes" for the run of the series. He *hated* those damn shoes with the 6-inch soles.

Freberg: "We rehearsed four hours every day, sometimes five. We were dripping wet by the time we went on the air, so we had to go in a kind of decompression chamber afterward or else we'd get pneumonia when we went out into the night air after the show. We would sit in Oblath's Café across from Paramount to cool off from hot lights and write the script on a portable typewriter and legal pads. Sometimes we sat in a parked car that nobody was using at the time and ran people's batteries down by turning on the ceiling light and typing up the scripts. When a guy would come close to the car and ask, 'Hey, what are you guys doing in my car?' Bob Clampett would say, 'Oh, I thought Warren Foster had this car.' Foster was a writer for Warner Brothers' cartoons. He'd apologize and we'd get out, but the car owner just couldn't believe it. Finally, we got an office and after that we'd go home, get a few hours sleep then come back and do the whole thing over again the next day. But it was the Golden Age of television.

"We devised this system whereby the sets would be held up with C clamps, so that while the camera was over on the left shooting, the stage hands are unloosing the C clamps, taking down the scene to the right which is off camera now, and putting a whole new scene up in a matter of ten or twelve seconds. Then we would rush out of the scene on the left into the one on the right, then they'd repeat the dismantling. Normally, it would all be nailed up with nails, but you didn't want to hear all that noise on the air because we were *live*, man.

"Daws and I were on that show, together every afternoon and night, five days a week, 52 weeks a year, for five years. I learned from Daws how to be a better actor. It wasn't just a matter of doing the voices but getting into the character itself and really being that character... very much like the Actor's Studio kind of thing where you really *become* that character. That sounds kind of ridiculous to think that you could do that not as an actor standing on stage but as actor talking up through your arm into the puppet itself and having that puppet become the character that you're

Daws & Stan - live!

doing down below out of the sight of the cameras. Even to this day whenever I do a voice, whenever I act, there's fragments in what I do just automatically from what I learned from Daws Butler. He was the greatest voice magician I've ever worked with."

Daws' own thoughts about the Beany and Cecil characters were that the love and their touching was very important. He considered it to be a *positive* show, especially as talk of television violence continued on the upswing. To Daws, the feature quality of *Time for Beany* was the relationship between Beany and Cecil, a boy and his "dog." He found the innocence marvelous, something he would acutely miss in later children's entertainment.

The series premiered on February 28, 1949 and contained the same animated puppet magic that would make *Sesame Street* and *The Muppet Show* such megahits.

The rigorous schedule of writing required additional writers later: Lloyd Turner and the future voice of Bullwinkle J. Moose himself, Bill Scott. Bill Oberlin, Clampett's old Warner Bros. buddy, created the often-complimented sets and served as art and stage director. Oberlin admitted that everyone on the crew would chip in with voices from time to time and contribute to the script. KTLA cameramen included Gordon Minter, Jimmy Morris and Lloyd Bockaus. Maurice Levy, Jr., a longtime associate of Clampett's, functioned as the show's personal business representative.

Another *Beany* cohort was proficient voice man Walker Edmiston. "I started with Daws on *Time for Beany* in 1949. Freberg resented me greatly. Stan and Daws had been on for eight weeks or so and Clampett needed somebody else, he needed more people. They gave me one of Freberg's characters to do, Clowny, but then I ended up doing Mouth Fulla Teeth Keith, the Lion and Clowny. Freberg and Clampett did not get along and Stan gave him static all the time. So Clampett wanted it covered so that I could match Cecil almost dead-on with Freberg's voice. So when Freberg didn't show up or something, I would do Cecil on the show. And he still resents that to this day. I covered for him quite a bit. Finally when he left, I took over Cecil, but I was doing several of the other characters, like the Wolf.

"Clampett had this stand built that was about four feet high upon which was his director's chair, with a little ladder to climb up. It was a logical idea for him to look straight at the puppets instead of looking up at them."

Things did not always go swimmingly, however. In *Close Shave Cave*, Stan was puppeteering Fat Bat, the guard of the entrance, which was actually a balloon. Fat Bat was supposed to take some diet pills from Beany so they could reduce Bat and get him out of the cave. The air was supposed to have been let out of the balloon, but the lights had melted the Bat's balloon airway together, and blew up. BLAM! Pieces of the Bat landed everywhere, including on Beany's beanie and Cecil's face. Daws instantly adlibbed, "There goes a good kid." The PTA, mothers, and teachers wrote in to vent their horrified outrage: "You don't blow up animals on the air!"

"Bob Clampett was a very interesting character," said Freberg. "He thought in terms of animation, and that's why this action-adventure show had that quality about it. He would come out with his famous yellow legal pad at the end of every show with all these notes for us. He was very good at creating

Jerry Lewis, Stan, Daws, Bob Clampett, Beany and Dean Martin.

weird adventures for the characters. The best thing he did was to bring Daws and I together. It was one of the great marriages of early television."

He told Clampett that some conflict was needed in the story, so thinking about a car dealer in Glendale, CA called Honest John ("who was *not*"), Stan suggested "Dishonest John."

"Everyone from bus drivers to movie stars was a fan. I met Lana Turner at a party once who said, 'Oh! You're the voice and arm of Cecil the Sea Serpent. Oh, I see you every night.' Lana Turner? I couldn't believe it. She watched because of her children, of course. We were responsible for selling more television sets than anyone else I can think of."

Lionel Barrymore was a great fan of *Beany* and would race back home to watch, allegedly sometimes stopping at a nearby house if he couldn't make it home in time so his chauffeur could watch with the family and report to Barrymore, waiting in the car, what happened.

A scientist at Cal-Tech told of Einstein leaving a jet propulsion meeting. He looked at his pocketwatch, said, "Gentlemen, you will have to excuse me. It is time for *Beany*," and shuffled off to his little apartment.

In the book *Harpo Speaks*, Harpo Marx's son, William, wrote of his dad: "He was an unabashed fan, a worshipper of excellence in sports, the arts, literature. But his all-time favorite was… *Time for Beany*. If any one of us dared break into the den while Dad was watching Beany and Cecil, we got grounded. Certain areas of our father's domain were unalterably sacred."

Groucho Marx also once wrote a fan letter, which was then printed in a newspaper: "*Beany* is one of the few things I watch on TV, and it's a must with daughter Melinda."

In 1993, Frank Zappa told *TV Guide* that his favorite show was *Beany*.

The first newspaper mention of *Beany* came on February 16, 1949 in California's "The Gadabout" column, simply stating "Daws Butler, Stan Freberg and Bob Clampett's preview of their original 'Huffenpuff' puppet show (for video ONLY)…" The first TV listing came in the *Daily News* of Monday, February 28, 1949, on KTLA Channel 5 (part of the Paramount Television Network) at 6:30 p.m., sandwiched in between *Telescout Club* (another children's show) and *Shopping at Home*.

One episode of what was known as *The Huffenpuff Show* had a rather short script, comprising of

Characters
Cookie the Clown   Beanie
Captain Huffenpuff   Cecil
Cecelia   Voice Chorus
Announcer

Songs
The Huffenpuff Song (Blow the Man Down, in D flat)
Sailing, Sailing (in E flat)
Gargle Song and Blue Danube (B flat minor/ D flat)
Miss My Mammy (Camptown Races) (B flat)

Sets
On board ship
Stage front

Props
Lightning
Lightning flasher
Bass viol

Sound Effects
Wind
Chicken laying egg
Stormy wind and thunder
Water gargling for Cecil's goodbye
String bass
Brake screech

    The show began with letters appearing and a Voice Chorus singing "H U F F E N P U F F! Huffenpuff!" The announcer then cheerily announced, "Yessiree, this is the Huffenpuff Show starring Daws Butler with Stan Free [sic] and Nancy Martin," and introduced Cookie the Clown as emcee. Cookie introduced his little shipmate, Beanie, to the Chorus, then Beanie's uncle, the fearless big-game hunter, Captain Huffenpuff. Cookie announced that they were all going to sail to Africa to make a million dollars. But first they had to get past the biggest, most ferocious bear in the world – the Horrible Honey Bear. If they can do that, they'll lay claim to his bubblegum mine, teaming with enough honey-flavored bubblegum to make a bubble as big as the moon.
    They cast off as the Captain sings his pleasure with a "Yo Ho and a bubble of gum." He continues various verses so much that Beany can't get a word in. For dinner they're all having cookies and a fried egg. The Captain calls for thirty-two pounds of air pressure in the sails and regales Beany with false tales of his fighting exploits. When being struck by light-

ning for his fibs threatens, the Captain goes below, leaving Beany free to stroll the deck singing "Sailing, Sailing." After a few choruses, Beany spots a hiccuping Cecil, the Sea Sick Sea Serpent. Beany suggests holding his breath and humming to get rid of the annoying hiccups, which turns into a hiccup & gargle version of "The Blue Danube." The Captain arrives too late to meet the sickly serpent, and claims there was no such thing. Lightning doesn't strike, proving it. When Captain orders Beany to wipe that smile off his face, he sounds just like Capt. Bligh. "I didn't know you could do impersonations," the little nephew says. That's a good cue for the Captain going into his Jolson impression, singing "Miss My Mammy." Thunder, lightning and boat rocking stops the song.

The Lena keeps sailing toward the LaBrea Tar Pits, hoping to capture the two-headed Freep, the last living species of prehistoric origin, with the aid of the Captain's Freep Map.

(Thousands of kids sent in drawings of what they thought the Freep would look like in eager anticipation. Parents and kids alike loved the series. One local housewife phoned the station to say her husband didn't want to leave town if he was going to miss the unveiling of the Freep, so she inquired about the next week's stories.

Parents were especially proud of the way Beany always handled himself and the situations he encountered, marking his conduct down to one of positive reinforcement, good fellowship and proper moral conduct! Its lack of comic brutality, a la Bugs Bunny and clan, was also constantly applauded.)

Sailing ever further, our gang of heroes continued on for the elusive two-headed Freep ... meeting the hazards of Boo-Hoo Bay and Lake Ha-Ho (bordered by the giggly Laughing Grass) and into the infamous Straits of Jacket. Cecil was dense, but if he had trouble with a question, sometimes he would visit his friend, psychiatrist Smarty Pants the frog, otherwise known as "the Brain." Other painfully puny characters included Hopalong Wong the Chinese cook, Clowny the clown, Crowy the crow, Tear-Along the Dotted Lion, the invisible (save for umbrella) Mr. Nobody, Flush Garden, Ping Pong the giant ape (containing either George Barris, Walker Edmiston or Bill Oberlin in a giant ape costume), the Jimmy Durante-sounding Inca Dinca Doo Bird, Dizzy Lou and Dizzy Too (punning Desilu Studios), and Moon Mad Tiger (voiced by "ah, yes!" Jerry Colonna). Celebrities such as Jerry Lewis, Liberace and Spike Jones also made onscreen guest appearances.

Stories were written so that kids would have to tune in the next day to see what happened next. Episode 50, which aired on November 8, 1949, contin-

"Gentlemen," Einstein said, "it's *Time for Beany*"

Beany, the Captain and Daws.

ued the storyline of trying to raise the sunken Leakin' Lena. Beany gets no help from Cecil who, suffering from a blow on the head, thinks he's Christopher Columbus. A passing hammerhead shark gives him another bang on the head, but it only helps the sea serpent remember that he's really Hopalong Cassidy. Beany overcomes his shyness to hit Cecil on the head again, but when asked to lay his head on the ship and relax, Cecil asks, "But would Hopalong Cassidy do a thing like this?" "I don't know," answers Beany, "but let's stretch a point and lay yer head down." He's fine! But in wanting to wreak revenge against that shark, he's banged on the noggin again, and in the final moment of the episode, confesses to being Bugs Bunny.

Later, in episode 281 (September 27, 1950), Beany and the gang are in Washington where Cecil sees an "Uncle Sam Wants You" poster and signs up at the F.I.B. to be Professor X's bodyguard. X is given a million dollars and 98 cents expense money for his "very secret mission" at Lookout Island, which Dishonest John attempts to steal with his hand-cranked sheep counting machine. Though he puts X out with it, luckily Cecil arrives and can't count beyond three, so it's John who counts for him and slumbers before he can make off with the black bag full of cash.

The 15-minute program was aired five times a week, live, and recorded by Paramount Video Transcription System, with 35mm and 16mm safety film prints available for distribution to other stations.

The series was a hit, preceded by two short kiddie programs: *Cowboy Slim* (6-6:20 p.m.) and *Telescout Club* (6:20-6:30 p.m.), all broadcast five days a week. The kids considered Beany and the other characters as real people. In April of 1949, there was a contest for the best pictures of the characters drawn by children. The PRIZE: a Freep gun! Even though they hadn't seen the Crow in the crow's nest, pictures of what kids thought he looked like were even sent in.

In the May 1, 1949 "Reviewing TV" column of *Hollywood Radio-Television Topics*, the six-week-old *Beany* was heralded for its "humor, sharp characterization and more nobility than most other shows of this type." Again Daws was named as the "well-known vaudeville and radio entertainer" before the lesser-known Freberg. A magazine article of June 10, 1949 listed the eighteen most popular shows for children. Beany came in at number two, just after Shirley Dinsdale's *Judy Splinters*, who also worked with a puppet, on station KNBH.

Meantime, Klaus Landesberg had been pitching his shows for syndication and East coast showings. *Movietown, RSVP, The Spade Cooley Program, Meet Me in Hollywood* and *Time for Beany* were all under heavy consideration as early as May 26, 1949.

At the four Broadway stores in southern California a child could plunk his $3.95 down and get himself his very own Beany puppet, or use the coupon in the newspaper and send away for one. "He's that little guy who winks, sticks his tongue out, laughs, looks embarrassed, plays pat-a-cake—depending on how you wiggle your fingers inside of him! He's a PUPPET, made of Lastic-Plastic. Everybody loves him!"

As time marched on through the summer of '49 *Beany* began picking up articles in magazines and promotional tools like magnetism. As of December 6, 1949, *Beany* (which somewhere underwent a spelling change from Beanie to Beany) was still a top-ranked local show. In a new poll, Milton Berle was on top, while Beany came in at #6, just ahead of Ed Wynn, and three ahead of *Yer Ol' Buddy*. And in the Tele-Views program poll (collecting 29,168 individual votes), *Time for Beany* claimed the #1 spots in the Hollywood and Combine Coast-To-Coast polls. While in *The Big Time*, another local magazine, *Beany* just made the top ten, right after Wrestling on the selfsame KTLA station. It was the Howdy Doody equivalent for the West coast.

The Hooper rating (measuring Los Angeles audiences) was even more astounding. It gave the show a 3.7 rating, which was the equivalent to a TV or Telerating of 39.6%, and indicated that *Beany* was claiming a 10.7% share of the combine radio-TV audience. Considering it was battling against seven other multi-weekly children's shows programmed by the five other Los Angeles TV stations, this was high praise indeed. Soon the fever spread, and *Beany* was seen in Dallas, Chicago, Tulsa, and San Francisco. Of the many celebrities who were captivated, *The Los Angeles Times* quoted Lana Turner and Bob Topping (married at the time) as speaking to no one while *Time for Beany* was on. "They go into hysterics over Cecil."

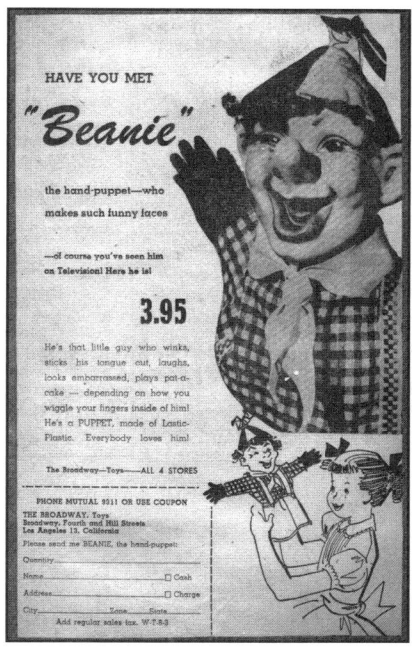

"The show was fun for the whole family," Stan said, "but it was also terrifying. This was the ground floor of television, under extremely hot lights. In fact, on one show, one of the characters actually melted on my hand! I had third-degree burns!

"The audience could sense that these were sweet characters. Cecil wouldn't hurt a flea. Beany boy loved his Uncle. The characters were good role models for other sea serpents watching the show.

"Two or three months after the show started, Charlie Shows, this wonderful writer I'd known from Paramount, began writing for us. Around those scripts Daws and I ad-libbed, constantly. The humor was just lapped up by everyone who watched it. Charlie also got us into some great adventures, all around the world. In one show, we might be in the Sahara Desert, and the next scene we might be at the North Pole, and after that, on the high seas!

"In the early days, Bob Clampett decided we'd handle the script by putting up a stack of index cards in a clip. A man below would take off each card as we finished it. That's what he was supposed to do. The first night we did that, he tried to pull the first one off and *all* the cards fell on the floor! So Daws and I had to ad-lib the whole show! The people in the booth kept saying, 'Please stick to the script.' They didn't know what happened.

"So then we devised the first teleprompter, but no one thought of copyrighting it. We scotch taped the pages together and devised a roller and Ralph Loretz would crank the roller, following us as we talked. It was really an ingenious thing. At some point we also had the scripts scotch taped up on the plywood back there. Later, we had monitors up above so we could coordinate with the booth. I still can't believe we managed to win three Emmys and do this every night, in exactly fifteen minutes.

"It's a good thing Daws and I really loved each other, being in each other's faces all that time. If we hated the other person, it never would've worked at all. We had such great respect for each other."

In 1952 Beany and Cecil even appeared in the first 3-D feature film, *Bwana Devil* starring Robert Stack, but was cut from the final version.

Time for Jack Benny.

The Beany gang with their Cecil Awards.

There would later be a 1962 cartoon series called *Beany and Cecil* which replicated Daws and Stan's voices, but did not use the original cast. While staunch fans of the puppet show tend to write these off as inferior, the satire and writing were often very fine, nearing *Rocky and Bullwinkle* quality in that only adults would get most of the jokes.

Though *Time for Beany* was essentially a West coast creation, it is one of the 1950s most revered children's shows to this day. The *Beany* DVD contains 12 of the best cartoons from the 1962 animated series, and four original *Time for Beany* shows, including audio interviews with Clampett, Freberg and Walker Edmiston. Bob Clampett, Jr. has plans to release more of his father's work in future.

Steady puppet work kept food on the table, and supplied a new home in Beverly Hills (where some of the Butlers still reside) in 1950, but did little to change the daily habits of a houseful of Butler boys. Donald Martin was born on August 31, 1946, Paul Dawson on March 7, 1950 and Charles Allen on October 15, 1953.

Daws would do voices at the drop of a hat, much to the pleasure of the little friends of the Butler children. But to young David, Don, Paul and Chas, it was something very normal, an ordinary occupation that was hardly worth excitement.

Paul: "This is just what my dad did, but for all the other kids whose dads had workaday jobs, they were just blown away by it. That's just what we viewed as normal."

Chas: "I'd have friends over and he'd go immediately into character. He was very free with his talent. No ego or anything like that, he was very humble about what it was he did. He was pretty open to perform at any time. He could get hurt that way too—giving his time to people, and kind of being taken advantage of."

David: "I didn't go to many of his recording sessions—I was usually in school. However, I did go down to the *Time for Beany* set at KTLA on one or two occasions. The organist was an east Indian named Korla Pandit. My mother recalls me saying on one of our visits to the studio, 'I wish Korla Pandit wouldn't play such sad music.' But I do remember a birthday party I had shortly after we moved to Beverly Hills (1950-ish), at which dad put on a puppet show for my friends using the actual *Beany* puppets."

Don: "When I was really young, I knew I wouldn't have any time with Dad at night because he always had to go to work. In the beginning I didn't associate his work with *Beany and Cecil*, until I was about six years old, then I became aware that Beany and Capt. Horatio Huffenpuff and I think Hopalong Wong the Cook were his voices. Back then, I kind of took it for granted that that's what Dad did for a living. And it wasn't until what I call his real golden age, when he worked with Hanna-Barbera, that I really became aware of the real significance of his talent."

With Daws away daily, more of the home life responsibilities fell to Myrtis, delegated with grandparents. Myrtis: "Grandpa was always willing to drive the boys to their swimming, dancing and horseback riding lessons. Our son, Don, being the middle one for a while, was always over to their house. In fact, neighbors thought him to be their son born rather late in life! They turned their vacant garage into a play area for the boys. Ruth was a doting grandmother, with only one child of her own. She never tired of their being at their house, whereas Charles would go to his room and lock the door when he had had enough. At Mass, Don always would know his grandfather was at that Mass—he had a clearing of his throat that was unique."

But even during the long days of those *Beany* years, Daws kept his hand in the family way with some love, discipline and a few pancakes.

Don Butler recalled, "He was always singing the praises of good old-fashioned discipline with a switch, but he never did it himself. He thought us kids were abnormal because we were so noisy. But I think the reason for that was that he himself was an only child, and didn't grow up with siblings, so it was much quieter in his childhood. 'When I was a child, I would never think of talking back to my parents,' he would say. But I couldn't help thinking to myself that you were also an only child and didn't have sibling support. But you did have other passive means of resistance.

"I guess we did our share of talking back, as much as we dared. But when he was hard on us, he would always make it a point to come back to us later and apologize, if he considered he had been too hard, and assured us that he loved us, that he only had our best interests at heart. When we were younger, he would resort to a certain amount of spanking. Then taking away our allowance. Mom was the one who would have us stand in the corner. They shared the responsibility."

Paul: "We went to the Hollywood Bowl to see the Nutcracker Suite, and Charles and I were cutting up the whole time. He had to separate us. But three days later I was in the living room humming something from it, so it wasn't a total write-off."

Sibling rivalry had its share of blame for the noise in the Daws Butler household. Don admitted, "I think David, the older brother, resented my having come into the world, to upstage him. And Paul may have resented Charles upstaging him. For a while, Paul was the real darling of the family. My mom would let his hair grow long and curled, and people would often mistake him for a girl, and he would protest! He's the family gourmet. And the funny thing is he was the only one who didn't like anything that was put before him as a kid. Very finicky."

Sometimes it was tough for Daws—and Myrtis—to assert themselves in a home overrun by such male engines. But when Daws took to cooking, everyone was attentive.

Chas: "My father was a gourmet chef, not an actual professional, just for the family. He would've loved having The Daws Butler Cooking Hour. That would've been the perfect thing for him. We are all little brats, and everything that he made we turned our noses up at. If I had any regrets, it's that we didn't appreciate what he was doing when he was cooking. He'd put Gruyere cheese in stuff and just experiment with an eight-year-old that way. My brother Paul would complain, 'These cookies are too bendy.' Stupid kid stuff.

"So Sunday morning would usually be our pancake or waffle breakfast. He would do a caricature out of the batter. The way he would pour it onto the skillet, he would form it into the shape of Popeye or some of his weird little caricatures that he'd draw while he was on the phone. He would've been a great animator. He always said, 'if I didn't get in on the voice side I think I would've gone into animation.'"

Daws would try giving the kids real maple syrup, but all they wanted was Log Cabin or some store brand. It drove Daws crazy. When eating out, he would take his own bottle of real maple syrup with him; a practice now handed down to his son Paul.

Sunday nights would see Daws making barbecue steaks or some such middle-class delight. And Myrtis admitted, "He was a great salad maker. He liked to mix a salad and try new ingredients. He was very good in the kitchen. He didn't hesitate from helping in the kitchen. I think it came from his parents when they were both working, he would do that when he came home from school, so it wasn't foreign to him at all."

Chas: "We used to have the family dinner on Friday nights. The plan was to gather everyone. This particular night my mom had decided to make Jell-O in wine glasses. Raspberry. So it had kind of a winey-looking texture to it. And we're sitting at dinner, and dad always liked to have a couple of glasses of wine at dinner, maybe even a martini as he was making dinner. By the time we were eating, he wasn't drunk, but definitely affected by the alcohol. He took the wine glass in his hand, leans back, and looks at the Jell-O in the glass—but nothing's happening. And it finally dawns on him that this isn't wine, it's Jell-O. We're all cracking up!"

Sometimes Daws would throw a baseball or football around with Dave or Paul or Don but no one would call him a sports nut. Not the man who preferred collecting and listening to records of classical music.

Don: "He was very proud of his collection of classical music. Particularly Mozart. When the movie *Amadeus* came out, he literally had to be dragged kicking and screaming to see it, because of the way it depicted the character of Mozart. Beethoven came a close second."

From the age of five or six, he also collected animals, especially bronze ones sculpted out of silver which he kept in a case. Alas, as time went on

Voice men recognized.

in the house of little boys, things got broken.

Myrtis: "Daws was a lecturer and usher at Good Shepherd Catholic Church here in Beverly Hills. We socialized with the ushers at nine o'clock mass, then go out and have breakfast afterwards, go to each others' home, but it was mostly church-connected friends. Our children went to Catholic schools. I myself am a convert, I grew up Methodist. I would say he was an Irish-Catholic-type of religious person. He did go to Mass every Sunday. I remember long before the readings and so on at Mass got looser, so to speak, on one St. Patrick's Day Sunday at the last part of Mass, Daws went into an Irish accent. I don't think the Monsignor was very pleased with it."

Beany ended its long run on September 7, 1954, but during early shows Stan started writing novelty songs and comedy material for performers like Scatman Crothers and Rose Marie. It was this love for musical comedy that would lead Stan and Daws to even greater notoriety and financial gain.

Stan had worked with bandleader Cliffie Stone who made novelty records. Since Stan and Daws had been voice actors on Capitol Records' children's albums, it was only natural the three of them should eventually team up. Stan's first (surprise) hit had been 1950's "John and Marsha." The title said it all, literally, gaining in sexual fervor as it continued.

Alan Livingston conducts while Daws, June and Stan record.

After other humor singles, Stan brought Daws in to work on their most successful record ever. In 1953 Jack Webb's *Dragnet*, a monotone detective series, was still running strong, transferred from radio. It was a natural for satire.

When they got the idea for a *Dragnet* spoof called "St. George and the Dragonet," they took it to music director Alan Livingston who had worked on Freberg's "John and Martha" skit and his Eartha Kitt takeoff. But first they had to get Jack Webb's permission, which took three hours of convincing. Webb had used Freberg on his show a couple times and he'd met Daws during the long and busy radio years. Webb felt safe, and with a cut of the profits, the go ahead was granted.

The three-and-a-half minutes of brilliance began with Freberg's Jack Webb-type monotone narration introducing himself: he's St. George, a knight. Soon he's called into the Chief's (Daws) office. who gives him the report about a dragon that's been devouring maidens. St. George documents every step as he goes, giving the time and activity. First stop, interview one of the maidens who escaped. June Foray, in her best Brooklyn accent, sounds like she has a head cold. "He was breathin' fire—he boined me already!" Next, the trail took the armored copper to a nasally knave (Daws) who describes the offending dragon: orange polka dots, purple feet, breathing fire and smoke, and a big bloodshot eye in the middle of his forehead. The only thing that would catch this creature: a dragonet. So, with his .45 caliber sword, St. George comes upon the large-voiced dragon (Daws) who protests to high heaven, leaving himself wide open to the charge of a 412. Overacting.

The single's flip side contained "Little Blue Riding Hood," with June Foray in the lead role. After the usual *Dragnet* vamp, the announcer seriously states that the title was changed from Red to Blue "to prevent an investigation." Narrated by Wednesday, a homicide officer whose beat was The Woods, the story begins with his meeting Blue. Wednesday basically frisks the basket she's taking to Grandma's. It contains nothing suspicious: sawed-off shotgun, bludgeon, box of dum-dums. But he doesn't let on that he found the secret compartment containing just what he expected. Goodies. So he takes a strawberry shortcut through the strawberry patch and beats her to Grandma's. Riding Hood gets there and runs down the list of big stuff Wednesday (in a grandma suit) has: eyes, for getting the facts, ma'am; subpoena, to serve you with; and police special, the better to take her downtown. Busted, the Hood deflates, knowing she should've been suspicious, since the copper didn't have a mustache like grandma has.

The ending was a bit flat with no real punchline, but it was great b-side material, with a mere two lines at the end going to Daws, again as the Chief.

Collaborating together, it took Daws and Stan about 15 hours to come up with the material for both sides of the single ("Riding Hood" consumed about four hours of that). Some of the gags were borrowed from a proposed radio show which the duo had been peddling around without success. The record was cut on August 26, with Walter Schumann in attendance, and as composer of the *Dragnet* theme, he shared in the record's royalties. Jack Webb didn't even ask for a demo recording before the record was mass pressed.

Freberg explained, "It looked good right away. Capitol played it next morning for some of its personnel and everyone was enthusiastic." When Stan brought the record down to the *Dragnet* set, Webb stopped production for the whole cast and crew to listen to it. Everyone laughed like crazy.

The record came out on the weekend of September 12, 1953. Played on *Juke Box Jury* that Saturday, Jimmy Boyd, Dorothy Malone and Bob Crosby voted it a miss (wouldn't sell 200,000), while Al Martino, Polly Bergen and Bob's daughter Kathy Crosby voted it a hit. That's just what it was. Within 24 hours it had sold an incredible 250,000 copies. "Dragonet" was released nationally that Monday, September 14, and by the end of the week, record totals were over the half million mark. Critics and crowds loved it. It sold bags of copies even in countries where *Dragnet* wasn't airing. Daws was thrilled that the single was hailed as biting, intelligent satire.

Little Blue Riding herself, June Foray, flew to New York to appear with the boys on Ed Sullivan's show. They all came in costume to perform the routine, but moments prior to the live broadcast, Stan came backstage and told Daws and June that he was going on alone and they had to stay off-camera and do their parts on a mike. The show was broadcast with Stan in the spotlight playing the Jack Webb part and poor Daws and June doing all the other characters off-camera. Stan claimed that it was Ed Sullivan who insisted it be done this way but Daws felt that Stan just wanted the limelight for himself and let it happen without standing up for them.

23 days after the record was first released, it had sold over 900,000 and was nearing the million mark, which is quickly passed. It was the first comedy record to achieve such distinction.

"Doors are opening right and left," Freberg commented at the time. "They want us at New York's Paramount. In Chicago. At Las Vegas. They want us to go on *The Perry Como Show*." But Bob Clampett wasn't having that. They couldn't get time off from *Beany* for the many appearances they would've liked to have given. They would have to wait for their Clampett contracts to expire that February.

It made an incredible amount of money but what Daws thought most important was that they proved themselves as performers. The psychological aspect was uplifting. It also lifted Stan and Daws into recording star status. They were immediately contracted for more.

Daws helped with the writing of Freberg's "The Worst of the Town (The Toast of the Town, Ed Sullivan)," and co-wrote and performed "That's Right, Arthur." The title referred to Arthur Godfrey's yes-man (Daws) who says that to everything, even to Godfrey's throat clearing; and when he's busy eating noodle soup, Daws does the next best thing and gargles his expected laughs. Daws is also heard as the intimidated bandleader "Frink" who, like everyone else, fears for his job.

"Christmas Dragnet (Yulenet)" was the inevitable sequel single (taking up both sides) starring Freberg again as monotoning Wednesday, and Daws as his partner who knows his green onions ("they're really called scallions"). "Grudge," brought into the station for not believing in Santa Claus, is voiced by Daws in the ol' dragon voice. It wasn't his first offence: he was brought in on a 1492 previously for not believing in Columbus. Confessing he doesn't believe in Cleveland or Cincinnati either, Wednesday is determined to prove to the guy there is a Santa. By helicopter, they make it up to the North Pole where a southern Brownie (Daws) tells Grudge of the pile of presents still unclaimed by the one guy, Grudge, who doesn't believe. The moment he believes, he gets 'em. Grudge breaks down and believes.

This was followed by Daws' favorite Capitol record (possibly because it was the only Freberg recording in which *Daws* was the star), "Person to Pearson." Edward N. Nonymous (Freberg) interviews J. Pierpont Pearson (Daws) who lives behind the A&P store. He has a clock rat, Brailsworth, that bites him awake every morning because he's gotta be quick to avoid being thrown out of the alley by the A&P man. It was Daws' shining single, telling in a tiny, aging, lost voice of how he put his rat through Cal-Tech (Brailsworth chose the school by eating the brochure).

It was actually the b-side to "Point of Order," a hilarious satire on the witch hunting McCarthy trials. The announcer introduces: "Ladies and gentlemen, we take you now to the committee room where Baa Baa Black Sheep is being investigated at the Subcommittee Sheerings. He is accused of receiving a special sheering instead of being clipped with the rest of the flock." Daws appears as the southern Senator asking the questions of the freezing, sheered sheep (Freberg), while another Senator (Freberg again) keeps monotoning (on key!) "Point of order."

In 1953 Stan and Daws had begun a comedy series for CBS radio. The pilot for *That's Rich* was broadcast on November 21, 1953, and the series ran from January 8 to September 23, 1954. Freberg played the lead character Rich who had a vocal delivery much like Jack Benny, while Daws, Hans Conried, Alan Reed (A.K.A. Fred Flintstone) and others ably supported.

Daws on *That's Rich*: "Stan played a young guy who was trying to make it in the world. He was very stuffy and funny to the audience but

Stan and Daws.

not to himself. A very serious, Harold Lloyd-type character. I played his southern sidekick, Hugh McQ, one of the first southern characters I did. It was pretty funny. Stan and I had the ability to do cold readings. If it's written well at all, all the little marks for laughs are there, like a roadmap. You would just feel the way the characters would be, and sometimes your first table reading was the way it would go out on the air. Most of the direction was done from the standpoint of time—you had to get the whole thing done in a half-hour. Stan and I, and Don Messick and I, had the greatest working relationships. They were like musical duets. Our timing, our respect for each other, we adlibbed together."

Daws also wrote some of the episodes, such as the *High Noon* spoof, written with *Beany* writer Charlie Shows, produced and directed by Homer Canfield. The series was created by Frank and Doris Hursley.

"Yes, *That's Rich*, starring Stan Freberg as Rich," says the announcer between a simple, homey theme tune reminiscent of *The Life of Riley*. In the "Fortune Teller" episode, the narrator began, "On warm summer evenings, some folks like to drive down to the beach where they can eat popcorn, drink soda pop and ride the roller coaster. Others prefer to get sick in different ways." Rich, his girlfriend Susan and friends are "fanning themselves with hot dogs that can *only* be put together at the beach." Daws gives his southern all as slow-witted Hugh McQ in a pre-Huckleberry drawl: "Once I took a girl on a ride through the Tunnel of Love and *man*, did we have fun! Wowee! My boat beat hers by two *minutes*!" (The audience was primed and Daws got some of the biggest laughs in the show, showing off his versatility and ability to wring every syllable out of a line.) They get a kick out of the towel-headed swami who tells Rich's future in a cheap crystal ball: he'll be murdered by his best friend. When the smaller predictions come true (to a modest extent), Rich becomes panicked that Flash or Hugh have it in for him. "You want to kill me because of my social standing?" "Social standing?" queries Flash. "In the social register, buddy, you're strictly small change." He stays away from them. "I wanna die a natural death, like crossing Sunset and Vine." He gives himself up to a cop, wanting to be locked up, but the policeman wants to know what he's guilty of. "I don't know, what's open today?" But in trying to find their friend, the trio are arrested for jaywalking and thrown into Rich's cell. Luckily, the fake swami is in one of the nearby cells where they find out that he's a con man, relieving Rich's mind.

The clever series is undeservingly forgotten in the wake of *The Stan Freberg Show*'s shadow, but had real charm, as well some solid gag-writing and top voices, such as Paul Frees, weaving in and out of episodes. The at-times hilarious show caused a lot of work offers to flood in for Stan and Daws. But *Time for Beany*'s daily schedule still loomed heavily and did not allow a lot of off-hours. It's surprising that Daws and Stan accomplished as much as they did during their Clampett contracts.

Somehow, Daws also found time during the *Beany* run to do more cartoon work. He finally cracked Mel Blanc's workplace and found himself in 1950 voicing the Tweety and Sylvester short *Gift Wrapped* (released in 1952). Other Sylvester cartoons followed, usually with Daws supplying the voices of Syl's cohorts. He also performed a few impressions or villain voices in Bugs Bunny cartoons, and after the original voice of Elmer Fudd, Arthur Q. Bryan, passed away, Daws lisped the famous hunter's role at least once, according to legend. Perhaps in *Pre-Hysterical Hare* in 1958 (though Bryan died in 1959) – albeit it may have been Mel Blanc or the new Fudd for Capitol Records: Dave Barry.

Cashing in, or paying homage to the great television success of *The Honeymooners*, in 1956, Warner Brothers cartoons for once chose Daws Butler over Mel Blanc, fitting him perfectly into two lead roles. He portrayed both Ralph and Norton – A.K.A. Jackie Gleason and Art Carney – in two cartoon shorts: *The Honeymousers*, and *Mice Follies*. Longtime WB witch-voice June Foray took on the Audrey Meadows role.

Neither June nor Daws received screen credit. Only Mel Blanc ever really held that honor, though even voice pros like Stan Freberg and Hal Smith would continually work for the famed cartoon studio. Freberg received onscreen credit only once, for Friz Freleng's *Three Little Bops*, a send-up of the Three Little Pigs with Freberg warbling in the rock'n'roll style of Bill Haley.

Time for Beany ended on September 7, 1954. When the performers' contracts ran out, both men jumped into other work immediately. Daws aimed his hated Frankenstein shoes at the wall – and threw. They shattered, so great was the force.

On May 13, 1985, Daws, Stan and a host of others who got their television start on Klaus Landsberg's KTLA station, Channel 5, reunited to pay belated tribute to Landsberg who had died of cancer in 1956.

As Freberg began to branch out into the highly lucrative arena of copyrighting/advertising in 1956, beginning with his Contadina tomato paste radio spots, he and Daws began to come to a parting of the ways and would rarely work together again. But apart from the hit Capitol records, there was one last hurrah. First, they would together achieve the high anti-honor of killing radio.

Chapter 4
Time After *Beany*

In his too-short autobiography, Daws wrote: "After the 'Beany' thing, I found that the thinking in town had now classified me as a puppeteer, and it was tough to shake them off this opinion. The success of the Capitol Records added to my self-confidence about writing so I decided to crack the commercial field.

"I sat down and wrote a batch of letters to all the Production Companies, citing my writing and acting credits, and that I thought I would have a true affinity for writing copy. Each letter was an original and I tried to make it amusing (which was a devious way of showing the comedy expertise I had). It took some time (as does everything worthwhile) and it paid off handsomely. I always say that if you've got to start somewhere, the top ain't bad!

"I got the nod from a production company for whom I had done voice work, and my first assignment was writing the spots (to be animated) for a Ford campaign. I wrote them and did most of the voices. It was lucrative and it got me off and running in this new field. I did this for a couple years, writing radio spots as well. Stan had also gotten into commercials and wrote some terrific stuff.

"This was the golden age of TV animation commercials; we hadn't divulged all of our secrets to the ad agencies yet, so they let us have artistic control. They figured we were the bright boys who had it and we did. Later, after we'd taught them the tricks, they took over, but they forgot to take the freshness and spontaneity and they added something else. Too bad. But I had the great good fortune to be a big part of what I called before and still do: The Golden Age of Animation, from about 1958 to

1965. Then the networks stepped in. We had taught them all the tricks and proper moves, and now they began calling the shots, which wasn't so bad except that they'd lost sight of the target, which was, and should always be, viable, provocative, imaginative entertainment."

Daws, like Stan, loved the work and found it a challenge to inform and entertain in such short spurts. Several of his written & voiced commercials employed his four sons. At the time he admitted to *Catholic Digest*, "I don't believe in pushing them. It was their own idea to work with me. They did a first-rate job and loved every minute of it, even the two youngest, who had to memorize all of their lines because they were too young to read at the time."

One of his early commercials featured the world's youngest automobile dealer. Six-year-old Fremantle, had a $5,000 a week allowance and threw birthday parties at which he would give cars filled with jelly beans as party favors. Another of these had the little sweetheart presenting his dear old dad with six station wagons, explaining that after all, *his* father is an *only* father.

Daws' commercials were so popular local stations were harassed by viewers to know when they could be seen; the TV studios finally had to list the times for the commercials alongside the times for the programs.

Longer commercials were more frequent back then so often Daws would have an entire minute to get his gags and sponsor messages in. One of his cleverest radio creations was a minute-long magic trick for National Bohemian Beer, all given in one continuous spot without *any* kind of pause, even for breath. "It's an actor's secret how I did it, but it's kind of interesting."

Another humorous spot was for Larry's Sandwiches, about a songwriter trying to get *just* the right jingle for the client.

Don Messick and Daws teamed up for some funny Chevrolet radio commercials around 1960: Don woke Daws up in the middle of the night to tell him about cars. One of the most imaginative had Don as Mr. Bear phoning southern California Chevy dealer Daws because he was told on the phone someone *would* be calling and hasn't yet. Mr. Bear went on to explain that he and the family went for a walk to let their porridge cool (presumably they would've been back quicker if they'd had a car), and the food was eaten. When Daws alludes that the thief might still be upstairs, in bed, off goes Mr. Bear to see.

Another went thus:

DAWS: (Whispering) Hey. You a Chevrolet salesman?
DON: Yes?
DAWS: Well I seen your Chevrolet commercials on TV. You know, where they say you got *immediate* delivery?
DON: That's right. Immediate.
DAWS: Well, I gotta have *immediate* immediate delivery. Hurry!
DON: Any particular model?
DAWS: You pick one out. Surprise me.
DON: Color?
DAWS: Yeah, color. Hurry, hurry!
DON: How about a heater?
DAWS: I'm carryin' one. Hey, ya better gimme bulletproof glass.
DON: Okay…Now, let me write this down. First, your name?

DAWS: 6675435.

DON: Beg your pardon?

DAWS.   That's my pen name. Better put down Garvey Trumm.

DON: Address?

DAWS: Just put down General Delivery, San Quentin. I'm in and out.

DON: Occupation?

DAWS: Crook.

DON: Now, uh, reference. What bank do you do business with?

DAWS: All of 'em! Here, here's your money. Now quick, open the trunk of my new Chevy so I can get in.

DON: What?

DAWS: Look, I gotta hide out someplace, don't I?

In another spot for Marlboro Cigarettes, he played both characters: a put-upon announcer in the Jim Jordan-style of voice as he attempted to get the big lug of a football player called Juggernaut Jones to push the cigarettes. Said Jones didn't know a cig from a shaver, and sported a dopey voice somewhere in Daws' Mr. Jinx range.

He also wrote and voiced at least one spot for National Bohemian Beer (Boh Beer), which set his Cap'n Crunch voice to commercials several years before the Cap'n bowed. As usual, it was a clever spot with an absurdist's twist: one character asks how it was the other guy was able to walk across the sky and draw a bottle of beer – the other guy, the Cap'n's voice, demonstrates that it's not sky, it's a piece of paper, and then goes on to inform his dopey friend that they are both cartoons, "we're just figments in some guy's imagination."

One early animated Thunderbird ad used an Edgar Bergen/Charlie McCarthy set up: after the pitch is given, the dummy jumps off the ventriloquist's lap, lets the air out of the big guy and jumps off the stage to visit his local Ford dealer.

His commercials were clever, and had at least as much punch as the average Freberg spot without lulling into formula or hard-sell. He would most often provide voices (his own, as well as casting other parts) for his clients of MJB Coffee, National Bohemian (doing Phil Silvers to Messick's Wallace Wimple voice), Solo, Bosco (complete with bouncing cartoon rabbit), and others. He would continue doing commercials for his entire career.

Foremost, the maker of Solo milk once employed Daws for a series of funny cartoons about a low-key cow who once got into a conversation with a Solo delivery man who was having trouble with his truck. After the milk was discussed, the cow mentioned to the driver (Daws) that it sounded like his distributor points were dirty. They were. The truck started right up.

Paul Frees as narrator joined Daws on a Quisp commercial or two produced by the Jay Ward studio, whose main client through the years seemed to be Cap'n Crunch for Quaker Oats. But there were also a few oddities, like an Aesop and Son relating the Uneager Beaver and His Brothers for Cheerios. Daws played both parts, including the father, usually done by Charlie Ruggles.

One of the cleverest of Daws' commercials involved a Cheeseburger coming into a tailor's shop. "I'm looking for something to go with my sesame seed bun while still highlighting my cheese." Of course he was a tight fit, being a double patty. The fitter had the perfect thing – something light that wouldn't clash: 7-Up, the Un-cola. The 30-second spot won an award, one of many Daws would attain in the advertising world.

In the early 1970s he worked again for Kellogg's, this time as an energetic sun who gives the grapes enough light to become grapes during a simple folk-like song. One had a feeling the sun would've been happier as a raisin.

Later in his career, Daws appeared as Professor Goody, in a very different voice from Cap'n Crunch yet retaining the fuddy quality, fighting a strange looking "goose" called the Waffle-Whiffer who was always after his Aunt Jemima Frozen Waffles. It was a popular character, though it didn't last long, and sold a lot of people on this new kind of fast breakfast.

Life after *Beany* was like being released from a tiring but hit Broadway show. The world of possibilities was open—but not completely. Much of the industry considered Daws and Stan not as voice men, but puppeteers, which was the opposite of what they knew they were. Like the funniest cartoons, they considered *Beany* like radio comedy shows, but with visuals on the ends of their hands. It was actually tough for both men to slip into more cartoon acting. Luckily, there was Walter Lantz.

When the creator of Andy Panda and the phenomenal Woody Woodpecker, was searching for a voice for his once-mute Chilly Willy, Daws was called upon for a high, clipped vocal that immediately heightened the little penguin's comic effect. Lantz: "Daws was a great actor, which you have to be to play a cartoon character, like my wife Gracie (voice of Woody Woodpecker)."

To secure more work, Daws recorded a six-minute demo, which began: "To recoin a cliche, first thing's first. First of all, this is me. Daws Butler. This is my tonality, this is the way I talk. This is my speech pattern. This is the lower end of my register. And the upper end is brighter and has more energy! Now I'm going to barge into character voices so you probably won't hear me anymore. (A whisper) I'm gonna miss me . . . " He goes into his lesser-known voices, but comes back as himself. It is a very literate demo, seemingly done in a single sitting, rather than an immediate punch into Yogi Bear, etc. He even begins to describe and perform his "dialect by degree," almost teaching how to do Irish and others. Even in his demo, he just couldn't resist instructing. Only at the very end does a Huckleberry Hound-sounding character (not even named) come on to say, "You had your chance to have me talk, but now it's too late, sorry."

Radio had never been out of Daws' mind. He would consistently be asked back by radio directors and producers, even though the pay was nothing compared with television. On August 31, 1956, he joined Stan Freberg again on "Colloquy 3: An Analysis of Satire" for *CBS Radio Workshop*. The now-classic recording began with Alan Reed presiding over chaotic delegates from states spouting their slogans during the 1964 Presidential convention. Daws is listening to the interesting Stan Freberg program when wife June Foray turns it off. After the credits, Freberg attempts to explain what satire is when Parley Baer, as society's Censor, interrupts to complain about kidding politics. Though it was more of a commercial for Freberg's recordings, it did provide Daws with a few brief spots, including a Fred Allen impersonation. Freberg and writer/producer William N. Robson collaborated on the script. Sam Pierce, Larry Thor, Bill Thompson also appeared.

When it came to parodying the lucrative advertising industry, Freberg had nothing on Daws. But they did share a Freberg-type love-hate relationship with advertising work, and letting off steam in a rare moment, Daws wrote and performed a record "for Quartet Films, one of the production companies in town. They used it for a promotional stunt when they were starting out. It was sent to every agency in the country under the title *All That Jazz*. It kidded the pants off the ad boys—but judging from the hundreds of letters received, none of which were negative, they got the point and who knows, maybe it made better ad boys out of them. On the record I do Miltown Jag, Shep Menken does Maury, Hershel Bernardi (Sgt. Jacoby) does Chuck and John Harmon does George."

All That Jazz was "a non-musical experience composed by Daws Butler, distributed as a non-public service by Quartet Films, Inc." Maury Siduals (Shep Menken) only has to say "Blooper Soap is real good," but wants to get into a character and funnies up the line in many directions. It was a fantastic spoof on commercial sessions and the unending mind changes of sponsors, in which Daws plays agreeable director Miltown who tries to ring every ounce of "pride" and "undersell" possible out of the actor's delivery.

The accompanying promo sheet with this demo reel read, "Whether originating a visual idea, or executing an agency-developed storyboard, the Quartet staff provides equal finesse ... and puts either idea on film

A Child's Garden of Versus
(Daws Butler Advertising)

Higgledy Piggledy
Chuck knows what Julie knows.
They've peddled papers
(Seems like a year)
Pure dedication to
Commerciality . . .
Actors all over should
Buy them a beer!

We are programmed – we're not free.
We're soft-sold – subliminally.
Though ADS and ADMEN go together,
I persist in wondering whether
(at the CLIENT'S instigation)
Are ADS born through inspiration
Or the ADMAN'S DESPERATION?
Like a tragic SCRABBLE GAME
"Find the words!!" – or put the blame
On art departments – copy chiefs . . .
No one's sacred! – Hold no briefs!
Get it on the air! – in print!
Pay whatever – Do not stint!
The CLIENT'S "all" – we must not fail!
(But try to get it done for scale.)

*

It is necez-SARA LEE-so!
Her cakes top your own, don't you know.
So stop with the mixes
(Jewish mothers and Shiksehs)
Buy her stock to make your own dough.

*

I tell of a jingle-ad fellow
Who sang songs to immortalize JELLO
With martinis at hand
To inspire the band
(They passed out – so he sang a cappella)

*

A cannibal, just on a hunch
Invited somebody to lunch . . .
No missionaries
Or Tom, Dick or Harrys . . .
He feasted on CAP'N CRUNCH.

Higgledy Piggledy
Life is a "CATTLE-CALL"
Many are called but then . . .
(You know the bit!)
Off or on-camera
(Characteristically)
Just be yourself and then . . .
"CALL BACK!" – you're it.

A clever young actress named PAT
Would "read" at the drop of a hat.
She auditioned in PARIS
For a big wheel named Ferris . . .
Now they're going around – and that's that

*

Sing a song of selling,
The jingle's "out of sight!"
Four-and-twenty ADMEN
Finally got it right.
When it came to credit
They stood up very tall . . .
When accolades were handed out
The A.E.* took 'em all!!
*A.E. – Account Executive

*

Higgledy Piggledy
Madison Avenue
Copy-chiefs avid for
Others' accounts . . .
Sometimes grow careless in
Superduplicity . . .
End up "out-clevered" and
They get the bounce!

*

Georgie Porgie
Puddin'n' Pie . . .
Kissed the girls and made them cry.
(Not so, Morris – LAVORIS.)

*

I think that I shall never see
An AD that has its way with me . . .
An AD that makes me change my ways
(Eat frozen food that comes on trays)
To say that they have my belief
Is true, because – I'm copy-chief!

CUSTOM VOICE-OVERS
Daws Butler

Representation by
MILES BOHM AUER
HO 2-6416

A press release for Daws and Don's commercials.

within a price pattern that is unusual for such quality. The talents on this recording are reflections of the fresh, spontaneous creative skills in the graphic, writing and musical arts that Quartet has attracted. The recording itself is a reflection of the unique equipment possessed by Quartet Films to devise and deliver the brightest, bounciest and most beguiling TV spots."

Blooper's Soap Revisited was a sequel with purpose. Over quaint, documentary-type music, Daws (as director) and Don Messick (as writer) pitch their follow-up commercial to Colonel Blooper. "Is real good—is real good—is real good!" shouts a man. A woman asks, "What's real good?" "Blooper's Soap!" They put a lot of time in on that spot—research, miles of statistics, but it's no soap. For the shampoo spot, Daws and June Foray do an incredibly funny, careless commercial spoof that proves that it's better to have looks and money than clean hair. Next up is a short spot for Wheat Chaff, which contains no food value, but fills you up and keeps you quiet so mom can get her work done. Blooper himself decides to join SAG and record the damn line himself, just as he said it. Besides, he's intrigued by the possibilities of residuals.

Equally intelligent was November 11, 1956's *CBS Radio Workshop* ("dedicated to man's imagination; theatre of the mind") broadcast of "Report on the Weans." Robert Nathan's script was an inventive, highly literate satire on scholars of the far future deciphering the ancient (then modern) USA in terms of Egyptian tombs and religion. A report from a posh June Foray on the site of the ruins of Holy Wood provides proof of sacrifices to the god Os-kar, in which glasses, nose and feet are preserved in the floor next to gibberish hieroglyphics such as Harold Lloyd, Jimmy Durante and Gloria Swanson. Daws played cheery announcer Dinar Geb reporting live from the Great Hall of the Ethnical Museum of Antiquity in the year 7954 A.D. for Radio Rhodesia.

On February 3, 1957, Daws joined Margaret Whiting, Shep Menken, Jay Novello, and Joe DiSantis for *Suspense*'s "Frankie and Johnny." "Master of Mystery" host William N. Robson began, "There is more than one kind of mystery. In addition to the whodunits, there are the howdunits and the whydunits." Everyone knew whodunit—Frankie—"and everyone knows why she done it: cuz Johnny done her wrong. But we feel that how she done it, with Ms. Margaret Whiting starring as Frankie, makes a story well-calculated to keep you in (Music)... Suspense." Hot New Orleans singer Frankie raises the roof throughout the story with the famed jazz tune, sandwiched between dialogue with no-good, clarinet-playing Johnny (Shep Menken) or trying to chase down the two-timer. She gets involved with blonde Nellie Bly and lets Nellie buy him a diamond ring, new shoes and suit, while Frankie bought a gun for him. Johnny is too handsome and too stupid, just living for the ladies: this time, it's Nellie Bly. "That man took all of my money," sings Frankie. "That man took all

of my love. He left me so sad and so lonely, my heart's a broken-winged dove. He's my man, but he's doin' me wrong." She shoots him and is locked up, but everyone looks at her with sympathy. Daws Butler provides some of the voices during her journey to find her love, and receives last billing on the credits.

Exactly one month later he returned to *Suspense* to support Vincent Price, Jack Kruschen, Sam Pierce, and Joe DiSantis in "Present Tense" by James Poe. In this overly-narrative episode, Daws is first heard as the cab driver who takes Vincent Price from the train station. Price, convicted for killing his wife, is saved twice from his own death when his train is wrecked killing a hundred others. He goes back home to learn that his wife and her lover framed him for her fake death. "Here on the wall by the stove... the cleaver...!" He kills them, but unfortunately it only takes him back to reality: on the train, handcuffed to the same officer. It was a poetic, almost surreal episode that eloquently chronicled the delusions of Price's rekilling his wife and her lover, and his escapes from death, even from the afterlife itself.

One of Daws' most intriguing *Suspense* show was "Flesh Peddler," narrated by a "bright young actor" DeForrest Kelly (who would go on to play Dr. McCoy on the original *Star Trek*) and told the story of a determined talent agent (Kelly) who wants to sign up a ventriloquist in a two-bit carnival he comes across. But the finale uncovers a dark, deadly secret ... Daws is heard as the barker near the beginning and definitely glows as Arthur, a slow-minded knife thrower, with a voice that is a cross between Frankie Fontaine's Crazy Guggenhiem character and the one Daws would soon use for an orange cat who "hated meeses to pieces" — Mr. Jinx.

On that same series, John McIntire starred in "The Big Day," written by Sam Pearce. Daws had little to do as the TV announcer who gives updates on the plot: a man, with the aid of his reluctant helper, pilots his Stanley Steamer on a 500-mile journey on the day of the Indianapolis 500 to prove that his much-insulted pride and joy can lick any gas-guzzling roadster out there. And they do indeed beat the time of all cars in the famous race.

Daws: "We received a double fee for sometimes doing two shows in the same day: for the West coast and the East coast. The one you would do for Los Angeles, which could mean more jobs if they liked you, would be the dog. The one for East, where you didn't know anybody and they couldn't cast you for anything, would be perfect. *You* know when you're good. The audience can approve of you, but if you know you're not good, you're depressed. Two actors working together can give each other so much. Some actors turn off completely through fear; they've learned it a certain way, and that's the way they're going to go with it."

1957 also brought one of Daws' greatest achievements.

The pinnacle in the art of radio comedy was the summer of that year, not during network radio's heyday but years after its supposed death at the hands of television. Joyous and inventive, hilarious and provocative, *The Stan Freberg Show* lept to the airwaves of the CBS Radio Network on Sunday, June 14, 1957 at 7:00 p.m. Bill Froug, West coast VP of CBS, called up Stan that year to ask him to devise a replacement series for Jack Benny's radio show, now that the maestro was leaving the airwaves for TV. The Freberg broadcasts were a wild mix of sketch comedy, social satire, and music, and featured an ensemble of crazy characters supplied by the usual Freberg gang: Daws Butler, June Foray, Peter Leeds, and Freberg himself.

June Foray is best known as the voice of Rocket J. Squirrel and Natasha on *The Bullwinkle Show* and the voice of Granny in the "Sylvester and Tweety" cartoons. Leeds continued to work as Freberg's straight man in a variety of sketches and commercial ads, while frequently appearing on camera as well.

Daws thought the combined talent was perfect. "Stan wrote a lot of it, but he was buying sketches from all the good writers in town. The terrific thing that only another actor can understand is that we had a sense of rapport. We could look at each other and almost sense when someone was coming up with an ad-lib. It was very delightful. Stan was a great guy to work with. And of course some of the biggest laughs were the ad-libs and mistakes—same way with *Beany*."

For fifteen weeks, audiences howled with glee. Sponsors did not. The cult series Daws called "a respectable failure" never did gain a sponsor. But it is considered the last network comedy radio show.

Stan Freberg built upon some very sound radio comedy traditions: a solid ensemble cast like that of Jack Benny; satirical sketches with a social perspective like the best of Fred Allen; inventive use of sound effects that would make Fibber McGee and Molly proud; with a little of *Your Hit Parade* thrown in for good measure. Stan made it all uniquely his own, like nothing heard on radio before or since.

The musical direction was supplied by the great Billy May, who orchestrated some of Frank Sinatra's greatest Capitol recordings. There were songs by Peggy Taylor, a chorus known as The Jud Conlon Rhythmaires (who did chorus work in Disney's *Peter Pan*, among others), and appearances by the likes of Hans Conried, Herb Vigran, and other surprise voices. Bill James and Gene Twombly were the great sound effects men Freberg inherited from Jack Benny. The scripts were crafted by Freberg himself, along with ample writing help from Daws Butler and the show's producer, Pete Barnum.

The first show almost did not get on the air. An extended routine entitled "Incident at Los Voraces" was a savage piece of satire which took up nearly two-thirds of the show. It was specifically an attack on the excess of Las Vegas and in general a comment on current social events including the Cold War and nuclear arms race. The original version included references to the Gaza Strip in a chorus girls song and ended with a hydrogen

bomb going off. It was perhaps Freberg's most brilliant work for the entire run of the series and almost got the show canceled before it began. The show had been pre-taped in Hollywood and fed to CBS in New York the Friday prior to the broadcast. When network executives heard the show, they flipped, and Freberg and producer Barnum had to stay up all night rewriting the script and re-recorded it on Saturday with a new audience, with the all references to the Gaza Strip removed and an earthquake ending replacing the hydrogen bomb.

It starts with a brilliant premise: Freberg as himself talking with the many characters he had created on records. The rebel yell "Yeeeee-ha!" blares from the bombastic Texan. "Dayyyyyyyyyy-oh!" shouts his Harry Belafonte sound-alike. Other characters from other records jump in. Soon an argument breaks out as to which one is the real Stan Freberg until they shout in unison, "We're ALL Stan Freberg." "Frightening," says Freberg. Next, Freberg interviews a Frenchman through an interpreter (Daws). The Frenchman has the unusual talent of playing "Lullaby of Birdland" on "tuned sheep" by having them ring the bells around their necks every time he hits them on their heads with his crook. The remainder of the program is given over to Freberg's fierce satirical fantasy on Las Vegas: "Incident at Las Varoces," about two Nevada hotels The El Sodom and the Rancho Gammorah. Originally intended as a running installment in something he called "Freberg's Fables," nothing like it was attempted on the series again. The controversy over the ending insured Freberg would stick to somewhat safer territory.

The second show, broadcast on July 21, features a slight hint at the beginnings of Freberg's classic *United States of America* album, a very short bit about historical figure Barbara Frietche (Foray) ending with a surprise tag line that would become a running gag throughout the series. Next, Freberg interviews the Abominable Snowman, playing both parts himself. His Snowman is a lovable, if loud, monster in sneakers that speaks with a strange vibrato. The character proved so popular, Freberg brought him back several times later in the series. A piece about "Mount Rushmore" uses sound effects to get laughs and create a wonderful visual image. "Max's Delicatessen" is more like a mini-sitcom, than one of Freberg's sketches. In fact, it plays much like an episode of *Seinfeld* with a series of confusions on the telephone leading to a big comic payoff. It is performed by Freberg and Peggy Taylor (in a rare appearance as anything other than the show's resident singer). The show closes with Freberg performing his rock & roll spoof "Rock Around Steven Foster," a twist on his popular "Sha-boom" spoof recording. The voice Freberg uses in both these routines is said to have started as a takeoff on Marlon Brando's "marble mouth"-style of acting. Daws Butler later borrowed the voice from Freberg for the Hanna-Barbera cartoon character, Mr. Jinx.

Program three, broadcast on July 28, 1957, began with the fair premise that the Miss Universe contest should include beauties from other planets. "Miss Jupiter," brilliantly played in Brooklyn dialect by June Foray, is outraged because she was not admitted to enter the Miss Universe contest. "Skin Divers and Mandolins" is another great use of sound effects and a comic combining of two unlikely pastimes to create an odd audio travelogue-style portrait. June Foray, as the haughty birdwatcher Mrs. Prill, proves a formidable adversary to Freberg in "Upward and Onward Girls!"

The show ends with "The Flying Zazlophs," which uses the limitation of the radio medium to comic effect. After all, if ventriloquist Edgar Bergen could be a success on radio, if Major Bowes could present tap dancers, why couldn't Freberg present a family of circus acrobats?

The fourth program brought Freberg another step closer to his *United States of America* album, when he presents "Great Moments in History" and the ride of Paul Revere. Next, the first installment of "Herman Horn on Hi-fi" is presented with Freberg doing a slightly different "prototype" voice for his creation. Freberg, Butler, Leeds and Foray plus guest Hans Conried are featured in a "Lox Audio Theater" presentation of "Rock Around My Nose." "Good evening from Hollywood!" chimes Conried, who is best known as Snidely Whiplash in the *Dudley Do-Right* cartoons. This routine is such a marvelous piece of work, one wonders why it was not chosen to be part of *The Best of Stan Freberg* Capitol releases. It is simultaneously a spoof on radio's *Lux Radio Theater* and a twisted tale of man who could not get close to his son because his nose was too big. The son is brilliantly portrayed by Daws Butler using the voice that would become Elroy Jetson on *The Jetsons*. Lastly, Freberg's famous record "The Yellow Rose of Texas" is performed live, along with the rebel yell and an upstart snare drummer played by Peter Leeds.

In a brilliant piece of "visual" radio, the Zazaloph Family of acrobats returns to the eighth program for a second time. Reminiscent of the use of sound that marked Fred Allen's broadcasts twenty years before, Freberg teases the listening audience with descriptions of the incredible acrobatic feats they are missing by not being able to actually see the radio broadcast, with each description falling just short of telling what is actually happening. This is followed by one of the least known and funniest pieces of the series: "Uninterrupted Melody: The Story of the Good Humor Men." Stan and Daws both introduce the sketch, affording a rare opportunity to hear Daws in his natural speaking voice. Next, all hell breaks loose once again in a second installment of "Face the Funnies," a parody of news discussion programs that remains as timely today as it was in 1957. The program closes with a perfect recreation of the classic comedy record, *St. George and the Dragonet*.

In the ninth program, Stan goes off to the Himalayas again for another visit with the Abominable Snowman (also played by Stan in an eerie vibrato) and is introduced to Abominable's fiancée (Foray). Next, Robert E. Tainter (Daws) introduces yet another scandal of history — the "true" story behind Washington Crossing the Delaware. Throughout the series, Stan toyed with various ways of spoofing history and with this one he finally hits the mark. The program closes with a recreation of Stan's record spoof of *The Honeymooners*, featuring Stan as Ralph, Daws Butler as Norton (an early stage of Yogi Bear), and June Foray as Alice in "The HoneyEARTHERS" — the first television broadcast from the moon! Similar in style to the Bob McKimson/Warner Brothers series cartoon spoofs, *The Honeymousers* (in which Daws played both Ralph and Norton), "The Honeyearthers" is a clever one-joke twist on Jackie Gleason's most enduring creation.

Daws began the original "Honeyearthers" comedy record with "Flash! Through a new electronic discovery, we are able to pick up the first television program actually being broadcast by Moonpeople!" June is Alice and Stan is crabby Ralph who eats the new atomic cereal, Nuclear Nibbles, that comes in the lead box. "One of these light-years, Alice, one of these light-years, POW! Right in the antenna!"

As they recorded *The Stan Freberg Show*, Stan and Daws were continuing their bestselling comedy singles. Daws narrated "The Lone Psychiatrist" and played Pronto, another southern character, and the various characters TLP meets on his travels to Grandpa Snyder's house. Grandpa thinks he's a Great Dane.

On "Elderly Man River," Daws is the annoying, well-intentioned Censor who toots his little horn with anything offensive. "Old" goes in favor of "elderly"; "somethin'" retains its g to become "something"; the double negative has to go, too: "he don't know nothin'."

For the musical "Green Christmas," Daws plays Bob Cratchet to Stan's humbugging ad man Scrooge. Bob just wants to wish people a Merry Christmas, without tying every waking jingle to bells.

Back to radio, the tenth Freberg program starts with a short bit in which Stan pits audience members (Leeds, Foray) against the inventor of the freeway, Henry Cloverleaf. Next, June (playing herself but in her funny stock Brooklyn voice) and Stan build the Freberg Do-It-Yourself Grand Piano. This sketch is a great example of what radio did best and what Stan excelled at: using inventive sound effects to paint the scene and get the laughs. In the days when prerecorded open reel tape was a fairly new technology, it is interesting to hear some of the sound effects being played backwards, something the Beatles used to great effect ten years later. The next sketch, an interview with Fortune Cookie Writer Albert T. Wong (played in Chinese dialect by Daws) would not have gotten on the air if this show had been produced in the later politically correct era. It is nevertheless a very funny conceit to present a fortune cookie writer as an applause-getting art form. This is followed by a third visit from Herman Horne presenting yet another silly symposium on hi-fi and yet another brilliant use of sound effects to get laughs ("the sound of James Cagney removing his makeup," a reference to Cagney starring in the Lon Chaney, Sr. bio-pic, *Man of a Thousand Faces*.) The program ends with a recreation of Stan's dead-on Elvis Presley impression in "Heartbreak Hotel," plus questions about Elvis from the audience.

The eleventh program aired on September 22, 1957. In his introduction, Stan states he is really getting over a cold or flu; he uses this to his comic advantage and opportunity for the "Swiss ... this way we don't offend anyone" running gag. The first routine finds verbose Cliff Les Huntley (Freberg) interviewing terse College Footballer Francis "Butch" Sharmley (Leeds). This is followed by Stan performing Hoagy Carmichael's bizarre scat song "The Monkey Song." Next, Daws Butler uses his Cap'n Crunch voice again, this time for Foster Pelt, Theatrical Agent for Dog Acts. With unbelievable acts like a trombone-playing dog, an audience member protests, "I'm so bored my *trunk* has gone to sleep!" The program concludes with one of the greatest sketches of the entire series, "Bang Gunleigh, U.S. Marshall Fields." Sponsored by Puffed Grass, this parody of *Gunsmoke* generates enormous laughs with very little dialogue and extended sound-only scenes (mostly walking in brush and horse hooves on dirt).

In program twelve, reporter Herman Busby (Leeds) interviews Leroy Strattle (Freberg) as he records the sounds of an Army colonel (Daws) as he rides a rocket sled. Like many of Stan's funniest routines, this one evokes cartoonish images such Leroy Strattle becoming a human satellite followed closely behind by his white sneakers. The second piece takes a potentially traditional comedy sketch (with Stan and June Foray in a domestic battle to fix a leaky faucet) and builds it into a wild fantasy of science gone awry. Daws Butler plays the salesman in a mild version of his Phil Silvers impression, a voice he would later use for the Hanna-Barbera cartoon character, Hokey Wolf. Daws Butler returns as Bob Tainter in the next segment. This time Tainter has sunk even lower than in his previous historical exposes; he's become a labor racketeer. The show concludes with Stan recreating his hit comedy record parody "Sh-Boom!" which features June Foray as Stella.

The thirteenth program begins with Billy May and the Jud Conlon

Rhythmaires performing an "unusual" version of "Cocktails for Two." Billy nearly blows the joke by stumbling on his punchline (one of the few times he ever spoke on the series). Next, Stan poses the question "How to Improve the Circus" to his audience (June Foray in her Marjorie Main voice and Daws Butler in natural speaking tones). Daws confuses Stan with Steve Allen. The remainder of the program is given over to the brilliant Sci-Fi/Madison Avenue satire, "Gray Flannel Hat Full of Teenage Werewolves" (a title arrived at by combining three popular movies of that period, *The Man in the Gray Flannel Suit, A Hatful of Rain,* and *I Was a Teenage Werewolf*). The highlight of the piece is a commercial for "Food" (a bit very similar to one done by Ernie Kovacs on television). This routine was so successful, Capitol Records later released it as an album entitled "Madison Avenue Werewolf," which is still a favorite today and often played around Halloween on public radio stations. Comparing advertising men to werewolves did nothing, however, to help CBS with a big problem they were having: attracting sponsors to *The Stan Freberg Show*. Since its premiere the program had been sustained by CBS with the intention of attracting sponsors as the show gained ratings. This never happened. *The Stan Freberg Show* lasted only two more weeks.

In a later interview, Freberg recalled, "Well, there's a thing that Daws did that was very hilarious in the 'Gray Flannel Hat Full of Teenage Werewolves' sketch where he bursts into the office just as my secretary and I have discovered that we are both werewolves. He says, 'What a riot you guys are in those costumes.' Then he suddenly realizes that they're not costumes. And he does this hilarious nervous laugh ... and this got a tremendous reaction from the audience. Now imagine that the laughter coming from the audience was caused not by a joke at all but from Daws's terrific performance as an actor."

Once Stan knew his show was canceled and he no longer needed to look for a sponsor, he pulled out all the stops and made fun of the advertising world full force by ... sponsoring himself in the fourteenth program. With the help of "The World Advertising Agency," it skewered nearly every possible advertising convention all in one show, which features a funny detective story spoof, "Sam Spillade." About the lack of sponsors for his show, Stan wrote in his autobiography, "First, I hadn't let them (CBS) sell 'spots' in the show, holding out for one or two sponsors to buy the whole show, as (Jack) Benny had been sponsored by Jell-O, State Farm Insurance, and American Tobacco. Speaking of tobacco, I also had written into my con-

Relaxing between sessions.

tract that they couldn't sell the show to sponsors that I felt were undesirable, like underarm deodorants and cigarettes, among others. As a result, CBS had to turn down two different cigarette companies who wanted to sponsor me. That didn't put them in the best frame of mind, considering that in 1957 radio was fading fast on the network level, and most sponsors were putting the big bucks into television."

The last program of the last great radio comedy series included special encore performances of "Elderly Man River," "Bang Gunleigh," "Banana Boat Song," "Wun'erful, Wun'erful" and "Abominable Snowman."

"This is the fifteenth show of the series of a konked-out radio series," Stan sings at the opening. Two weeks earlier when Stan announced on the air that *The Stan Freberg Show* would be ending, he asked listeners to write in and tell him what they would like to hear on the last program. The mail that poured in was enormous and resulted in this program of encore performances of sketches from earlier episodes. After the series left the air, Stan ran a full-page ad in *Variety* and *The Hollywood Reporter* in which he appeared as a white-coated doctor with a stethoscope administering to a sick radio with a headline from the *New York Daily News* that read: "RADIO'S TIRED BLOOD REVITALIZED BY DR. FREBERG." In the picture, Stan's head was severed by an ax that was labeled "CBS." In spite of an audience of six million radio listeners, CBS pulled the plug on the show.

Stan immediately began negotiations with CBS for a television pilot for a visual comedy show called *Frebergland*, but the series never got off the ground because CBS executives found Stan's humor too bizarre. Ironically, for several years prior, Ernie Kovacs had tried something similar with his *Ernie in Kovacsland* on NBC and in 1961 on ABC Kovaks gained the national television audience that would forever elude the equally brilliant Stan Freberg.

In 1958, Capitol Records released two recordings of selected sketches from the radio broadcasts under the title *The Best of Stan Freberg*, which won a Grammy award and was among Capitol's biggest sellers up to that time. The complete fifteen programs were finally released on two Smithsonian collections years later, with a new audio introduction by Freberg, Foray and Leeds.

After CBS rejected his off-the-wall pilot script for TV, Stan immersed himself in advertising, incorporating Freberg, Ltd., though he and Daws did continue to make comedy singles for a few years. As Daws later admitted, the two great comics found themselves slipping into different directions. Stan just stopped calling him in for sessions around the time of the first *USA* album in 1961. Daws thought Stan did not like his singing voice and since there were a lot of songs on the album, he refused to use him. Of course, Daws had a great comedy singing voice, and since Daws was busy anyway with all the Hanna-Barbera cartoons by then, he stopped trying to get Stan to use him. By then, of course, the dynamic of their relationship had deteriorated from equal collaborators to Stan as boss/genius and Daws as hired voice with no input, which hurt Daws tremendously.

Stan Freberg had been a frequent Butler houseguest during the *Beany* years. But there were times that the two actors just didn't see eye-to-eye (even with "Frankenstein shoes"). Chas Butler remembers one such incident.

"At Raleigh's Studios, they were doing a commercial that had to do with a faucet, and Stan wanted it to drip a specific way. They had these plumbers and all these people in the soundstage working on this faucet to make it drip. And I remember my dad sitting there, probably for 12 hours, maybe longer than that. He just sat there the whole day. I remember him getting really annoyed at Stan. And then he just left. It was that kind of stuff that he got really annoyed at and it was some of that animosity that built up and was why they hadn't seen each other for a number of years."

Even as late as November 5, 1979, Daws wrote to Joe Bevilacqua, "Here is Stan Freberg's address. Good luck. He's a hard man to reach—I haven't bothered for years. I like him—I love him, actually, I guess—but we don't have that much in common anymore. I never could relate to him on a one-to-one basis, and I wouldn't want to work with him under any circumstances. We're on different wavelengths altho we did have a glorious collaborative honeymoon!"

Hair Bear · Quisp · The Sun · Funky Phantom · Capt. Skyhook · Bumble · Lambsy
Chilly Willy · Cap'n Crunch · Loopy-de-Loop · Baba Looey · Quick-Draw McGraw
Mr. Jinks · Snagglepuss · Dixie · Yogi Bear · Fibber Fox · Augie Doggie
Henry Orbit · Huckleberry Hound · Hokey Wolf · Blabber Mouse · Super Snooper
Lippy the Lion · Elroy · Cogswell · Wally Gator · Peter Potamus

Chapter 5
Hanna, Barbera & Yogi

Radio was dying. So was the theatrical cartoon industry. Both were rapidly replaced with television's all-consuming appetite for more and more "stock," often regardless of quality.

While Disney continued with their animated feature films, at other studios the cartoon departments were closing fast. MGM's award-winning animation wing folded so quickly, it left at least two industrious workers seriously wondering about their futures. But then Bill Hanna and Joe Barbera had too much drive for self-pity.

Bill Hanna was born in Melrose, New Mexico on July 14, 1910: the year William Howard Taft was President, and the Boy Scouts of America, which would come to mean a lot to the cartoon man, was founded in Washington, D.C. Hanna's first job was as janitor for Hugh Harman and Rudolph Ising who had just begun producing "Looney Tunes" and "Merrie Melodies" cartoons for Leon Schlesinger to sell to Warner Brothers Studio. The job paid $18 a week, but in those tough days of 1930 Bill was happy just to work. His smiling attitude and staunch loyalty to friends would be his trademarks as he moved up the ladder to contributing gags and little songs that would find their way into early Tunes and Melodies. It was this love of music which gave Hanna the knack for timing cartoons: aligning visuals with all audio cues to produce a tight, well-paced and *in synch* story.

"Hugh and Rudy were both extremely generous," Hanna wrote in his autobiography, *A Cast of Friends*, "giving me opportunities to gain a growing hands-on knowledge of animation production. I learned a lot from both men regarding the mechanics of making cartoons as well as an increased appreciation of the many subtle artistic and humorous nuances involved in creating appealing characters for personality animation."

MGM had become Harman-Ising's main cartoon purchaser, but in 1937 that studio decided to cut costs and establish its own cartoon studio. Many of the proficient creative people were recruited by MGM's cartoon department, headed by Fred Quimby. Hanna also came over. It was there that he met his future partner, Joe Barbera.

Artist Joe Barbera was born on March 11, 1911 on the Lower East Side of New York, at 10 Delancey Street in Little Italy, then moved to Flatbush, Brooklyn when he was four months old. His father was a barber who liked to play the track so much his family rarely saw him. Joe first worked for Fleischer Studios for four days, then for the Van Beuren Studio, then for Paul Terry, creator of *Terrytoons* (Mighty Mouse, Heckle & Jeckle).

From 1939, Hanna and Barbera began collaborating in one of MGM's animation units, under the supervision of producer Rudy Ising, who was then developing his Barney Bear character. Two years later, when Bill and Joe had their own Tom & Jerry unit, the infamous animation director Tex Avery joined MGM cartoons after six years at Schlesinger Productions.

"Whenever time permitted," wrote Barbera in his autobiography *My Life in 'toons*, "I would take the opportunity to run one of Avery's latest cartoons and study it on the movieola, frame by frame, in order to hone my own skills in timing."

Meanwhile Bill and Joe were pretty much left on their own to create characters and stories, since producer Fred Quimby seemed neither interested nor understanding of the cartoon business and its creative personnel. Left to their own devices, the Hanna/Barbera team came up with a cat and mouse which they called Jinks and Jasper, later to be their Oscar-winning Tom and Jerry.

For all of their huge success, Hanna and Barbera were two very different personalities. "Joe is a streetwise New Yorker," said Bill, "with a stylish, self-assured flamboyance." Joe Barbera loved the Hollywood life with its parties and people; Bill Hanna preferred "regular" guys and the outdoor life. But together in the studio they were an unbeatable team that went on, with the help of one uncredited voice guy, to create history.

Eventually Bill and Joe's Tom and Jerry won seven Oscars—which all sat on Fred Quimby's desk. As producer (who actually had nothing to do with assembling the cartoons), Quimby was the one who was credited for and received the esteemed Academy Awards. A fact which the two anima-

Bill Hanna, Joe Barbera and Daws Butler.

tors resented and lived with for years. Also, oddly enough, Hanna and Barbera didn't receive screen credit for all their diligent, time-consuming work. Even before the move to television, their thoughts were forming to "what if we worked for ourselves?"

When the ax finally fell on MGM's cartoon studio in early 1957, it ushered in the Hanna-Barbera era of "limited-animation" television. A coin was tossed: heads, the company would be called Barbera-Hanna, or tails, Hanna-Barbera. It was tails.

In a 1990 interview with Joe Bevilacqua for WNYC, New York Public Radio, Joe Barbera explained: "It was from desperation. They found out they could reissue our old Tom and Jerrys and do almost as well as spending money on new ones."

"By the late 1950s," Barbera once wrote, "television was cutting deep inroads into traditional Hollywood's bottom line. MGM was no exception, and, floundering in red ink, studio heads were desperately groping for corners to cut. One corner they found was ours. Television was in its infancy and very, very hungry for children's programming, and if Hanna-Barbera was not there to feed it, a lot of others would start getting the idea that *they* could."

Bill Hanna: "What could we do? Well, we could have elected to go out in a blaze of glory with a swan-song, big-screen cartoon that saluted the demise of the animation business. One final Tom and Jerry picture for the road and then maybe a career in real estate. Forget it. That was never a serious option for either Joe Barbera or me."

On December 14, 1957, their first TV production appeared, on NBC. The five 5-minute *Ruff and Reddy* cartoons were slated to open and close a half-hour children's show for Screen Gems (Columbia Pictures' TV division) on Saturday afternoons. The budgets were between $2,700 and $3,000, whereas H-B's Tom and Jerry budget at MGM was usually at around $35,000 (some sources claim $65,000) for each 7-minute cartoon! The necessity of limited animation had been born.

Production supervisor Art Scott explained that "because of time and budget we couldn't use a lot of animation. So we borrowed from radio the concept of using a lot of jokes and satire. The characters created were

Ruff and Ready.

more like stand-up comics than slapstick clowns."

"We did it in limited animation," Barbera explained to Bevilacqua, "and got as many laughs as we had before in the Tom and Jerrys. We were actually able to put over the business but by using the knowledge you had of twenty years in animation and by using the drawings and by timing it correctly, you were able to get the same effect."

"In my mind," Bill Hanna stated, "that phrase has always been somewhat of a paradox in terms. Limited may have meant fewer drawings per foot of film, but the concept that Joe and I launched was hardly restrictive in either its creative or commercial potential."

If anything, their new paradoxical cartoons had to be *better* than feature cartoons. In order to combat the relative cheapness of those early TV cartoons, more emphasis had to be given to character, not just luscious surroundings and action. The quality of the voices was a key issue.

"The Tom and Jerrys never had any voices in them," said Barbera, "except a loud scream when a safe fell on Tom once in a while. But I suddenly found myself in a position of having to do something we never had to do before and that was voices.

Enter stage left, Daws Butler and Don Messick.

"This little fellow walked in, and I said I want a Southern voice for Reddy. Not a New York or a Brooklyn but a Southern. Well, he took about a half-hour: 'Well. North Carolina would sound like that and South Carolina would be a little slower, like that, and the Cracker, oh, the Cracker voice down in Florida, the Everglades, and then if we go over into Atlanta…'

"It was Daws who suggested a guy named Don Messick."

"At the advent of television cartoons," said Messick, "one of the pioneers in that area was Hanna-Barbera after MGM in its infinite wisdom decided there was no future for cartoons in television. Too expensive to produce. But Bill and Joe came up with a method of short-cutting and doing what was then known as limited animation. Looking at some of those even today on reruns … those old ones to me, they hold up. There's a certain simplicity about them, which to me is beautiful. The backgrounds don't get in the way of the foreground, the characters. Bill and Joe put the emphasis on voice characterization, one reason being due to limited animation, that the character had to be strong to carry the impact of the characters. Daws and I worked together on so many of those series."

Daws also explained: "I had entered the new world of limited animation. And for five years I did most of the characters they dreamed up, along with Don Messick whom I had introduced to Bill and Joe at MGM as being a very talented actor. Don and I did all of it except for the feminine characters. I did Yogi Bear, Huckleberry Hound, Snagglepuss, Quick-Draw McGraw and Babba Looey, Super Snooper and Blabbermouse, Augie Doggie, Mr. Jinks and Dixie, Wally Gator, Peter Potamus, Elroy Jetson, Lippy the Lion, as well as a whole raft of characters for Jay Ward's *Fractured Fairy Tales* as well as the son in *Aesop and Son*. For the past twenty years I've been the voice of Cap'n Crunch for Quaker Oats. I guess I was everybody's babysitter."

Daws may not have known it at the time, but the work he did with Don Messick would perhaps be his favorite of Daws' long career. "We could work remarkably fast. Don and I would do 4 four-minute cartoons in about two hours."

In movie cartoons, voice tracks were recorded line by line, but in the new medium of television, there was interaction, with all lines recorded together. Daws found it like radio: more honest and exciting.

As a former ventriloquist who had also worked on a puppet show, Messick complemented Daws perfectly. Their dialogues were recorded quickly, which Daws felt enhanced their performances, even though budget constraints were probably the main reason this was done. And female roles were kept to a minimum to keep the dual cast small.

Daws was originally hired to be the voices of Reddy and Scary Harry

Daws Butler, Don Messick and Doug Young.

A scene from Ruff and Ready.

Safari (according to *TV Guide*, 1962) in 1957. *Ruff and Reddy* was a highly narrative, alliterative comedy full of puns and clever lines that longed to rhyme and just enjoy the sound of words.

Ruff and Reddy premiered on NBC on December 14, 1957. "Get set! Get ready! Here comes Ruff and Reddy!" sang the opening chorus as dog and cat gaily roamed the country in their little scooter. Daws voiced Reddy, the big, dumb, white dog with the black ears, in a precursor to his Huck voice, while Don Messick took the other four characters: Ruff (the tiny, brown cat), the narrator, Professor Gismo (in Droopy's voice) and Ubble-Ubble.

Originally sponsored by General Foods' Post Cereals, the short new material was programmed along with old Columbia cartoons such as *Color Rhapsodies, Fox and the Crow,* and *Li'l Abner*. Telecast in black and white, until June 1959, the series included a live host and emanated from WNBC-TV, New York.

The series lasted until October 1960 when production ceased, but the serialized stories had been proof enough to NBC of H-B's reliability to produce quality work. The network signed them to a five-year contract.

Next stop, a complete half-hour show. A half-hour pilot for *The Huckleberry Hound Show* was completed in the spring of 1958.

"Suddenly," said Barbera, "I found myself in the position of trying to

sell the show to advertisers, something I never had to do at MGM." The idea was sold to sponsor Kellogg's cereal over the phone. "Then I flew to Chicago, to play the first Huck show for the Kellogg's executives, done in limited animation, and we got as many laughs as we did with the Tom and Jerrys. They screamed!"

As with any new medium, the rules of the previous one were still in force: Bill and Joe were still thinking in seven-minute terms, just as their features for MGM had suggested. So along with Huck they had to come up with other clever characters for the short segments within the half-hour series. Enter stage right, Pixie and Dixie and Mr. Jinks, and Yogi Bear and Boo Boo.

> The biggest show in town
> is Huckleberry Hound
> for all you guys and gals.
> The biggest clown in town
> is Huckleberry Hound
> with all his car-toon pals.
> It's Huckleberry fun.
> It's for everyone,
> so come on, gather round!
> Get yourself all set,

tune up your TV set
for Huckleberry Hound.
That oh so merry, chuckleberry Huckleberry Hound!

"Kellogg's Cornflakes," energized the announcer, "the get going cereal, presents (chorus sings) Huckleberry Hound!" After which Daws/Huck would introduce himself with "And a Huckleberry hooooooounddog howdy!"

When originally brainstorming what Huck should sound like, Bill and Joe first requested a voice he'd once used for a big, scaredy-cat wolf. But Daws drew upon Myrtis' old North Carolina neighbor and drawled, "Man, the fearful wolf wouldn't be right. What we need for our series is a

Tennessee Ernie kind of character—amusing, persevering, and optimistic." It was basically the same voice he had used for Tex Avery's laconic but ultimately evil wolf and H-B's upbeat but not too bright Reddy...with a personality shift.

Within a half-hour, Bill and Joe were ready for the writers and animators. Daws was shown sketches for some of Huck's sidekicks and was given suggestions for which parts he could do and which could be done by Don Messick's specialized skills.

The Huckleberry Hound Show premiered on WPIX in New York on October 2, 1958 and was a smash hit. Sponsored by Kellogg's Cereals, it became the first cartoon to win an Emmy for Best Children's Program. It was also a phenomenal success with kids and parents alike. Everyone enjoyed the blue dog with the lazy eyes, the red bow tie and the Daws Butler drawl.

Hanna: "The laid-back, sow-belly-and-greens accent that Daws Butler endowed the character complemented perfectly the visual image of our unflappable little idealist." A large percentage of the 16- million viewers were college students and adults, grateful for a change from the 20 westerns and 12+ detective shows currently sharing the airwaves. Huck's slow-talking delivery was also a surprise novelty, smashing the stereotype that *everything* in a cartoon had to be fast to keep hold of fans' attention spans.

Clever comedy writing from Warren Foster and Mike Maltese (who left their long association with Warner Brothers to work for Hanna-Barbera in 1958), and Charlie Shows (who had co-written many of the *Time for Beany* shows with Clampett, Freberg and Butler), distinctive character design by Ed Benedict(extra fat lines, bulbous noses and rings around the mouths) and expert animation from Irv Spence and Ray Patterson (who had worked with Hanna-Barbera on the Tom and Jerry cartoons) helped the series become an instant classic. "I think of Huck as human," said Warren Foster. "He's the fall guy, and a large part of his humor is the way he shrugs off misfortune. To Huck, nobody is really bad."

Huck became so popular that fan clubs cropped up around the country. A Huck fan club in Seattle boasted some twenty thousand members. "It sure surprised me," Daws told Bill Weaver in a 1959 interview on KNX-TV, the former channel 2 in Los Angeles. "There was even a bar in Seattle named Huckleberry Hound. And on Tuesday nights," Daws continued, "It's like election night...they don't serve any booze...for a half an

hour before *Huckleberry Hound* comes on…that's out of respect…and then instead of watching the fights, they watch 'Huck' which I think is great."

Daws's star was rising. In 1960, Daws showed off his H-B voices and actually *appeared* on *You Bet Your Life* with old *Beany* fan Groucho Marx, first winning $500 with a French lady, and by a spin of the wheel, had a crack at $10,000. "What was the name of the act which enforced the 18th amendment (prohibition)?" Daws answered the Volstead Act and won! "See, it's not so bad bein' a dog after all," he quipped in character. With his half, Daws promised to set aside trust funds for his four boys. Groucho was comically upset, as he didn't have to give away that kind of cash often. "Well, I'm glad you won the money even though you won't get it."

Daws was invited to be a guest on other TV shows including Art Linkletter's *House Party*, and *Truth or Consequences* with Bob Barker. For each TV appearance, Daws would write special material for Huck, Yogi and the gang:

Huck: When I was a little kid pup, I was poor, you know. My momma, she was poor. And my daddy was poor. And we dint have no money and that's the worst kinda poor.

Yogi: I remember we was very poor too, and we didn't have no butter in the house...so what we used to do, we used to wear yellow sunglasses and eat lard! I come from a big family of bears. We had so many kids, momma used to make Jell-O in the bathtub.

In 1962 *Parents Magazine* gave the *Hound* show an "acceptable" rating, reviewing, "Although there is considerable action in the Hanna-Barbera scripts, they are not frightening. They never use a vicious character, not even for purposes of villainy. They never use violence for the sake of violence."

But remembering their solid, 18-year career with MGM which had folded so unexpectedly and quickly, Hanna and Barbera were not eager to rest on their laurels. Joe Barbera was eagerly sketching out new ideas and pitching them. By 1960 their company had nine shows in syndication and was by far the premiere studio producing cartoons for television. Not even Disney Studios could match their speed or success.

It was their personal and artistic philosophies, as well as their strong business sense, which led Hanna-Barbera Productions to glory. They believed in likeable, *cute* characters that would never cause fear or revulsion, but which could be eagerly embraced (even via tie-in dolls and toys) by impressionable young children. Luckily for parents, the stories and voice work also so impressed as to keep a staple adult audience.

The Huckleberry Hound Show was divided into three segments: Huck, Pixie and Dixie, and Yogi Bear. Pixie (Messick) and Dixie (Daws) were fun-loving mice menaced by an articulate, laid-back cat, Mr. Jinks (Daws), who "hated meeces to pieces." The voice Daws used for Jinks was his own take on a voice Stan Freberg used for his Capitol recording, "Sh-Boom" in which Stan lampoons not only early rock 'n' roll but Marlon Brando's mumbled performing as Stanley Kowalski in *A Streetcar Named Desire*.

When Mr. Jinks and the meeces took to showcasing Kellogg's Raisin Bran, one episode found Pixie and Dixie winding up a robot lady cat to get the illustrious breakfast food away from him. And in 1963 Jinksy literally flipped his Beatles wig when he and the mice sang a rock 'n' roll number,

Beatles-style, on Jinks' raisin ranch. Daws and H-B knew how to sell cereal.

The Damon Runyon-like articulation that Jinks employed kept it as one of Daws' top three favorite characters throughout his life. "Mr. Jinks calls for my lowest register and not much push. This cat is pretty limited, reminiscent of the sort of actor who enrolls in a New York method school and comes out with the sweat shirt but no talent." He called it a very loose and somewhat intelligent sound, while Dixie was "nasal, wistful and innocent."

The other half of the mouse team was Pixie (the mouse with the bow tie) done by Messick in an appropriately high elf voice. Daws' Dixie (the mouse with the vest) was a Southerner like Huck but with a voice that Daws pushed into a higher register; "a back of the head voice," Daws used to call it. He would use variations of this small head voice for many characters: Dixie (Southern), Augie Doggy (a shaky vibrato), Elroy Jetson (self-assured), Blabbermouse (a side of the mouth lisp), Lambsy (added diphthongs where there were none: "It's the wool-uf!"), Beany (a bit deeper in tone than Augie Doggy), Aesop's son (the deepest and smartest of his kid voices), and others. By giving each their own unique inflections and rhythms, Daws made each an individual personality.

Daws later wrote, "I did quite a lot of adlibbing. Interpolation. The line would be there, but I would talk around the line and loosen it up sometimes. Especially with Mr. Jinks and characters like that. Joe Barbera respected my ability to ad-lib and let me get away with it a good percentage of the time. It wasn't what they call chewing scenery or padding your part. I wanted to make it as *funny* as I could, and by twisting or inverting a line, sometimes it made even the writer look better. Don Messick on the other hand is very straight and reads exactly what he's got to read and is very disciplined. I used to take chances and sometimes got away with it!"

It was Daws who added the phrase "You dig" to many of Jinks' lines, giving him a sort of '50s beatnik quality.

The third *Huckleberry Hound* segment made history. Yogi Bear. Messick was Boo Boo and the Ranger. Yogi, voiced by Daws, became such a huge star (H-B's first true superstar), he had his own spin-off series.

Daws later said that H-B remembered a dog voice that Daws had done for some of their MGM cartoons, and built the Yogi character around that. When Don Messick and Daws would view model (cartoon) sheets of the characters, they would pitch around voice ideas until something clicked with all concerned. Joe Barbera had wanted an Ed Norton (*The Honeymooners*) sound-alike, but Daws fought to pull the character into its own direction as the series progressed.

Daws: "I was doing a little dog character once in a while for Hanna-Barbera's theatrical cartoons, and I had that kind of a voice, based on Art

Carney, but Art was a much lighter voice. I added diaphragm, vowel spreads, all kind of things, pumped air into it. Little by little it became my own style."

Daws knew that every voice should have the element of a real person behind it. "If the sound you are hearing is funny but doesn't evoke a certain type of character, the voice actor isn't doing a good job." And he knew that strength and vitality were the keys to winning the audience over to the characters. The voices of the characters had to be larger than life. It made them memorable.

He knew his unreal family well. As much as Hanna and Barbera were the originators of the looks of these animal friends, Daws voiced the personalities, created the subtleties and nuances that were so important to every other facet of the cartooning process, from scripts to merchandising. He could tell anyone how "his" characters would act in any given situation.

He wasn't a static performer of vocalization. When Daws voiced Yogi Bear he would stand on tiptoe, roll his eyes and posi-tively enunciate his catchphrase, "I'm smarter than the a-ver-age bear!" Letting all the air out of himself for a sluggish and sage blue Huckleberry Hound, his laconic syrupy tones would almost monotone a completely different personality.

When the ever-popular Yogi Bear got his own show, Hokey Wolf (Daws in his brightest, pushiest Phil Silvers-Sgt. Bilko voice) filled the slot left vacant on *Huckleberry Hound*. Daws explained that the voice was "an upper baritone, a head tone for a fast-talking operator who dazzles you with his bridgework." Doug Young voiced Ding-a-ling.

Yogi's show, meanwhile, featured new Daws creations, including Daws' favorite H-B character, Snagglepuss.

Don Butler remembered a significant event: "I sat in at a couple of Hanna-Barbera sessions in 1960, with Dad and Don Messick, doing a

Yogi Bear cartoon. And I do remember specifically in Dad's recording studio, my brother Paul and I witnessed the birth of Snagglepuss. It was a *Huckleberry Hound* cartoon, the premise of which was that Huckleberry Hound was a shepherd-tending sheep, and Snagglepuss is the mountain lion that Huckleberry Hound is guarding the sheep against. And Dad was in there in the recording studio experimenting with all kinds of different voices for the voice of Snagglepuss. He was zeroing in on Bert Lahr, singing a song, 'I'm going to the fa-re, 'cause Willy boy is the-re!' Ending the way Bert Lahr sang the 'King of the Forest' in *The Wizard of Oz*."

Daws' vocalization of Snagglepuss was a direct imitation of Lahr when Snag was a supporting character in the Quick-Draw, Snooper, and Auggie Doggie cartoons from 1959. Don Messick, and others, thought it Daws' best vocal characterization. But when Snag was given his own cartoon in 1960, Daws completely changed the voice, pushing it into a higher range, making the voice breathy, taking out the guttural sounds (the trademark Bert Lahr "yong-yong" sound), but kept the personality and the rhythm.

There was one Snagglepuss line, which read in the script as "I don't agree with ya." Daws changed that to "I beg to differ. I'm a differ begger." It was just those sorts of improv characterizations, which kept Daws always on form and at the top of the voice world. "I wasn't always going for laughs, but it had to be individual, to fit the character."

Putting in extra syllables helped Snagglepuss' unpredictability and freshness. When working on a Kellogg's Cocoa Krispies commercial, Daws/Snag would not say "crunchy" as written. He would claim it's "Ka-runchy, even!" It helped Yogi too, who didn't steal picnic baskets. They were "pic-a-nic baskets" he was after.

Snagglepuss' catch phrases were instantly snapped up by kids and adults both. Once while waiting to be seated in a restaurant, Daws heard the man in front of him give a bad Snagglepuss impression, "Exit, stage left into the dining room." Daws instantly turned to the man he was with (writer Mark Evanier) and did the real voice, "Heavens to trademark violations! I'm being plagiarized!"

"Snagglepuss was Mike Maltese favorite character," Daws told Joe Bevilacqua in 1979. "Mike couldn't wait to come into the studio with his latest story," Joe Barbera told Bevilacqua in 1990. "He loved reading it out loud and imitating Daws."

Though Snagglepuss was a recurring character on *Quick-Draw McGraw*, his voice changed with every appearance. Only when he decided on Lahr did the character retain its lasting grace. But Lahr didn't feel complimented, suing H-B and sponsor Kellogg's. The infamous Lahr suit came from Snagglepuss' Cocoa Krispies commercials, which had the lion playing the banjo and singing to a happy audience (inserting "Heavens to Murgatroyd!" at just the right moments) who eventually stampede him to attain the delicious cereal. Lahr said he was insulted to think he would stoop to selling cereal; meantime, he was selling Lay's Potato Chips. Therefore, all Cocoa Krispies commercials soon carried a superimposed line of credit: "Snagglepuss voice by Daws Butler." Daws didn't mind the extra credit. It made up for all those Warner Bros. years when only Mel Blanc had his name onscreen.

It was the commercials that kept H-B, and all of television, going. In addition to the commercials, there were short interstitial segments where all the characters would interact between the cartoon and the commercials. Sometimes the cartoon shows seemed like almost seamless programs, hard to tell when the cartoon stopped and the commercials began. Characters would walk on, suddenly eating Kellogg's Cornflakes.

One of Daws' many H-B cartoon commercials for Kellogg's had Quick-Draw McGraw and Babba Looey making a Rice Krispies commercial. Unfortunately, Babba Looey throws the real Quick-Draw over the cliff instead of the stunt dummy, so the cowboy horse only has a few seconds remaining to sing the Krispies' praises before hitting the earth (a tree branch, actually). A bigger sponsor budget gave a greater range of motion to this one-minute spot than the series itself.

His name may have been enveloped in the too-fast credits at the end of the shows, but Daws reportedly made $150,000 in 1960 doing H-B voices. The great thing was that he was a star without being a star. "There's something to be said for anonymity, too. I mean, a head waiter can be as rude to me as anybody. They don't know who the hell Daws Butler is. It's only the people who look at the titles, those are the people that really dig you."

While fan mail poured in by the hundreds weekly for Huck, Yogi and others, Daws was free to roam the streets without inciting that sort of attention. Some knew who he was, though. In 1959, Seattle radio station, KING, phoned him after a bear had escaped from their local zoo. They asked Daws to sooth the listening public and keep them from panicking. Daws improvised a bit of Yogi: "Uhhh, it's not me, folks. It's some kind of imposter!"

A year after *Huckleberry Hound*, came the horse with the cowboy hat, holster, gun, tin star and blue bandana—*Quick-Draw McGraw*.

> Yippee yi-o ki-a,
> Galloping all the way
> Here comes Quick-Draw McGraw.
>
> Yippee yi-o ki-a,
> Galloping all the way
> Great big star on his chest.
> Outdraws all of the rest.
> Fastest gun in the west.
>
> Yippee yi-o ki-a,
> Riding around your way,
> Here comes Quick-Draw McGraw.
> The high-falutin'est,
> Fastest shooin'est,
> Cowboy you ever saw.
> That's Quick-Draw McGraw.

The voice talent did include the occasional Peter Leeds, Jean Vander Pyl, Don Messick, Doug Young and Hal Smith—but mostly, it was all Daws. From Quick-Draw and sidekick Babba Looey, to the art-ic-ulate tough guy patter of Super Snooper ("worlds' greatest detective and winner of this year's Modesty Award") and Blabbermouse (his lisping sidekick), Daws had a gas talking to himself in the staring roles. (Later, Paul Frees substituted as Super Snooper on the *Monster Shindig* album, because Daws was under contract to Columbia's Colpix Records. The weirdest and least successful of these LP re-castings was Allan Melvin as Yogi Bear and June Foray as Boo Boo! "We [Don Messick and I] weren't doing anything, but we were *signed* to them.")

Daws originally wanted to use his Charles Butterworth voice for the honest and fearless Quick-Draw, but Joe Barbera wanted him to sound more Western, so Daws added a twang to his Butterworth voice and it became Quick-Draw McGraw.

In an audio tape he made for Joe Bevilacqua in 1975, Daws explained, "Quick-Draw McGraw is a dope character...and it's very hard paletted

and I am keeping my jaw very tight. The tongue inside of my mouth is doing a lot of articulating but basically the lips are doing most of it. I'm forcing out the articulation. So the lips and the nerve endings are doing are the hard work, all the journeyman acting."

For Super Snooper, Daws chose a New York dialect gleaned from his impression of one of his favorite actors, Ed Gardner, who played Archie on radio's *Duffy's Tavern*, and combined it with another character actor, Tom D'Andrea, who played Jim Gillis on TV's *Life of Riley*. The result is one of animation's most sly and subtle characters to ever appear in animated cartoons.

The third segment came in the guise of Augie Doggie and Doggie Daddy, based on *Spike and Tyke*, two dogs that recurred in HB-produced MGM

cartoons. Joe Barbera wanted Daws in both leads, and was desperate to have Doggie Daddy like Spike—a Jimmy Durante clone. But Daws feared his throat wouldn't be able to take the strain of Durante's guttural deepness, and recommended Doug Young. The great exchanges between the two—plus Michael Maltese's fine writing—made the cartoon another hit.

"Around 1950 radio started fading out and television was coming in," recalled Young. "Everyone was sort of scrounging around, and I had a family to support so I got a job driving a truck and I figured, well, I'll see what's going to happen. I was in a bookstore browsing around one day, and Daws happened to come in. We hadn't seen each other for a while. Meantime, he had connected with Hanna-Barbera for some early stuff for

Blabbermouse, Super Snooper, Doggie Daddy, Augie Doggy, Quick Draw McGraw and Babba Looey.

them. He said you shouldn't be doing this, come on, you've got to come out to Hanna-Barbera with me and do some things there. It was one of those uncanny coincidences. He had a wonderful little studio out there in Beverly Hills behind his house. And we worked out a tape that I did, of my characters and all that.

"Hanna-Barbera was starting out with a series called *Quick-Draw McGraw* which involved various segments. One of them was called *Augie Doggie*, about this little dog. They were looking for someone to play Augie Doggie's father, so he said come down here. And Daws himself talked to Joe Barbera. So they held an audition. Myself and several other people read for it. And they liked what I did. So I got hired to do the character voice of Doggie Daddy. Daws loved it.

"Miles was one of these agents who was always trying to get you more money. He saw to it that everyone got paid the right amount. I think it was around $150 per voice character per show. Which would add up quit a bit if you did a lot of roles.

"At that time a lot of the radio people were getting into the animation thing. So Daws got me going there, and from then on I got quite a lot of work. Daws was the one who did it. I said one time, 'You know, Daws, you were awfully good to me. What can I do to thank you?' And he said, 'The way to thank somebody is to help somebody else.' I always thought it was admirable of him to take that position.

"Joe Barbera was a pretty tough task master. He wanted things as right as could be. But at the same time he was open to suggestions. You had freedom to experiment. Daws was a very creative guy. He would always think of a different way to do the line or change it or the attitude.

"Daws was always doing some kind of character. Even walking down the hall. I always thought he was the best of the voice people. With all due respect to people like Mel Blanc. Daws would always do these different voice characters. And you were never sure if it was him doing it. Whereas I could always tell it was Mel Blanc, he had that certain sound. But Daws was just unbelievable. He would do five guys talking to each other, interrupting himself."

In his 1990 interview with Joe Bevilacqua, Barbera recalled his favorite Daws character was one that never said a line of dialogue. "We had a dog that worked with Quick-Draw McGraw, named Snuffles. Well, he was a two-faced dog. He wouldn't do anything unless they gave him a dog biscuit. He'd point at his open mouth and go, 'Uh-uh-uh!' and Quick-

Draw would say, 'No way are you gonna get another dog biscuit.' Snuffles would just shrug and not move. 'OK. Here's another dog biscuit.' And Snuffles would go off and meet the heavy. But the heavy would give him three dog biscuits. Each time he ate a biscuit he'd float up in the air with a sigh and float gently back to earth. I gotta tell you kids would come into my office and hug themselves and imitate that dog. The funniest thing was when Quick- Draw McGraw, trying to figure out what was the ecstasy that he got out of the dog biscuits, ate one himself and he did the same thing."

Quick Draw was another smash. H-B now had the money and track record to move into prime time television with *The Flintsones*, and produce another series of cartoon shorts: *Loopy DeLoop*, which was filmed in wide-screen format and distributed to movie theaters by Columbia Pictures. It gave Daws another chance to be outrageous, via his flavorful French-Canadian dialect. Loopy DeLoop was a good-hearted wolf that donned a wool cap, whose attempts to help those he met in his travels always went awry.

Daws and Don were also given many record album projects to do as each series attracted higher ratings:

Ruff and Reddy's Adventure in Space (1958)

With only an organ for music, Don Messick announces and voiced Ruff, while Daws pulled his weight through a few tongue-twisters as Ready (and others). "Reports of a strange saucer-shaped ship" were denied by the media, but were in fact true: the ship sought out and acquired two Earth people (R&R, of course, though they aren't people) to bring back to their planet to study. The animals try to steer the ship back to the earth, finding the control room deserted, but soon the spacemen come with their Whamma-Bamma-Gamma Gun to burn a hole through the door. Through a mishap, the spacemen are tossed into outer space when everything goes weightless, but R&R still can't veer the craft from its destination: the metal planet Munimula. ("That's aluminum spelled backwards," helps the narrator.) There, they meet the two-faced, two-voiced Big Thinker (Daws) who is going to build an army of robots based on R&R—and will invade the Earth! The aluminum men place them in the replication chamber called the Big Squeeze ("placing them between an irresistible force and an immovable object"), are painted, then get a thinking cap (an electronic brain, under control of the Big Thinker).

Cat and dog extricate themselves from the robots' clutches, only to later find that what they think is the Big Thinker is a Wizard of Oz by the name of Professor Gizmo (Messick), an inventor, who built the first interplanetary rocket ship (the *S.S. Gizmo*) on Mount Cucamunga. Now he too is a prisoner, who speaks like Bill Thompson's Wallace Wimple from *Fibber McGee and Molly* and Droopy Dog. The *real* Big Thinker sends his Munimulamen after the trio in a sequel rocket the Prof. managed to build in his spare time. With the help of Gizmo's bag of tricks, they shake off the pursuing spacemen and just barely make it back to Earth in the out of control rocket. Prof. Gizmo immediately puts the wasted rocket up for sale with Hard-Sell O'Dell. "For sale: slightly used rocket ship. Used only by an elderly Cucamunga professor. Cheap." Ruff and Ready journey back to Mount Cucamunga with Gizmo to build the 3rd edition of the rocket ship.

The script was written by Charlie Shows. The voice track was taken directly from the first season of the *Ruff and Reddy* TV show, with the Capitol stock music replaced with organ music.

Huckleberry Hound—Kellogg's Great TV Show (1959)

To organ music, Huck narrates the tale of "Yogi Bear and the Missing Ele-fent." An elephant, done in Droopy-style voice by Messick, escapes from a circus truck and comes upon Yogi's cave, waking the poor bear up. Yogi hides his chubby new friend from the two fiendish circus drivers. Next up, he relates "It Ain't So Easy to Catch a Measy," a Pixie & Dixie

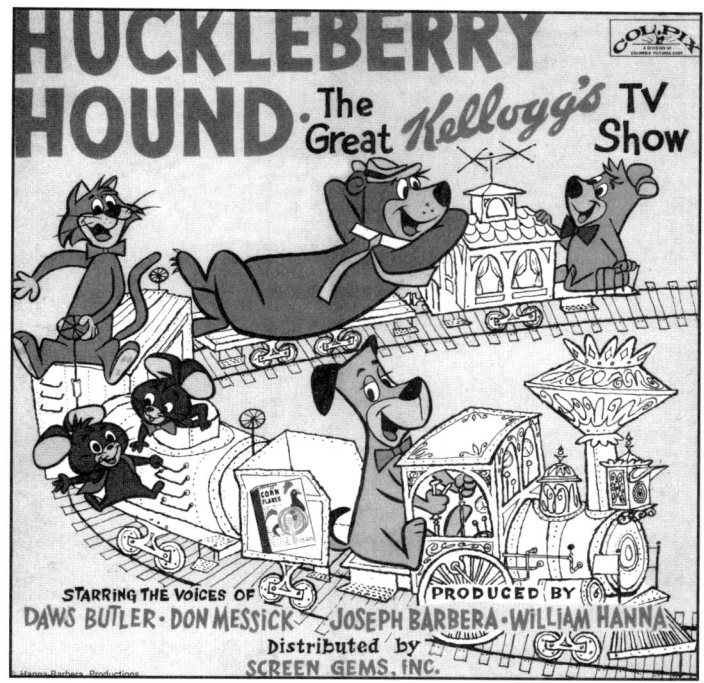

adventure in which Mr. Jinks teaches his little kitten son how to catch meeces. Trouble is, junior gets along with everyone: mice, puppies, and he even likes cheese. "Dinky Dalton and the Showdown at Howdown Corale" tells of Huck's own slam-bang tale of bringing in huge, mean Dinky, last of the Dalton Gang. His handcuffs were barely big enough to handcuff the guy's pinky, but, as usual, the blue dog always gets his man.

Once again, this LP is made up of voice tacks from the TV shows with the organ music replacing the Capitol stock music H-B were using at the time.

Quick-Draw McGraw (1959)

McGraw tells a few stories to "you" and Babba Looey. First up is "In the Picnic of Time," starring Doggy Daddy and Augie Doggy who befriends an ant at their father & son picnic. When Daddy lashes one ant for running away with some cake (a mistake, since Augie *gave* it to his little friend), the whole ant community declares war on poor Daddy. Next: "The Case of If the Shoe Fits, Wear It," starring the vacationing Snooper and Blabbermouse. Mission: to find the girl who lost a glass slipper at a party last night. All voices were by Daws except Jean Vander Pyl as the fairy Godmother and other females. Then, Quick-Draw's own "The Story of El Kabong vs. El Tabasco." The off-key singer croons between fighting villains and bullfighting, "Oh, I have not slept in twenty days. I should look an awful sight. But it does not bother me at all, 'cause I always sleep at night."

Doug Young recalled that "Daws got an actor who was down on his luck to direct that record. He said, 'I want you in the booth, making sure we're doing it right.'"

Mr. Jinks "Lend-Lease Meece" (1961)

Mr. Jinks, ably interrupted by Pixie and Dixie, tells the story of the time he lent out the meeces. This is another use of the actual TV show voice tracks, with the Capitol stock music replaced with new underscore music written by Hoyt Curtin for the *Loopy DeLoop* series.

In the first story, Jinksy, to ingratiate himself to the new next-door cat lends his meece to Charlie until he can get some mice of his own. After all, the owners might wonder what's the sense in having a cat around if there are no meece? But after two weeks, Mr. Jinks proclaims himself perturbed since his little friends are treated so nicely over there (they even have their own mice house); they don't wanna leave. After a few bang-on-the-head fights, all is resolved when a minuscule, hungry, homeless mouse wanders into Charlie's world. Jinksy scoops up his friends pronto, and new cat and mouse live together as soul mates.

For a second story, the tale of mouse Judo Jack (voiced like Charlie Chan by Daws) tells of Pixie and Dixie's revenge on Jinksy for treating them to frying pans on the noggin and whatnot. With a violent "Ah—*so!*" Judo Jack beats the catnip out of the pussy. Before leaving, he gives the meeces a lesson in leverage, plus do-it-yourself judo kits (Judo Jack suits), which are *just* enough to keep Mr. Jinks in line to the end of the episode.

Pixie and Dixie start the cat off on a third tale next—about the time Jinksy tried to impress a butler (Daws Butler) in a mansion, caught the meeces and mailed the guys off to the North Pole. Alas, the butler informs the cat that since his livelihood is posted, "we deduct you" from the household. "Let's, uh, take it from the top, sir," queries Mr. Jinks. "I missed some o' the last quotes." To insure a life of employment, the pussy cat zooms off to the North Pole to bring his "friends" back, and proceeds to milk their presence for all its worth. Trouble is, the owner of the place had to sack the butler due to rising costs, and the only way the poor snooty soul could retain his needed standing was to chase the mice. Off went

Jinksy again to the North Pole, hopeful to find more meeces.

The final story, "Goldfish Fever," told of Mr. Jinks' obsession with panning for goldfish in the next door neighbor's house, risking life and teeth against the aggressive bulldog (Daws) they have. When the goldfish turn out to be equally tough, it puts Mr. Jinks off fish for good. Except for canned sardines, since they don't fight back.

Huckleberry Hound and the Ghost Ship (1962)

This LP release by Colpix, which was a division of Columbia Pictures, was one of only two that Daws had the opportunity to write himself. And it shows. The writing is much more fluid and complex than the TV cartoons, the jokes sharper, the word-play more intricate. And the characters better integrated into each other's lives. Huck, Yogi, Boo, Jinks, the meeces, Hokey Wolf, Ding-ling, and even Snooper and Blabber appear together in the story of Huck and the gang's travels at sea. All the voices are performed by Butler and Messick, except for Doug Young's Ding-ling, and Messick is given co-writing credit.

"One day, Huckleberry Hound and his friends decided to get together for a little fishing trip," began Messick's narrative. Pixie, Dixie, Mr. Jinks, Yogi Bear, Boo Boo, "and yours truly, Lemuel Fropneg (Daws loved the name Lemuel and would later use it for a character in his "Sherlock Holmes in Trouble" script produced for NPR in 1982 by Joe Bevilacqua). Huh, huh. I was just joshin'. I'm really Huckleberry Hound." They rent a boat from Hokey Wolf and his assistant, Ding-ling. "I got a special going this week. A one- cent sale. You buy one yacht for $50,000, you get a second one for a penny." Boo Boo offers him a penny. "We'll just take the second one." But they end up taking a row boat for a dollar an hour.

At sea, the fish don't bite, but the sky darkens and the wind whispers a scary "Beware…the Black Swan…" Huge waves capsize their boat, but a passing ship comes along to rescue them. The Black Swan! Ghostly screams and noises terrify the others to run, but Huck calms them. Unfortunately, Mr. Jinks has vanished. Pixie and Dixie sing a short lament, ending with "We realize now what our friendship meant. He wasn't all bad, only 90 percent."

Mr. Jinks is lost in the bottom of the ship, wishing he had a flash-type light. That's all Hokey has to hear: "Flashlight? Flashlight? I have a special going on flashlights today, one for the price of two. Quickly, quickly!" With it, he finds a phone and a dime to call up Super Snooper, but the

sleuth is "otherpied occuwised with another case." Jinksy is captured by Captain Kidd and is forced to call up to his friends on the ship's loudspeaker. Ghosts, led by a definite Cap'n Crunch voice (Daws), appear to the gang, because they've been sentenced to 500 years aboard this musty old ship. "We're banished banshees, real gone ghosts," says the lead ghost. "As spooks we have a problem that annoys us quite a bit." Another ghost (Messick) continues the poem, "It's hard to keep our ghostly sheets away from grime and grit." Alternating they finish: "Our victims, when we holler BOO!, just laugh at us and shout, 'Go wash your dirty shirts and get that tattletale gray out! Clean sheets! Clean sheets! We want clean sheets! White or pink or green sheets, as long as they are clean sheets!" That's all Hokey Wolf has to hear. He rushes upstairs to give the ghost his card for Hokey's Laundromat. The ghosts are overjoyed and fly away.

Sneaking around the spooky ship, our heroes find a cockney rat (Young). "I shower each day, and eat chlorophyll cheese, so I won't offend, and me breath will please." They make a deal with him: if he helps them find Mr. Jinks and get safely to shore, they'll take him with them and help him find a good job in the United States. "Patriotic rats are in demand now. For rockets, missiles and satellites."

Meanwhile, the Captain Kidd (Daws doing a Terry Thomas-type effeminate British voice) has tied Mr. Jinks up, and threatens the *scaredy* cat with leaving him on an island with cannibals. Mr. Jinks insults the ghost's bravery. "I bet they've even got you listed in the Yellow Pages." To prove he's got guts, the ghost unties him so he can tie him up again when Jinks is not unconscious; Jinks calls him a "dumb sock" and scrams. He's captured again and forced to walk the plank, but tricks the Captain into walking for him, to get the idea. The gang fishes him out and listens to his tale of a poor childhood, having to drink milk with mud in it. Hokey Wolfe again appears to convince the pirate that the aptitude test he took years ago was in error—he should be a TV actor. Kidd has no peg leg or eye patch, and his cardboard cutlass just doesn't cut it, so he might as well star in Captain Kidd's Kid Show.

The Treasure of Sarah's Mattress (1962)

That same year saw the release of a second gem, one that may have been one of the finest and funniest children's records to ever see the light of vinyl. The resourceful script filled with in-jokes, puns and other assorted, hidden gags stands up favorably against anything Hanna-Barbera ever produced, and could even give *The Simpsons* competition.

Over strings and a slow western cantor comes Don Messick's unmistakable narration: "No character of the old west is more exciting than that hero of countless hair-raising adventures—namely, Quick-Draw McGraw!" The great cartoon horse is bored by inactivity. "There's nothing left to fight. Even the catsup shakes out easier these days." He and Babba Looey spent their days sleeping on the side of a cliff. "If ya can't live dangerously," says McGraw, "ya might as well sleep dangerously."

Meantime, over at Tarantula Ranch, its new owners, Doggy Daddy (Doug Young) and Augie Doggie (Daws), are being terrorized by a sinister laughter, bats and other creepy creeps. The next day, they travel to the employment agency in town to select a foreman. The ever-ebullient Snagglepuss enters, stagestruck. "Heavens to Murgatroyd, an audition! I do card tricks. I tap dance! Even when I was a clerk, I juggled the books." But this cat is a bit too crazy for such a spooky job. Luckily, they meet McGraw who doesn't even know how to *spell* fear. He's hired.

The guest ranch opens for business, bringing in Snagglepuss via two old spinsters looking for husbands. Chief Crazy Coyote (Messick), the bubbly giggler, also enters with his exploding matches. After another night of terror, Daddy phones up broken-English detective Super Snooper

(Daws) who "will solve any crime or mystery for a phenomenal nominal fee." He shows up with his diminutive assistant Blabber Mouse as the ghosts return to scare everyone away into the desert night. Little do they know it is Snagglepuss and Chief Crazy Coyote who scare up the spooks in order to lay the area clear to hunt for the treasure they know is hidden in one of the 24 mattresses somewhere in the ranch's 12 bedrooms; not counting the 48 in the bunkhouse. "That," exclaims Snagglepuss, "is a lotta bunk!" Sarah Bellum was the brains of a gang of western outlaws who stashed her loot in a mattress somewhere nearby, so the story goes.

The screams that continue into the night develop a skip, telling the frightened animals that "the ghosts are on a record, being released at this more inconvenient time," says Snooper. "Somebody's been needlin' us, and needle us to say, only dumbbells would fall for that." In the ranch house, Coyote finds only feathers in Sarah's mattress. "Me thought you'd be tickled," he tells Snagglepuss. "Feathers in Sarah's mattress different. They Golden Eagle feathers!" Caught in the act, Doggy Daddy is "not one to bear a garage" and so takes $500 from Coyote for the mattress and contents. It's nothing to sneeze at, but Coyote does, realizing he's allergic to them.

Once again, written by Butler with help from Messick, there are some very clever moments of word-play such as when the two spinsters (Butler and Messick) arrive at the ranch:

Snooper: How old are you?

Spinster: 28.

Snooper: How old?

Spinster: 28.

Snooper: *How* old?

Spinster: I told you two times: 28.

Snooper: Two times 28 is 56. That's more like it.

Snagglepuss narrates The Wizard of Oz (1967)

After a "Snagglepuss" pop song and an intro by Daws/Ed Sullivan, the cat begins, "Oncest upon a time, as we say in the trade, there was a little orphan gal. Her name was Dorothy. And it still *is*, even." The narration was heavy, but every word an enunciated treasure, lit with plenty of H-B sound effects and music. Penny Singleton provided the voice of Dorothy, with Daws showing off his vast bag of impressions along the way. Along her Golden Brick route she encounters the not-too-bright Scarecrow (in perfect Frankie Fontaine); the Tinman (rusty to the point of being parrot-like vocally), constructed by a non-union tinsmith, therefore without a heart; and the Lion (oddly not Snag, but sounding like Ed Wynn). Together they head for the Emerald City to get a dose of home, brains, heart and courage from the great Oz, retaining a faithful adaptation to the classic story. The script was original and not taken from the TV cartoons.

Ruff 'n' Reddy in Gulliver's Travels (1967)

Full of adventurous Hoyt Curtain underscore music (written originally for *Jonny Quest*) and plenty of stock H-B sound effects, the faithful but satirical adaptation of the famed satire may have been over the heads of kids, but there was plenty of action and Munchkin voices to keep the tykes interested. The script was original and not taken from the TV shows. Messick narrates, "After many exciting escapades all over the world, and many narrow escapes in outer space, those two swashbuckling adventurers, Ruff 'n' Reddy, have decided to relax!" Vacationing in the South Pacific in their small boat, *The Leaky Tiki*, they crash on the rocks of an "uninhibited" island stocked with little Lilliputians who tie them to the beach. Helping the islanders repel the evil invaders, Ruff and Reddy have fun playing baseball with enemy airplanes and are rewarded with a sail for their boat to get back home.

These rare LPs, no longer in print, are among the few examples of Daws writing for these characters and clearly show his tremendous talent for it. Daws' son, Chas, explained why his dad never got the chance to write for Hanna-Barbera: "Dad bugged Joe Barbera for years to let him try his hand at writing for the cartoons but Joe only saw him as a voice. Finally, in 1964, Joe relented and even gave Dad his own office at the studio. This lasted only a few weeks. One day, he came in to work and was told he was not needed. I blame the networks."

As H-B grew, the networks laid claim to more power within the organization. Art Scott: "In the early days we created our products and sold them. Now we're just a service. The network calls and tells us what is wanted. We give it to them at the lowest cost possible. Otherwise, they'll call someone else next time." Once H-B opened the limited-animation door, competition indeed swiftly walked through.

Daws was less than happy with the new layer of administration that cartoons had to soon go through. "Everything has to be approved. By the time that happens, it has to be rushed through, giving no time at all for consideration of comedy timing or rhythm."

Although locked out of the writing end of the business, Daws would interject his own unique phrase and ideas into the script when he could.

"We don't ad-lib when we're actually recording," said Daws, "but when we're reading it through for time, if we get any ideas, we interpolate them. But as you do a character, there are little nuances and shadings of meaning that only the actor, in many cases, can determine.

"Sometimes the characters that come in for just a line or two are harder to do than the lead characters. You always feel that when you're doing a voice that you shouldn't waste a good voice on a character that is too small. Joe Barbera and I will sometimes spend ten minutes figuring out what to do, so we don't waste anything good. If I do something straight, Joe might say 'Oh-ee, it sounds like Daws Butler.' Which is a crime."

Don Messick: "Daws would watch his own stuff with a critical eye. You could see when he was pleased, and when there was something he could improve upon, in his own mind. He also had no patience with inefficiency."

When asked for some background material on him for the purpose of writing up promotional material on H-B's voice, Daws wrote to Hal Humphrey of the *Los Angeles Mirror*: "I don't believe in Santa Claus, the Easter Bunny, or press-agents. To me, paid-for publicity is a pretty empty entity: a form of prostitution. In my naïve way, I always believed that publicity would come naturally as a sort of reward for honest work performed. Needless to say, I've bought the Brooklyn Bridge three times—and I'm dickering for it again right now.

"Not so you could notice it, but for the past two years I have been doing the majority of voices on the *Huckleberry Hound* and *Quick-Draw McGraw* programs, which have caused a small furor. So far, the publicity I've received has been nil, or so close to nil that 'nil' is still the qualifying word. I realize it's good business for Screen Gems to prefer the heavy play in the papers to be directed to their property, and not to the actors whose voices spark it. Being a patient man, it's just beginning to irritate me a little.

"To be honest about it, the lack of publicity doesn't particularly bother me. As the old Chinese philosopher said, 'Get the money.' What does bother me, is the fact that my wife and kids wonder about it. They see glowing write-ups about the two above-named shows and my name isn't even mentioned. (Even if it were mentioned in anger, I think they'd be pleased.)

"What all this rambling is about—is this. If you feel there might be a story in my background, something that your readers might find interesting, perhaps you'd set up an interview. It would give the kids something to talk about at school anyway."

Daws may have had talent, but he had no head for business. "I took care of the finances," Myrtis stated, "deposited all the checks and so on. When I started looking after the bills, we had a plumbing bill which he paid, and it came back next month, and it was just a small little thing, but I saw that he had paid the date instead of the amount. So he said, 'Well, you do it!' So from then on I did it. Miles was delighted about that!

"There were always residuals coming in, if not work. Miles was an excellent agent. Daws would've given it away free, more or less, had it not been for Miles who knew the business inside and out. He would always set the prices for Daws, always above scale, maybe even twice as much as scale. He was one of the highest paid voice-over actors. They would call him and Daws would tell whoever called to call his agent."

Daws did give away his talent a few times, which annoyed Miles to no end. Once he recorded a few safety announcements for the Las Vegas airport, without fee, in the voice of Yogi Bear. Up until a few years ago they were still being used.

But even though he loved the work, at times he loathed the endless meetings and rhetoric that would have to be a part of every creative session. The first meetings were often fine, but as Daws got more and more into the politics of voice work, the producers and directors weren't so great. Especially in his later life.

Don Messick was a frequent guest in the Butler home. In Daws' home recording studio he would frequently do some recording, and submit it at work. Sometimes Don Messick would come and record with him, or they would find themselves going out to movies, Don's great love. Sometimes Don would bring his son Timmy who would play with Chas out in the frontyard while they worked in Daws' studio.

Chas Butler recalled, "At that time I had no *clue* what they were doing—it wasn't until my early 20s that I really appreciated what my dad did. In fact, I didn't like anything my dad did when I was a kid. I liked Felix the Cat and things he didn't have anything to do with. When my friends came over he'd ask what my favorite cartoon character was and I'd always say Felix the Cat. It got to the point where he didn't ask anymore because he didn't want to be embarrassed. I was that kind of a kid! When I look back on it, most of the Hanna-Barbera shows, and the *Bullwinkle* shows, were filled with pretty adult dialogue and a lot of the stuff they were talking about when I was 8 or 9 years old just went right over my head. I liked the characters visually, but much of the time what they were *saying* I had no idea.

"We didn't socialize much with other voice actors, except for Don Messick. He was the closest to Dad. I remember once Timmy and I having a contest on who could drink the most glasses of water at the dinner table. And of course we couldn't eat our food when it finally came to the table. And I remember my dad being very annoyed at me, and Don being very annoyed at Timmy."

Daws' granddaughter Annie recalled, "G-pa (which is what my sister and I called him) had a set of puppets—Yogi Bear and Huckleberry Hound.

He used to do little shows with them at my birthday parties when I was a kid. One year he came to my 3rd or 4th grade class to do one of his shows. When the other teachers got wind of it, they were a bit annoyed that their classes missed out, so the next year he came back to do puppet shows for *all* of the classes. So, every year I was rather popular for about a week.

"He was always happy to do his voices on command for my friends and me—even when I was a teenager. If you asked him to do a particular one, he'd carry on an entire conversation with you in that voice.

"G-pa also invented a game called 'You Pass.' He'd come up with some nonsense words and phrases, then I'd have to repeat them. If I repeated them all, he'd pat me on the head and say, 'You pass.' My husband once asked me what the 'reward' was and I looked at

Chas and Daws.

him like he was nuts and said, 'I passed. That was reward enough.' I have an audiotape of the game that G-pa made for me as a gift at least 25 years ago. My husband and I put in the tape and play along with it quite often."

The anonymity anomaly of being a cartoon star was quite wonderful. Myrtis: "He was always very appreciative of someone recognizing him and so on. But he didn't pursue it. I remember once we were in a drugstore, and we were just purchasing something, and someone recognized Daws' speaking voice, I don't know how, and said, 'Aren't you Daws Butler?' I thought I recognized your voice. And he appreciated that type of thing, but he didn't really seek out that kind of recognition. That's the only time I can remember that happening, too."

The constant Hanna-Barbera work led to talks at other studios like Disney, but little came of it. Daws did have his heart set on being a Peanuts character, and met with cartoonist Charles M. Schultz to discuss it, but again the meeting led to nothing. Possibly Schultz was too much seeking voices by "real, ordinary" kids to have been impressed with Daws' acting skills. But Daws' range of characters and constant TV series was making a name for himself that far outweighed even his *Beany* years.

One thing Daws tired of during this golden age and beyond was being asked how many voices he could do. In a later [Dr. Demento] interview, he succinctly set the record straight. "They're not voices. They're characters. There are only so many voices, like only so many notes in a pattern. That's all you got, you can write a whole symphony with that! By the same token, there are only a few voices. I have head tones, I have chest tones, I have a combination of both, which is like a stereo pattern. I have textures where I tighten the jaw. I spread vowels, I use stresses. I get a character out of a lot of little mechanical things, what I call working through a conflict, which establishes the speech pattern of a particular individual. Elroy Jetson is a straight-forward thing. Augie Doggie is the same thing, with a tremolo. It's still the same basic voice." To illustrate he also did Babba Looey, then Dixie. "It's one voice, but I've done four characters. As far as characters, I probably have done several hundred. But the voices that I use may have broken down to about 30."

"Hanna was ear-deep most of the time in production of the ongoing shows," wrote Barbera in his autobiography. "My days were mostly consumed in working on these also, as well as developing and/or pitching new ones. Then, in the evening, I'd direct the recording sessions for *Quick-Draw, Huckleberry,* and the rest."

Daws later told *Starlog* magazine, "I would change a line occasionally, and I was good enough, apparently, that the writers wouldn't get mad. I always wanted to say it the way the character would."

He didn't consider Joe Barbera a very good or flexible director. The busy executive/artist/pitch man often had preconceived notions on how the character should definitely sound before Daws even opened his mouth. The gist of the struggle was a constant tug of war: Joe wanted a voice, Daws wanted a character. It was a difficulty he would come across many times in his career.

One of the earliest conflicts Joe and Daws had was with the voice of Yogi Bear, originally typecast on Art Carney's individual delivery. Through time, Daws managed to remove Art's personality from Yogi's (a comparison that was easily discernable when Daws would perform first Art's version of Yogi to Yogi's version of Yogi, back to back), but in the early days of the character, Joe kept wanting the Art Carney cadence left in. Daws sought the more flexible and subtle rhythm that the bear character kept focusing him to adopt. "The extended vowels, the expansiveness, exuberance, diaphragm control, ebullience, and the bigness, the massiveness of a bear.

"When I do a character, it grows. It has a life of its own." Unfortunately for Daws, the man who co-owned the studio eventually had to be appeased, and the uneven collaboration was usually tipped in Joe's favor.

The same held true for the rhythm of Mr. Jinks' speech patterns—and others. But however many fights Daws would lose, he would never stop fighting for the rights of his characters, often winning significant victories.

It was perhaps for these reasons that Daws welcomed the opportunities to showcase his talents elsewhere.

Sometime in the 1950s Daws and Don Messick got together for a radio show called *The Christmas That Almost Never Was*. Written by and starring Daws and directed by Chuck Benedict, it also included Marian Richman as David & Mrs. Santa Claus, Don Messick as Bubble, and was narrated by John T. Smith. Music for this Standard Radio Production was by Eddie Dunsteader.

The ambrosial kiddie music begins this show for youngsters. "It's a story for boys and girls," says narrator Butler, "and the ... not quite grown up. You see the North Pole has a rule. A rule that says: to have a place in that wonderful world of Santa Claus, you must be either a child, or not quite ... grown up." Amidst the organ music, you're instructed to imagine yourself at the North Pole, on Christmas Eve. Santa is awaiting the he or she who gets to ride with him in his sleigh on his present-giving trip this year—but each year he or she must be good for 364 days. So far, there have been no takers. But *this* year, David shows up. Santa introduces him to the various elves, including a South Henry Pole, another Daws variation on Huckleberry Hound, who was the highest elf in his class of toy makin' and ribbon tyin' (12 inches high). Daws talks to himself in a funny scene in which Pole lists to Santa the toys he's made: 71,011 watermelon seed stoves (they burn 'em) and 99,006 jars of tangerine polish. But he was just joshin'; he didn't have a list of his own and didn't like to be left outa the conversation. When Santa is hit on the head with a batch of crotchet balls, he loses "his remembery." The elves decide to put on a radio quiz program to help Santa regain his memory, but he answers incorrectly (horses, he says, pull a sleigh, not reindeer). Eventually, Santa bumps his head again and Christmas lives!

The Alphabet Conspiracy was a 1959 educational film in which Dr. Frank Baxter explains linguistics. Hans Conried appeared as the Mad Hatter in live action with Daws as the voice of Wolfgang von Kempelen in an animated segment directed by Friz Freleng.

It was also around this time that Daws joined producer Jay Ward's Vocal Dream Team: June Foray, Paul Frees, Bill Scott, Hans Conried, Walter Tetley, Edward Everett Horton, Charlie Ruggles. When ABC began broadcasting the first season of the now-classic *Rocky and His Friends*, Daws had a role in most of the *Fractured Fairy Tales*, featuring witty scripts most times by George Atkins. He loved coming up with a plethora of voices for each episode, but usually Jay Ward insisted on the effeminate Prince voice he loved. Jay also kept June Foray rather stifled with her Brooklyn accent, cackling witch and Marjorie Main belting voices, great though they were.

When *Rocky and His Friends* became *The Bullwinkle Show*, *Fractured Fairy Tales* was often replaced with *Aesop and Son*, in which Daws was heard as many of the male characters, as well as playing Aesop's son to kindly father, voiced by Charlie Ruggles. Aesop would narrate an animal tale (he thought) guaranteed to produce the perfect morale, only to have his son whip out his own scroll and pun away a better one.

Daws, like everyone else associated with the series, loved his time on the Jay Ward clock. "*Aesop and Son* was some of the most brilliant writing material," Daws admitted to an interviewer. "Bill Scott did a lot of it, and I never knew what I was going to do. Jay would never let us look at the script. We knew we'd have to do five parts, but he said just read it. So you got to the end of the page and you'd have to grab onto a character! And with these people it was like jazz! It was one of the most delightful experiences of my life."

Though his Bullwinkle work was limited to the *Aesop* and *Fractured Fairytales* segments, these made up some of the greatest work of the show. Clever stories abounded, such as the reversal of *FF*'s Little Red Riding Hood in which Red (Foray), who owned an exclusive shop in the Holly Woods where she sold riding hoods, stalks Walter the wolf (Daws via Frank Fontaine) for his skin, which is worth a lot of money to a rich lady customer. Red offered 10% for that skin, but Walter knew it was worth 90% right where it was. After Red pretends to be Grandma in a bearskin rug, Walter sells

"Grandma" to the rich lady and goes in the fur biz himself.

Another inventive story had the Wicked Queen consulting her coin-operated Magic Mirror for the usual question ("Who's the fairest of them all?") which received the usual answer ("Snow White"), but this time the Queen was the victim, hoodwinked into joining a health club, a charm school, taking a health food plan, and dancing lessons by six dwarves (led by Daws as a Phil Silvers con man) who ultimately strip her of everything and trick her into eating her own poison apples. Of course, the seventh dwarf was inside the Magic Mirror all the time.

Later, Daws played villains and extra characters in *George of the Jungle* and *Super Chicken*, as well as Clutcher in the *Tom Slick* bits. In order not to offend H-B, Daws always declined screen credit.

"We were like Jay Ward's toys," said Daws. "He would make us do recordings over just so he could hear it again."

Chapter 6
Unknown Superstar

Now that Hanna-Barbera Productions owned the keys to the cartoon kingdom, there was no place to go but prime time. "Now, with all those shows going," wrote Joe Barbera, "I found myself betting my future, my business, and the welfare of my wife and children on a family of Neanderthals in a Neolithic suburb called Bedrock."

It had been a dream of theirs to conquer a nighttime time slot, but the idea to get a series on prime time network TV took a lot of doing. Hanna, Barbera, their writers and artists toyed with Indians, pilgrims, gypsies, but nothing seemed right. In 1990, Barbera recalled, "Our sales guy came in one day and said, 'Why don't we try a prime time show,' which no one had ever dreamed of or dared, so we did endless drawings trying to create a family. Nothing was ringing. We tried a father with a business suit and a mother who was shorter and a little rounder and a teenaged son and a dog. Then, we went to overalls and country and a hillbilly family. Then, we went to athletic gear, sneakers and things. Then, one day a guy named Ed Benedict was drawing the characters and he decided to go caveman. Well, once we did that a piano became a Stoneway piano. We went on a roll. We had the Polarock camera. We had Ann Margrock. We had Cary Granite. We had Stoney Curtis. The cars had no gasoline so they did them with their feet."

Bill Hanna had been impressed by *The Honeymooners,* which he regularly watched. *The Flagstones,* later *The Flintstones* when it was discovered that the *Hi and Lois* comic strip used that name already, were born.

The voices for the Betty Rubble and Wilma Flintstone were easily cast, but not so for Fred and Barney. Bill Hanna wrote that "the actors first selected for the roles proved to be dismally miscast and had to be replaced at the cost of a considerably expensive settlement."

Before Alan Reed and Mel Blanc took up the granite gauntlets of Fred and Barney, Daws had a go at both roles.

He recorded a short demo film but was replaced almost instantly, as the Winston cigarette company who sponsored it didn't want the show sounding like other H-B shows. This series, loosely ripping off *The Honeymooners*, was meant for an adult audience. The network agreed.

The Flagstones, now finally released on DVD as part of *The Flintstones'* first season set, had a shaggier feel to its caveman look. Betty Rubble, voiced this time by June Foray, looked nothing like she later would (unless you count the hair color), while even Wilma's dress had a woolly mammoth complexion. Fred and Barney looked similar to what they would become later, and though Barney's Ed Norton-type sound was remarkably close to the way Mel Blanc would do it (yet differing much from Daws' own higher-pitched substitutions later), Daws gave Fred a more guttural, New York truck driver sound, akin to a cross between the voice he used for his Jackie Gleason/*Honeymousers* voice and a Dead End Kid all grown up.

Hal Smith, Bill Thompson and two other actors more than likely attempted the roles, also. But they too were trashed. Daws' longtime friend June Foray again did her Audrey Meadows impression (as she had in *The Honeyearthers* and *The Honeymousers*), but Jean Vander Pyl was the final casting decision. Alan Reed (credited by Barbera for improvising the first "Yabba-dabba-doo!") and Mel Blanc were the final male selections.

Joe Barbera stated: "As important as the story, the gags, and the look of the characters are, if you don't have just the right voices, you don't have a successful cartoon. And with five shows done but yet to be telecast, I realized that we did not have the right voices."

It took eight weeks of Joe's pitching *The Flagstones* to agencies like Walter Thompson and William Esty and network executives before ABC finally took it up.

The Flintstones premiered on September 30, 1960 on ABC and ran for 166 episodes, ending in 1966. Though Daws found himself playing bit parts on several episodes, he did replace Mel Blanc when Mel was almost killed by a young driver on a hairpin turn. During Mel's lengthy, painful recovery, Daws stepped into the role of Barney for five episodes: "Droop Along Flintstone," "Fred Flintstone Woos Again," "The Hit Song

Writers," "The Rock Quarry Story" and "The Little White Lie." And it was Daws who may have inadvertently been responsible for Barney's noticeable change in voice after Mel returned to the role. The original voice Mel used for Barney was a guttural twangy voice similar to his impression of a punch-drunk prizefighter ("Dah! Gee, Fred"). When Daws briefly took over the role, he did a higher pitched and lighter version of his Art Carney voice for Barney. When Mel returned to work, he began doing a lighter voice closer to Daws' version, which he may have found less physically taxing during his long and uncomfortable recuperation in 1961, and the definitive Barney Rubble voice was born.

Obviously, the demotion to providing incidental and guest voices to the series never dampened Daws' spirit. Doug Young remembered a particular *Flintstones* episode. "I did a character on *The Flintstones* called the Grand Poobah. We did one of those shows with a comedic actor named Howard Morris. Daws was a drill sergeant. He said, 'Gosh I've got to get a laugh out of that guy.' So on one of his line readings, he said, 'All right men, forward, march!' Then another—'All right men, Fredric March!' Howard rolled on the floor and Daws was as happy as could be. He got a laugh out of Howard Morris. Those things were always happening, at rehearsals. Daws had a quick wit, was always cutting up. In fact, I think it was Daws who invented the phrase 'Yabba-dabba-doo.'"

The Flintstones was a huge hit due to its appeal to kids and adults alike, and is still regularly played on TV stations globally. Jackie Gleason once considered suing H-B for their prehistoric "updating" of his series, but finally decided not to bother. Joe Barbera found the "analogy" complimentary, though he was quick to point out that there were no foot-pedal-powered helicopters, nor any rolling rock bowling alleys associated with The Great One's hit series.

As of January 1961, H-B's near-monopoly of children's programming was staggering. Kellogg's *Huckleberry Hound* and *Quick-Draw McGraw* were both seen on 192 stations. *The Yogi Bear Show* was set to debut to universal fame on January 29, its half-hour format made up of three 7-minute cartoons starring Snagglepuss, Yakky Doodle Duck & Chopper, and, of course, Yogi Bear. Yogi was a superstar. H-B reported that the Knickerbocker Toy Company had already sold more than $7 million worth of Yogi stuffed dolls, and its Plastics Company continued to sell half a million Yogi Bear plastic banks each year. Dell was publishing 25 Yogi

Yogi and friend.

Bear books (cutout books, coloring books, punch-out books, comic books, and more), the comic book of which sold nearly 800,000 copies in less than a month. Even the Duke of Wellington's Regiment in Wales, England had adopted the not-so-average Bear as their mascot.

In September 1962, there was a *Pageant* article about Daws, with illustrations of him by a staff artist at Hanna-Barbera, which told his abridged story as well as telling of new shows like Wally Gator, Lippy the Lion and Touché Turtle, new for that fall. The premise of Wally Gator was that he was a young alligator who lived in a zoo, constantly trying to out think the zoo keeper and get back to the Everglades. The animal being from Florida,

Daws tried him out with a Southern accent with a lisp, then a smart-aleck tone. But he already had a southern Huck and a dynamic Hokey Wolf to contend with. He took another tack. Playing against-type, that Wally would be a typical Florida gator, lazing in the sun, Daws switched his vocal to make him a peppy alligator with a good-natured laugh. He sat up with a shake of the shoulders, his hands came up and out, his feet got frisky and his eyes lit up. Speaking with a lisping, thin, high, half-cracked voice, Daws iterated, "Well, like I always say, I wanta break outta here and go back to my ever lovin' Everglades..." Before he'd finished saying it, animators were sketching Wally's tail-a-twitchin', shaking movements. He later explained Wally's Ed Wynn delivery as "sloppy, like eating a sandwich through a picket fence."

Back on prime time, *The Flintstones'* flip side emerged to give Daws one of his most famous creations. Using the same basic formula of now-meets-then, *The Jetsons* premiered in September of 1962 on NBC. The vocal line-up was perfect: George O'Hanlon as George Jetson, Penny Singleton(Blondie in the successful film series) was "Jane, his wife." The kids were Judy, voiced by Janet Waldo, and little bitty Elroy, vocalized in high pitch by Daws Butler. Jean Vander Pyl returned from her Wilma days to portray Rosie the Robot, while Don Messick pitched his Scooby-Doo voice into a different key for Astro, the lovable pooch with an R problem – "Rots of ruck, Rorge!"

The prime time series was a marvel and an achievement in writing, gags and voice work. But coming up against two established family shows in the same time slot – *Dennis the Menace* and Walt Disney's *Wonderful World of Color* – *The Jetsons* just wouldn't fly. Perhaps audiences weren't yet ready for an ample supply of non-Saturday morning cartoons. *The Flintstones*, for all its prehistoric references, had been ahead of its time. *The Jetsons* may have been eons ahead. Regardless, the series produced enough of a cult following to bring it back in the 1980s when eventually 51 more episodes were produced, though without the clever writing and sharp characterizations of the original.

Daws thoroughly enjoyed taking his Beany sound into, literally, another dimension. "For me, it's like self-hypnosis. You must convince yourself you're nine years old again. Let it go through your whole body."

Daws never did exact impressions when developing his voices but he did use the facial expressions, body movements and voice "placements" of some of the favorite actors and comedians and then altered the voice and personality to come up with something unique. Both Lippy the Lion and Peter Potamus were based on the big mouthed 1930s movie comic Joe E.

Brown. In the Yakky Doodle cartoons, Daws looked to Shelley Berman's hilariously comic nasal whine as inspiration for Fibber Fox. Both Yahooey (*The Peter Potamus Show*) and Quisp (the Quaker Oats cereal commercials) had their origins in the question mark inflections of Jerry Lewis. He based Cogswell (*The Jetsons*) loosely on comedian actor Eddie Mayehoff. He used his W.C. Fields voice for the Warner Bros. theatrical short *Merlin, the Magic Mouse* in 1967 and again used his Augie Doggy voice for Merlin's young assistant. Both roles were later recast with Larry Storch (*F Troop*). Daws was also one of several actors who voiced Mr. Magoo's nephew Waldo (yet another Frank Fontaine variation) in the 1950s UPA theatricals.

Now that H-B found that nighttime cartoondom was entirely possible, they soon followed it up with other offerings. *Top Cat* based its main character on Phil Silvers' energetic con man character, Sgt. Ernest T. Bilko from *You'll Never Get Rich*. After demo-ing a few actors as Top Cat, Arnold Stang whined his way into the lead. Daws would play a few bit parts now and then, however, even once bringing that Hokey Wolf voice back into the fold as one of Top Cat's rivals.

On one *Top Cat* album, Daws narrates over "big city" music before starting his own Phil Silvers-type Top Cat, who gets the idea of becoming Robin Hoodlums from a book: they are the poor, ergo, they should "borrow" from the rich to give to themselves. Officer Dibble (Allen Jenkins) warns 'em not to contemplate robbery, but has to rush off to round up bank robbers. Homicide McBride (Daws) and his accomplice, er, "associate" Big Fats (Daws as E. G. Robinson) run into the alley looking for a hideout—uh, room. T.C. rents them their clubhouse for five bucks a day, but when he gets suspicious from a gun he finds, McBride suckers the cat into believing they're shooting a movie and casts T.C. and friends in a hold-up scene. The no-goodies hijack Dibble during their getaway, but T.C. and gang save him and the $10,000. T.C. faints at the end when he realizes how close he was to that ten grand ...

For the *Top Cat* audition, Daws used the same type of voice he'd done for Hokey Wolf, but again Daws was replaced on the series. Was it because of the previous desire to keep new H-B cartoons from sounding like old ones? There was more than likely a growing anxiety that Daws was becoming too powerful a crutch. What if something happened to Daws, or he wanted more money suddenly?

During *The Jetsons* era, the H-B-Daws team began to have their differences, usually over money. As the studio's business continued to boom, Miles Auer, Daws' agent, kept trying (like an agent should) to get his client more money. Since Daws was an integral part in their success, as well as being the majority of their famous characters' voices, he was worth it. Unfortunately, Joe and Bill were beginning to wonder at the wisdom of putting all their eggs in one very talented basket. "They were worried that if I went on strike, they'd have to recast almost everything they were doing."

The real disagreements were over commercials and records, when Daws was needed to replay his famed Yogi Bear, Huckleberry Hound or Snagglepuss. If no satisfactory deal could be struck, Allan Melvin or Hal Smith would be called in to tackle the characters. But the results were less than great.

When new roles came, Daw auditioned, but more and more of the roles were going to others. He did manage to find a few roles at H-B after the mid-60s. Peter Potamus in 1963. The evil Captain Skyhook in *Space Kidettes* from 1966. One of the Banana Splits, plus many of the contestants in *Wacky Races*, in 1968. 1969 saw him as Lambsy in the "It's the Wolf" segments on *Catanooga Cats*.

Luckily for Daws, in 1963 he began his 25-year career as the aged, good-natured voice of Cap'n Crunch, leader of *The Guppy* and its crew on an ever-wayward quest to battle the soggy villains who threatened to turn his beloved cereal into a less-than-crunchy breakfast. He of the blue admiral uniform, long white mustache, drooping eyebrows, and long face that went down to his chest, the Captain, sword in hand, was a doddering fool stuffed with puns and unintentional cleverness from the mind of Jay Ward writer Allan Burns. In the last twenty years of Ward's career, Cap'n Crunch commercials brought in much-needed income to cast and crew alike, sustaining the studio after its ultra-successful *Rocky & Bullwinkle* days. Charles Butterworth was the jumping board for the voice which eventually became 100% Daws Butler.

Daws called the character a combination of sincerity and stupidity. Quaker had been designing the cereal at the same time as the character. Jay Ward suggested Daws' "King" voice, and it continued to be one of Daws' favorite characters "because it lends itself to non sequiturs." The cartoon drawing had actually been inspired by Daws himself, who posed for sketches.

On July 25, 1986, Daws wrote a script for a pilot idea he had been hashing around with Jay Ward for years. The idea was to give Cap'n Crunch his own TV show. The script was typically satirical. Walter Crankcase is interviewing the president of Filmation, Lou Scheimer, about the TV special they are going to do on CC's life, when the Cap'n arrives to commandeer the parlay. During the course of the lengthy six-page commercial, Squish the Sogmaster and his minions arrive to wreck wetness on the earth. To be continued…

A few interesting changes were penciled into the script. Interviewer: "Everyone else only knows you for your wacky sense of humor. It's up to us to show another side of you they don't always see in the commercials." The Cap'n's line, "Frontal nudity is out of the question," was changed to "Rear nudity is negotiable."

Alas, a Cap'n Crunch TV show was never to be. "The networks wouldn't go for it," Daws told Joe Bevilaqua. "This was around the time Congress passed a law prohibiting such crossovers from product to series."

Daws with the Cap'n and the gang.

Daws was also the voice of Alfie in the Cap'n Crunch commercials, and had lengthy runs as other characters in animated commercials. Beginning in 1966, Daws was Quisp, for Quaker/Jay Ward. Quisp was a pink-skinned propeller-driven alien in a green jumpsuit. His eyes are permanently crossed. Quisp and Quake (William Conrad) fight over whose cereal is better, and who can "save the day" in a series of commercials. "Vitamin powered sugary cereal Quisp for Quazy energy." He was also The Blue Barron (the King Vitamin commercials), and Professor Goody (from the Aunt Jemima Waffles commercials). Professor Goody's voice was one of Daws' favorites, an adaptation of 1940s radio actor, Clarence Hartzell (Uncle Fletcher on *Vic and Sade*). For Kellogg's Rice Crispies, Daws was the voice of Snap! (Don Messick was Crackle! and Paul Winchell was Pop!) And he was the voice of the Sun in the long-running Raisin Bran TV ads (yet another Augie/Elroy/Beany voice; while these were similar voices, they weren't identical—the Kellogg's sun had an endearing crack in the voice absent from, say, Elroy's delivery).

By the middle of 1963, with an amassing fortune continuing to pour in from their various series, a new Hanna-Barbera cartoon studio had been erected at 3400 Cahuenga Boulevard. These were the "salad years" of the H-B legacy. Chas Butler worked at H-B for a time; among several of his jobs was "checking" cels, which is putting the individual inked and painted action drawings (on celluloid sheets) against the background artwork, in the correct order in which to be photographed.

In 1964 Hanna-Barbera, through Columbia Pictures, released the 89-minute feature film, *Hey There, It's Yogi Bear*, with the original voices and catchy songs from Ray Gilbert & Doug Goodwin (among others). Hanna and Barbera directed, collaborating with Warren Foster on the screenplay originally entitled

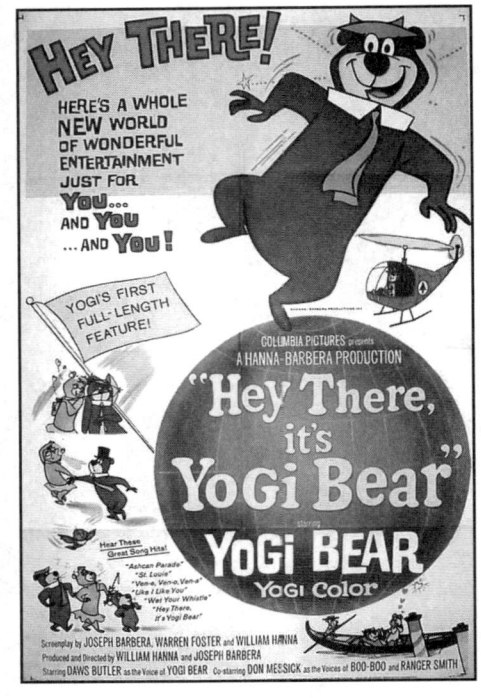

Whistle Your Way Back Home. Between numbers, Yogi's girlfriend Cindy (voiced by Julie Bennett) is abducted by the evil Chizzling Brothers Circus, forcing Yogi and Boo Boo to rescue her. But when they get lost on the way back to Jellystone Park, Ranger Smith sees them on the news and comes to lead his bears back home. Once again, Daws's singing talent was disregarded and he was replaced with another actor whenever Yogi sang in the movie. At one point, James Darren sings for Yogi (who even comments in the scene on how much he sounds like the pop idol.)

That same year Daws secured one of the few jobs he ever had for Disney, in that studio's biggest musical hit, *Mary Poppins*. Daws was hired for two small parts: a penguin, and the turtle that carries Poppins across the pond. But:

"The cartoon honeymoon ended circa 1965," Daws later said. "That's when it started to go downhill. Everything was an imitation of an imitation. Magilla Gorilla was an imitation of Yogi Bear. Ricochet Rabbit was a Huckleberry Hound."

He'd had an amazing decade, but now Daws found himself with more time on his hands. And more time for his family.

"He was a movie buff," said Chas Butler. "And we have tons of home movies downstairs. He liked to do that. I remember when we would watch the movies, because they were silent super 8, he would do vocal sound effects. I remember he shot one of Paul and his friend, who were so taken with *The Man From U.N.C.L.E.* and those spy shows, that my brother put together with dad's help. With chase scenes and the whole nine yards. I loved it."

"He loved taking home movies," agreed Don Butler. "He did it with exuberance and tremendous zeal, and did it so long I wouldn't call him an amateur. Although it took him a long time to figure out how to stop shooting pictures of me and my brothers at swimming lessons, doing the crawl stroke back and forth across the pool. The skill and instinct for editing he developed in time. As long as he was active, he did them. But in later years all of his time was dedicated to the voice class he conducted in the back house."

David Butler: "Dad was constantly taking home movies; and at the end of every 3-minute roll we'd see the same close-up of Dad's face, a cigar in his mouth, peering beneath the lens at the footage counter while he ran off the last foot or two of film.

"Occasionally, Dad used me (and two out of three of my brothers) as voices in commercials he would write as a freelancer. My younger brother Paul and I did a series of radio spots (7 or 8) for the Southern California Chevrolet Dealers. Paul played a kid named Fremont, the world's youngest Chevrolet Dealer. And I was his older friend, Tarwick. I was probably 11 or 12 and Paul was 5 or 6 and couldn't read. So Dad would stand next to him at the mike and feed him the lines one at a time. When they were all recorded, the engineer would cut them together with mine to create the spots."

Chas: "Even though he had a career and a lot of other stuff that took a *lot* of his time, he always made time to do things with us. He wasn't very

Daws and the boys.

adept with sports and stuff, but we would go out and play sports and we'd go out to movies. One of the things he loved to do was trick photography. Not just us, but he would gather all the neighbors' kids, all of our friends from the neighborhood and they would be part of these films as well. For instance, someone in the road would have bought a new refrigerator or something and there would be a huge box in the alley. We'd go drag the box into the front yard, and one at a time he'd have all of us get into the box, with stop-starting footage, so that when you put the whole thing together and show it, it looks like 35 people are coming out of this cardboard box. That kind of thing. Or we'd be hopping down the sidewalk. I would hop, then it would be my brother Paul hopping, then David and he would hop, all in a line, it looked like it was the same person but it was four different people. All sorts of weird things like that, he loved to do those.

"I've been in rock bands. I would have sessions down here in the studio. There was one particular night we were playing a little *too* late and we were playing a little *too* loud, and he came out, and said, 'Hey, good to see you, boys. How's it going?' and that kind of stuff. And I had snuck out and went into the other house to go to the bathroom, and he's coming back and muttering to himself, 'Assholes! They're all assholes!' It was somewhat semi-soundproof."

Don Butler recalled a difficult time for himself in Vietnam. But as always, somehow, Daws was there to help. "Around April 1968, about a month and a half after the Tet offensive, I was stationed up near the city of Pla-Cu in the central Highlands. I was CQ that night, which meant Charge of Quarters: I stayed awake in the command tent of our company to answer the phone and handle any emergency that might come up.

"It was 10 at night when I became aware of a lot of explosions and concussion sounds coming from across the valley, a very wide valley that separated where I was stationed from where the 1st Infantry Division was stationed, outside Pla-Cu. I stepped out of the command tent to look beyond the concertina wire into the darkness, and I could see little flashpoints and tracer bullets shooting back and forth across the valley. I

Daws Butler and the Butlers!

could see increasing lights of explosions going on there. We knew that there was going to be a second wave of assault after the first wave that took place in January during the Tet holiday.

"As I was becoming more and more apprehensive as I was watching, suddenly I saw what looked like a huge cauliflower shaped, red, orange, yellow, crimson fireball rise slowly from the base of the valley and assume the classic mushroom shape. I threw myself on the ground and put my fingers in my ears, knowing the concussion would be tremendous. I know if I hadn't already been on the ground, the shockwave would've knocked me down. And by this time I was in a state of near panic.

"The radio was playing in the command tent at this time. I rushed back into the tent, and it was just then that I heard the voice of my father on the radio. It was a commercial he was doing for Armed Forces Radio, the voice of a character called Private Floopert. These commercials would be aimed at the GIs to buy war bonds and other things the GIs would use in the course of their service. It was a voice very similar to Mr. Jinks. At that particular juncture in time, hearing my father's voice on the radio, it just suddenly filled me… I calmed down very quickly, and I was enveloped in a great peace. And I've always felt that it was providential that his voice should've come to my ears at that particular time."

When Don was on leave, Daws took him to a recording session at Jay Ward's studio. It was an amazing experience. And even though none of the Butler children opted to follow in their father's footsteps, Don was the nearest to be tempted.

"I'm a letter carrier for the postal service. I studied theatre arts in college, and I think that was very much due to my father's influence. He taught me to love good dialogue and good drama. Before I went into the postal service, I belonged to a community theatre and have done some acting in my time. Nowadays I guess I keep my hand in by doing dramatic readings here and there, and scriptural readings at church. My father didn't push me into acting, but he did encourage it. He was very supportive and encouraging to me when I pursued it. But it wasn't imperative to him."

What did matter was art—music and comedy. Paul Butler remembered the many comedy albums that could be found in their home. "Shelley Berman, Nichols & May, Bob Newhart. I remember one Christmas, '63 or '64, the Bill Cosby album *Why Is There Air?* was given as Christmas gifts four different times in a family of six!

"He worked like four or five hours a week. The rest of the time he'd drive around, listening to the classical music station on the radio. All the shopkeepers knew him by name.

"When I was in 7th grade, in a Catholic school, we had to put on a skit for the 8th-graders. He took dozens and dozens of hours of his time to write up skits for us and we put on a whole vaudeville-type show with one-liners and things like that, which was much appreciated by the nuns and the parish priests. He used to coach the parish priests on diction and speaking, honing their skills for giving sermons and such. He was very giving in that way."

His cousin was Brother Victorian of the Holy Cross Order and taught at Notre Dame Academy in Sherman Oaks. Daws once wrote an entire script of private jokes and personal references, performing it for the Notre Dame graduating class.

In the early '60s his shrewd agent curtailed his benefit appearances, insisting that Daws shouldn't just give his talent away. Though he reluctantly agreed, Daws was happy just performing and probably would have given his talent away to anyone who would ask. Somehow he managed to sneak in a regular performance at Los Angeles children's hospitals and give shows for the Junior Blind.

Mostly Daws' idea of a good time was home life, curled up with his vast collection of classical records or listening to the nonprofit FM station KPFK which he regularly supported.

His time with H-B's golden age may have been dwindling to a close, but its ramifications were historical. An issue of *Catholic Digest* ran a rare feature article on "The Voice of Yogi Bear. Daws Butler: Invisible Star," condensed from *View* magazine. Daws' three TV series had been watched by 50 million homes in the USA via 168 TV stations, and countless more in 33 foreign countries. Huckleberry Hound had received fan mail from little kids, college professors, invalid children and Los Alamos atomic scientists who were so pleased with the dog that they wanted the network to move his show to a more convenient broadcast time, so as not to conflict with lab schedules. Huck even had an island named after him by an Antarctic expedition.

In the 1960's election, Hawaiians found themselves voting more for Kennedy and Nixon when a team of actors dressed up like Huck, Yogi and Quick-Draw to tour the island and drum up political support. It worked for cereal, why not the Presidency?

Work *did* continue. One of the cleverest specials Daws had been a part of was Hanna-Barbera's delightfully satirical spin on *Alice in Wonderland*, broadcast on ABC on March 30, 1966. Taking the absurdity of the story even further, it contained characters like Humphrey Dumpty (voiced, naturally, like Bogart by Allan Melvin) and Hedda Hatter (Hedda Hopper) rather than the typical Mad Hatter. It was at least the seventh adaptation of Carroll's classic story, with solid songs from Lee Adams and *Annie* composer Charles Strouse.

Chuck Jones' *The Phantom Tollbooth*, based on Norman Juster's 1961 book, was one of Daws' oddest films. Released by MGM in 1970, the 90-minute feature combined a live-action beginning and end with an animated, musical middle that projected young Milo (Butch Patrick) into an almost Yellow Submarine-like surrealness stocked with the vocal talents of Mel Blanc, June Foray, Hans Conried, Candy Candido, Daws (as the indecisive Weather Man) and others.

Daws' most famous special of the 1970s was unquestionably *Dr. Seuss' The Cat in the Hat*, which premiered on CBS on March 10, 1971. Written by Seuss himself, with music by Dean Elliott and Eric Rogers, the rhyming half-hour musical bounced madcap Cat (voiced by Allan Sherman) into the lives of two bored, rainy day children. Daws played Mr. Krinklebein the Fish.

The following year on ABC Daws voiced the Sheriff of Nottingham's dog Scrounger and Richard the Iron-Hearted for H-B's *Robin Hoodnik*, an hour-long Saturday morning special broadcast on November 4.

The 1970s brought Daws a series of uninspired roles at H-B, none of which lasted more than one season. *Funky Phantom* premiered on Saturday morning, September 11, 1971 on ABC. In it, Daws recycled his Snagglepuss voice for crime-solving Revolutionary War-era ghost Jonathan Wellington Muddlemore. The cast also featured former "Monkee" Micky Dolenz. That same morning, *Help! It's the Hair Bear Bunch!* premiered on CBS with Daws doing his impression of comic actor Jack Oakie for the Afro-wearing Hair Bear. The following year, on September 9, 1972, *Roman Holidays* (an ancient Rome take on *The Flintstones*) premiered on NBC. In it, Daws played Brutus, the family's pet lion (again a Snagglepuss variation), as well as many guest roles. Daws used a variation on his Frank Fontaine/Crazy Guggenheim voice for Undercover Elephant, a segment on *C.B. Bears*, which premiered on NBC on September 10, 1977. Throughout the 70s and 80s, Daws also had the chance to revisit some of his most famous characters (Huck, Yogi, Snagglepuss, et al) in a string of badly conceived shows including *Yogi's Gang* (1972), *Yogi's Space Race* (1978), *Galaxy Goof-Ups* (1978), *Scooby's Laff-A-Lympics* (1980), and *Yogi's Treasure Hunt* (1985) and the Saturday morning special, *Yogi's Ark Lark* (1971).

Cartoon writer Mark Evanier called Daws "one of the dearest, sweetest people I have ever known… an opinion that is darn near unanimous among those who worked and/or studied with Daws. He was a man who loved talent, and not exclusively his own. He loved to see writers writing and actors acting and when you were with him, you just felt more like a writer or actor. He brought that out in everyone.

"What you got from Daws was the sage experience of someone who'd been there, done that and – most importantly – understood precisely where he'd been and what he'd done. There are some wonderful actors who haven't the foggiest notion as to what they do or how they do it.

"He was like Olivier, of whom it was said that he understood the reason for every inflection of every syllable he uttered. To add the slightest hint of sibilance to a word told us something about the character speaking it…said something about his background, his breeding, his intelligence. Daws, like Sir Laurence, always knew precisely why he was doing what he was doing. That made him the ideal tutor."

Daws had continued writing. But even for a voice genius with close connections, it was tough breaking into the writing arena of animation. Chas: "I don't think he ever sold a script at Hanna-Barbera and I don't think it had anything to do with Bill or Joe. After 1964, he just walked away and didn't bother Bill or Joe with it." Some decision makers liked to pigeonhole talent. A writer was a writer; a voice actor was a voice actor.

But in his precious workshop for voice actors, he would become one of the most prolific writers for voice the industry had ever seen.

Chapter 7
The Workshop

> *"I want you to understand the words. I want you to taste the words. I want you to love the words. Because the words are important. But they're only words. You leave them on the paper and you take the thoughts and put them into your mind and then you as an actor recreate them, as if the thoughts had suddenly occurred to you."*
>
> —Daws Butler

The 1970s didn't see Daws at Hanna-Barbera very much, except when reprising some of his earlier hits, as in *Yogi's Gang* in 1973 and *Yogi's Space Race* in 1978. He would later be asked back when *The Jetsons* was revived, or another Huckleberry Hound or Quick-Draw McGraw project. But few new characters were set before his plate. He revamped his Snagglepuss voice to play *The Funky Phantom* in 1971, and bestow his W.C. Fields impression upon J. Wellington Wimpy in the Saturday morning *Popeye* series in 1978. He was also heard as "Clumsy" in the half-hour special *B.C.—The First Thanksgiving*, an adaptation of the stone age comic strip *long* before pilgrims. It premiered on NBC on November 19, 1973. Generally, he was "forgotten" by the studio that depended on him so much before.

Now that he had the time for extra pursuits, Daws decided to give back what he'd taken from the comics who had given him a helping hand onstage: advice. Thus, was born The Workshop.

His first student was Brian Cummings. "Rod Serling was hosting and authoring part of *Zero Hour*, done for the last days of the Mutual Network, and I met Daws on that show. I had come out to California to study and summoned up enough courage at the end of the session to say I was looking for someone to teach me. I had signed up for a workshop with Mel Blanc, but he had a serious car accident and wasn't able to teach. Daws told me he'd thought about teaching often and had someone else who was interested, but hadn't really solidified anything. He gave me his number, told me to send him a tape and said he would be *brutally* frank. I learned later that Daws didn't know how to be brutal—I would do a terrible reading and he would say, 'It had some really good things in it.' He was always encouraging. So I sent him a tape, which in retrospect was sort of 'okay,' and he agreed to teach me. He made an appointment to teach me at the same time as another girl, to charge us both half-price, which was great because we were poor. But she never showed, and Daws charged me half-price anyway. Early on, after I'd just got married and was trying to stretch a dollar even more, Daws put me on what he called 'scholarship,' which meant he didn't charge at all. I know there were others he did that for.

"The wisdom of the man in what he did with his characters, because of the *love* of the characters, was just amazing to me. People studying with Daws got much more than voices—it was almost a Zen kind of thing, like studying a martial art. It's really a philosophy of life as much as a technique."

Once he had the teaching bug, it never left. Actually, for years in interviews he had been teaching the elements of acting with the voice, but never applied the techniques one-on-one to others. Now he had the time and will to focus that knowledge into actual application.

A separate building in the backyard was Daws' haven and home to his precious Workshop. It was also his trophy room, teeming with photos of himself as a young actor and a myriad of pictures of students and friends plastered all over the several rooms. In the largest area, amidst the Gold Record he and Stan received for *Dragonet* and his soon-to-come Annie Award, were the puppets he would use for school performances and the rare knickknacks he'd picked up from a life of animation service. This was where the magic happened every week, around the big table and folding chairs.

In the next smaller room Daws kept his beloved classical music records, more photos, the family cat, ancient radio microphones, videos and the occasional animation cel affixed to the wall. The third tiny chamber was

The Butler residence.

his recording studio which included a mixer and a turntable, much like Paul Frees' home microphone, set up where he could dash off letters to students, assemble demos and other nonprofessional audio recordings. "It serves its purpose. Mainly, I want to hear how people read and sound on a microphone, and teach them some mike technique, which seems to be a lost art. Now people wear a microphone on their tie or whatever and they just *talk*. But the mike as an instrument should be viable and alive and a helpmate so that when you walk up to it and talk like this, like silk—it's nice. It's soft and requires no energy at all. The mike helps you. So I try to clear up a lot of these misconceptions. I'm very egotistical, as you can see."

As an introduction to students, Daws composed the following handout:

To the Work-Shop

This is to be an open letter. I hope it will be an Open Sesame to your various psyches. There is another *you* in there and I mean to find it!

Try always to remember some of the precepts we're talking about. Okay, then, *I'm* talking about.

DON'T BE AFRAID TO BE LOUSY.

IT ALL STARTS WITH THE WORDS—Understand The Words
              Love The Words
              Taste The Words

The words are only marks on paper—they mean nothing—they take on meaning only when you have taken them from the page and transferred them to your computer—and they emerge as your thoughts *full-born.*

Pause only when a pause is necessary—no cosmetic reasons. The mind can think very quickly but the minute hesitation shows the audience that a particular and proper word has just popped into your mind and that you have selected it over all the other possibilities. Eye contact prompts the pause—distraction in the speaker's mind—when some other possibility has presented itself, only to be instantaneously discarded ... or used.

THE PRONOUN—When you speak of someone you love—or with whom you are simpatico—round the pronoun with personal acceptance. When the person is alien to you, express your feeling by the way you read the pronoun. The smile or the curl of the lip—not that easy but I'm sure you get my meaning—these are gauze shadings, but needed textures.

TUMBLE THE WORDS—Read several sentences, which are separated by commas, dashes and what have you, one on top of the other. That is the way we talk in everyday life—the excitement of getting our feelings *out* carries an undercurrent of immediacy—an energy—following this:

GLISSING—Start with an inverted elision. Difficult to explain. Example...

"But it's a marvelous idea!"

The only word that is really hit is "marvelous." "But it's a" is slurred, lightly articulated in a rising inflection...as the person getting the idea and expressing it—the computer has told you that it is "marvelous" so "marvelous" is the main thing you are saying. Ask me about this if you want.

INTERPOLATION—Don't overdo or you'll annoy the writer. (Not *this* writer, at this stage of the game, anyway.) Give freshness to the expression. Example:

"I felt so sorry for her. She was standing there, no idea of what to do—worried."

So you would do it...

"I felt so sorry for her...I just...She was standing there...*standing*...no idea of what to do...she was...*worried*."

Something like: the idea being that the expression of your concern with "her" is the important part, not a cosmetic exact reading of the line.

The emotional or physical expression of what the word implies but where the "word" is incidental to the physical meaning.

If this is confusing, try this:
The plot: this guy has been unfaithful to this gal. She has always forgiven him. Now he has asked for her forgiveness again. But she has had it. This is now a traumatic experience for her.

GUY: It'll be different this time! Try it with me!! Please, Cathy!
CATHY: No.

The "no" should be swallowed—it should be lost somewhere in the mucous on the vocal chords. The next physical reaction would be tears. But don't just say a sad little "No!" This won't make it.

DYNAMICS—In the sense I'm using it right now, I mean a "change of pace." You are talking along and then suddenly the old computer up there rams it home to you what the real point of your discussion is, and the excitement of this brings out the point with a vibrant emphasis. Example of sorts:

"...sure, Charlie had this old car. I forget now if it was that Chevy with the two-toned. (Up) *It was the Plymouth—the Plymouth you got flowers in now out in the side-yard!* The one Charlie won at the Kiwanis Raffle twenty years ago!"

The italicized words are the excitement of "remembering." The last line is sort of a "throw-away"—back to the mundane small talk.

SHAPING OF ONE WORD IN A SENTENCE—Sometimes only one word is important in a sentence. Don't be afraid to stress it above all the others. Sometimes you might pause before you say it to give it more meaning, or you might use emotion to say it. Sometime like this:

"...she didn't forget. She didn't call as a *deliberate* slight to me—getting even for that other time!"

Dynamics would be used in saying "deliberate." Tumbling, glissing, interpolation would all be used in the above, when the word is properly stressed and "shaped," we know the feeling between the characters.

He also explained that "what I run is a 'word-store'...a SENSITIVITY WORD-SHOP for actors and writers—people with an existent talent who explore the dynamics of dialogue. Both acting and writing are nourished by constant observation of the human comedy and imitation thereof.

"I teach how to 'orchestrate' copy...and perform it in a naturalistic way—by shaping and shading the words and sentences so that they become the actor's thoughts...resembling airplanes at LAX in a holding-pattern, waiting for permission to 'come in' for expression—yet, in a seemingly spontaneous manner.

"The rhythms of both acting and writing establish the individual performer's 'logo'...Be yourself!—but first, be what the copy *tells* you to be!!"

To the *West Side Herald*, he explained the true purpose of the new vocation. Others may have charged hundreds or thousands of dollars for this first-hand knowledge, but that was never the issue with Daws. "Because of what I've done for 40 years, it's like passing the wand. And it's exciting to get somebody who's really talented, see him make it and feel that I'm largely responsible for it. I'm not afraid of teaching people who can take jobs away from me. It's like having a gas station on four corners. Theoretically they can all make money."

To supplement his hands-on work, he also wrote and recorded a corresponding tape called *How to Do Dialects*, now published as part of *Scenes for Actors and Voices* by Daws Butler, in which he gave an overview of how to master any flavor of language:

"An accent is given out now and then in your normal voice, perhaps more dominant as you get mad or more extreme, but a dialect, I think, is constant, all the time.

"[On doing an Indian accent] Put the tongue on the roof of your mouth and just leave it there because you won't be able to say P's. Do everything through your lips. Now listen to the music. It's British and Hindu behind it."

One of the most significant by-products of the Workshop was that, in order not to have to keep repeating himself, Daws wrote a twelve-page autobiography to explain just who this new teacher was. "WHAT IS A DAWS BUTLER?" began: "That's the question that plagued me from the beginning. Who was I? In retrospect, I realize that I was born with raw talent and sensitivity. Good partners. I had the early desire to draw and write and act...and to find idols to emulate.

"The realization of this and the application which would give it cre-

dence took many years. What sustained me were the basics I mentioned. Raw talent and sensitivity.

"For the past seven years, I have been the mentor to many actors—dealing with each individual—helping to find the 'logo' which would set them apart—a way to fulfillment as a complete human being, if not the 'big star' they'd like to be.

"Now, when I'm encouraging students or insecure actors who need reassurance, I tell them: Don't worry about the audition all that much—whether you give the perfect, definitive reading—do the best you can—based on your track record, your technique and your sensitivity—and your ability to take direction—and then have confidence in yourself! The best thing that can happen is that the producer or casting director will recognize a 'something' in you—in your personal 'logo' and will decide to trust his judgment, and that you will come up with what they want at the recording or taping.

"Trust and confidence—it works both ways—have enough to spill over on them!

"Trust yourself to play hunches and to learn to love the words and the challenges they represent—as much as I do and it's a sensual thing with me—the shaping and shading of words—the tumbling of short sentences—dynamics—syncopation and the orchestration of dialogue and movement—change of pace. It's exciting! It isn't just 'reading the words' because the words can never do it for you—it's what you do to the words! You get no 'brownie points' for a good reading—a good interpretation—a thoughtful one—that's the ticket!"

After giving his personal and professional history, he concluded: "I'm not bitter—I just don't jump up and down as much as I used to. That's my track record. I'm grateful to the business. I had a career in nightclubs and theatres as an impersonator. A career in radio doing both heavy dramatic work and comedy. A career in TV with an award-winning children's puppet show, as well as TV animation and radio spots. And the Hanna-Barbera and Jay Ward experience. The business has been good to me.

"Which brings me to my present love. My Workshop. A sensitivity workshop for young actors and writers. My passion is words and I try to instill in my students a like passion; to intellectualize them. Performing for them the marriage of the cerebral and the visceral in artistic expression. I audition them and am generally able to detect that talent spark from just reading one of my pieces with them. I am attuned to whatever sense of timing they have, as well as the believability of their performance. Some with 'enhanced mediocrity' but whose enthusiasm, dedication and application do better than the lazier talented ones. Sensitivity is the core. I can draw much from a sensitive person. The ones who don't want to apply themselves as a musician does to his instrument, drop out after a few weeks. I work no magic, I only hand out the plans. They build their own destiny.

"If accepted, they become a member of my 'creative family.' As a non-cocktail-party enthusiast, I have my 'party' with the members of my workshop. We build and grow together.

"Remember when I said that writing was my first love? Well, I think it was the workshop that brought it into final, full flower. I realized that I never did like to 'slant' for commercials or established properties. I could write parodies of them, but at long last, it came home to me that I liked to write my own style, my own stuff, and in the short-form. I would resent giving up a few years to write a book. I write fast and usually have to do very little editing. What I am striving for is, in most cases, short, succinct relationship exercises for actors, and to demonstrate to the writers how to achieve dramatic and comedy rhythms and densities, and naturalistic dialogue. I hope that you will find the 'pieces' both provocative and compelling; that they will lead you to many diverse characterizations.

"Remember, the words can't do it for you. Your thoughts must make the words become realistic and viable.

"So that's what a Daws Butler is—and it's high time to pass that wand!!"

From a creative standpoint, the Workshop was the best thing Daws could have done for himself. The years of H-B frustration and his need for more artistic input finally had a release valve and a reason to do that which he loved perhaps even more than voice work. Writing. He would produce hundreds of scripts for students to use, study, flex. Most television scripts are never written by actors, but by writers, so Daws' combination of the two gave actors the ability to literally read both sides of the paper. And *understand* as well as just say the copy. It prompted him to put his own book together of scripts for actors. This sample from *Scenes for Actors and Voices*, published after his death, is typical of Daws' comic/dramatic style.

MARGERY DICKERSON (IRISH)
(2 Men or 1 Man, 1 Woman)

PADDY: Margery Dickerson…fell down one day…and never got up.

SEAN: Never got up?

PADDY: Never got up.

SEAN: Y'mean t'say she fell down an' never got up?

PADDY: Never got up.

SEAN: (*Pause*) Why?

PADDY: She jus' plain didn't want to!

SEAN: (*Beat*) She jus' lay there?

PADDY: She did.

SEAN: On the ground?...or on the floor?

PADDY: On the ground.

SEAN: Oh, the poor soul! (*Clucks tongue*)

PADDY: Well, at first, they swept around 'er...sometimes, they would lift up her skirt an' sweep the dirt under it...she never got up. (*Up*) They built a house around 'er...jacked a bed under her an' there she stayed...she never got up.

SEAN: (*Beat*) She...was a peculiar person!

PADDY: Why d'ya say that?

SEAN: (*Taken aback*) Fallin' down an' not gettin' up' (*Beat*} Did she hurt herself?

PADDY: She never said.

SEAN: Was she ever asked?

PADDY: Aye.

SEAN: ...and what'd she say?

PADDY: Nothin'

SEAN: Nothin'?...why'd she say...nothin'?

PADDY: Because she was asleep...an' when she woke up, she grew taciturn. Never surly...always co-operative was Margery Dickerson...but not 'word one' would she utter! She wrote down all her requests in a fine Spenserian hand. (*Up*) They're all bound now and kept in the museum by the main road's turnin'...(*Up*) You could go see 'em if you'd like!

SEAN: (*Beat*) So they...so they built a house around 'er?

PADDY: Not really a house...well, it was a wee house...only one room. (*Up*) There was only her, y'see.

SEAN: But how did she live? I mean...who took care of 'er?

PADDY: The townspeople. They drew lots every day...the loser, would look after Margery Dickerson's needs.

SEAN: On that particular day?

PADDY: On that particular day, aye. She would be fed what she desired.

SEAN: (*Beat*)...and what was that?

PADDY: It was always the same...barley cereal, with great chunks of fat...slightly browned in the skillet...an' a wee drop t'wash it down!

SEAN: That was her way of life, then?

PADDY: It was, indeed.

SEAN: (*Pause*) It is a strange tale.

PADDY: She was a strange woman, was Margery Dickerson.

SEAN: (*Concerned*) I wish I had known 'er...I would have been able to talk some sense into 'er! (*Up*) I woulda made her get up and become part of the world again!

PADDY: Others tried...they failed.

SEAN: (*Beat*) Why?

PADDY: (*Quickly*) She jus' plain didn't wanna get up...it was as simple as that! She lived in that wee house until the day she died.

SEAN: It were a tragedy, pure! Niver, to my sartain knowledge has there ever been one the like of it. (*Pause*) Margery Dickerson lived there till the day she died?

PADDY: She did.

SEAN: How old was she when she died?

PADDY: Ninety-two.

SEAN: Ninety-two!! The saints be praised! Ninety-two!

PADDY: Well, she was Old.

SEAN: Poor lost creature! (*Pause*) How old was she when she fell down?

PADDY: Ninety-two.

SEAN: (*Up*) Ninety-two!

PADDY: Well, she died three weeks later.

SEAN: Three weeks! But you made it sound as if she spent her whole great long life there—lyin' in a bed, in a one-room house! Whatta ya call this ramblin' argosy of words, that're now pointless and inane!??

PADDY: I call it…conversation.

"There's a good 500 to 600 scripts downstairs in filing cabinets still," says Chas Butler, "just sitting there doing nothing. The book he was trying to put out, it was like a handbook for actors. And he was going to have his scripts in there with representations of a woman and a man, 2 women and 2 men, etc., showing various situations men and women would be involved in. Serious, dramatic, comedy, whatever. He had a great representation of all different kinds of emotional situations. He even had the help of Ray Bradbury, and that didn't seem to help. I can't believe that there was nobody out here that didn't want to do anything with it. Using his name and still not be able to get anywhere blew me away—blew him away too I'm sure. In the mid-'70s to early '80s he even tried to sell some of his scripts to TV shows of the time. He sent one to *The Mary Tyler Moore Show*. To *The Waltons*. They were all rejected.

"He would sit at the typewriter in his studio, which was his work office, and it was at a time when he had had some surgery, and he had a bit of a memory loss, so rather than trying to remember stuff, he would write it down and type it out and then stick it up on the wall in front of his typewriter. And it got to the point when the entire wall, window, the

REVISED - 10/31/79

```
AUDITION        RE-REVISED MAY 30, 1986        By DAWS BUTLER

ARLIN:      (CLEARS THROAT)
(PAUSE)
ARLIN:      As they say in the cartoons - Ahem!
(PAUSE)
ARLIN:      (RISING INFLECTION) Something?
PATRICIA:   You're something!  What's that supposed to mean?
ARLIN:      (CHUCKLE) It's supposed to mean..something..I suppose.
PATRICIA:   Let's not have any games here .. I've been waiting for
            over an hour!
ARLIN:      Ah! A lady in waiting!
PATRICIA:   Knock it off!  I was down for 3:30 and it's almost five!
ARLIN:      It's the name of the game - I mean, if we were gonna have
            any games here .. you know what cattle-calls are.
PATRICIA:   Chattel calls.
ARLIN:      Nice!  This is still Hollywood where every girl is looking
            for the big break - nobody's forcing these interviews on
            you.
PATRICIA:   You're something!  Look, mister !.  I'm in no mood for (SIGH)
ARLIN:      (QUICKLY) No mood for what?
PATRICIA:   It happens every time .. I feel like such an absolute fool!
            I should have left - what was I trying to prove - just
            'sitting here!'
ARLIN:      (FLAT) That's why I said 'something' with a rising inflection.
PATRICIA:   It didn't rise.  Your inflection didn't rise.
ARLIN:      Not this time - but it did then.
PATRICIA:   (QUIETLY) You're something.
ARLIN:      Very true - I am something - I am composed of blood and bone
            and marrow - an imported jacket and revealing trousers.
```

shade that you pull down, had notes all over it. One of them would be something typed; instead of superstitious, it would be supercilious or something like that. It had to do with Mr. Jinks. Plays on words. Hundreds of these things all over the walls. I have them in a binder now."

Daws was very proud of his *Scenes* book, but as he began to solicit publishers through the years, it became obvious that they were more interested in Daws the voice, not Daws the writer. In a May 1978 audio letter to Keith Scott, Daws stated, "I finished my actor's handbook a long time ago, but as far as any commercial direction goes, it's questionable. It would be great for actors, but the publishers feel 'Who the hell are actors? They're not going to buy that many books, even in college bookstores.' So I'm going to have to fight through that."

Don Butler: "His mind was always in a whirl with new ideas, and sometimes it made him absentminded. He always had a notebook, and he would sit down at odd times to jot an idea down before he would forget it. I remember one time he and mom were discussing going to Europe for a vacation. In my own mind I could see Dad in the Louvre, using the Venus deMilo as a rest for his notebook as he jots down an idea. 90% of his concentration was on his craft and the art beneath it.

"When he was trying to get his voice class started, he may have been going through a mid-life crisis at his middle age, feeling that life was passing him by, but I think that was just in his own mind. That's the only low point in his life that I can remember."

The "low" did not last long. If cartoon work was slow in coming, students were not. His weekly class soon filled up with some of the best and hardest working voice actors of the present age. (Personal tributes from some of these are given in the next chapter.)

"It wasn't just his regular students who took part in the workshop," says Chas Butler, "it was actual working people who would come through the workshop and get some updated pointers. Ben Wright, Lucille Bliss and many others.

"I wasn't trying to become an actor, but I was there sometimes because I loved my dad. This one particular night he had invited Hans Conried. I got to do a reading with Hans Conried! And it was only myself and him. We had eye contact—that was one of Dad's main things—and I can tell by the way he's looking at me, Who the *hell* am I reading with?' And I'm thinking, 'I don't *care* what you think, because I'm reading with Hans Conried!' One of my all-time favorite actors! I couldn't believe it. I wish *that* could've been recorded. He would only record workshops when he had a specific plan, and wanted to show the students a specific thing. We have about ten 10-inch reel tapes of workshops here. He'd gather them into the studio and they'd stand around the mike and do some stuff with the mike technique."

One early student from Australia was Keith Scott (now the voice of Bullwinkle, and author of *The Moose That Roared*, the official biography of Jay Ward Productions), whom Daws would correspond with through taped and typed letters. On March 19, 1974, Daws wrote to Keith: "Do as much of your own stuff as you can. It is very difficult to come by decent material. Jay Ward's writers, viz Allan Burns, were an exception. Bill Scott writes creamily. I feel that material I write for myself is superior (in most cases) to the hired writers on cartoon shows. A writer-actor molds his words, sculpts them, forms them to the needs of his voice changes.

"One thing I should mention (and my dad drilled it into me when I was starting out) is to be very careful of enunciation and articulation.

Watch the change of pace in reading. Read one character slow and methodical, the other crisp and impatient (for example). Don't fall into the trap of using equal emphasis on two characters. Tempo is as important as the voice differential and builds character. Don't speak too quickly, especially with sharp material—the audience isn't as quick as they should be. They can miss some goodies. I get frantic when I listen to Gilbert and Sullivan and some smart-ass comic takes pride in how fast he can sing a lyric. He gets in all the words and stays on the beat, but I don't know what he said without a libretto. This is conceit. Do this for your friends, who will appreciate your voice control.

"Jay is still grinding out Cap'n Crunch's, Quisp and Quakes, Quangeroos, Prof. Goody and the Waffle Whiffer. He is working on a theatrical (or possibly TV special) film of the Robert Benchley shorts, with great animation inserts (caricatures of Benchley, etc.). Also, a Buster Keaton film.

"One thing that excites me is an animation series from Japan—half-hour in length with beautiful backgrounds and animation. The subject is Heidi, the little Austrian girl with her grandfather. Walter Lantz is trying to sell it here for the American market. June [Foray] and I looped the voices of Heidi and her little friend (older, though) Peter. Walter is trying to sell it now. I'm really up on it—the quality is so good—so keep your fingers crossed."

That October in an audio letter to Keith, Daws described his new workshop: "Every Thursday at 7 in the evening we have our little meeting for an hour and a half to two hours. I just charge them ten bucks for the whole evening, we make an evening out of it. We either have cold drinks or coffee, maybe a little hard candy wrapped in foil, but no messy food. I have a little deal out in back with lawn chairs and cover and some ivy and when the weather's nice they can sit out there and smoke. We take a break about every 20 minutes or so. I really enjoy this. I would say it's one of the most stimulating things I've ever done. Little by little I've stored up a lot of knowledge about a lot of things and now I'm able to give these things back to these young people who are all professionals, there are no amateurs. I don't take any amateurs. I'm hearing them grow. They're doing things now they couldn't have done four or five weeks ago.

"I give them a loose leaf binder and punch holes in all the scripts so they can keep track of everything they've done. Sometimes they might say, 'Oh, I'd like to try such-and-such a piece, I think I can do it better now.'

"I've also written a lot of poetry, like Dylan Thomas, where the words have a sound as well as a meaning. They flow. In everything I write I try to get a musical sense of flow and rhythm."

Every Thursday night was open session to all comers. Daws would open up his studio to help his students get their voices on tape. He also had private students off and on throughout the week who would cancel or set up appointments as jobs came or went.

Myrtis for one was supremely glad when Daws began his new vocation "because I could not really make a grocery list because he would always go out and get what little stuff I had on the grocery list without waiting for a long one!" He just had too much time on his hands. Between students and writing scripts for them—and the Workshop—to use, Daws was a kid again. He had found himself: as a mentor.

The main reason he fully engrossed himself in his workshop in the 1970s was to give up-and-coming actors and voice actors a sense of purpose and reality from one who had made it his business over the last 20+ years. Someone who would listen with a careful and professional ear and give encouragement or, when needed, fatherly advice about choosing another profession if he thought someone just wasn't cut out to be an actor.

To those with real talent, Daws would stick by them with a dedication that was seldom heard of. One such prodigy was young Whimsical Will who first met Daws while they were both doing a Winnie the Pooh recording session for Walt Disney Educational Media around 1975. Ten-year-old Will was Christopher Robin while Daws played Owl. Several of the stalwart Pooh voices were involved, including Sterling Holloway. There were about six films in all, with Larry Gross doing most of the music.

"I joined the class in 1975, and was the first kid in the room. I think I felt intimidated by all the adults in the room at first, but they were so receptive and so generous with their comments that I felt at ease after a while.

"From that time on he became sort of my mentor. He would advise me and guide me through my career as a child actor. He was always there for coaching and advice.

"He was an authority on regional accents and dialects. For example, if you would ask him for coaching on a Texas accent, he would ask you what part of Texas? He was loved by so many and was really the most sincere and the most generous with his time and with his caring. He didn't have to do all this—workshops and private lessons and all, because he wasn't making money off of it. He really truly enjoyed it and looked forward to it, and we certainly did the same."

Joe Bevilacqua was 16 years old and living with his parents in Iselin, New Jersey when he first wrote Daws Butler. Soon after hearing stories the teenager ad-libbed on a portable tape recorder, Daws dubbed himself Joe's mentor.

"The first time I visited the Workshop in the summer of 1975, I was nervous as hell!" recalled Bevilacqua. "Sitting at the table were Corey Burton, Tony Pope, Billy Simpson, Pat Parris, and about ten others, many of whom were already working in the business. Daws passed around copies of two very funny Uncle Dunkle scripts: *Sticky Wicket* (Cockney circus seals) and *Punky Possum and the Mud Bath* (Southern possums and a pig). He went around the table and each of us got to read one or two of the roles. He gave us some pointers and then, 'the Master' himself performed them, doing all the voices himself! My jaw dropped. I knew then I had a lot to learn."

The young protégé spent part of each summer staying with the Butlers, between 1975 and 1987, when the Workshop was disbanded due to Daws' health. "I slept in the guest room and everyone treated me like family. I even became friends with his sons, especially Chas. And I went on many of Daws' recording sessions. Daws and I would trade voices and ideas while Myrtis drove us around town."

One recording session Bevilacqua witnessed was for *The Jetsons* revival in the 1980s. "There I was at Hanna-Barbera studios in the very place where all those classic cartoons were created. All the actors were together sitting in a circle in this large room. There was a very high ceiling and near the top of the room a window that revealed the recording room where the engineer and director were. The director was Gordon Hunt (actress Helen Hunt's father). I sat right in the circle with the actors, in-between Mel Blanc (Mr. Spacely), who was the only one in the room allowed to smoke, and Howard Morris (reprising the role of a nervous bus driver from the original series), who was devilishly playing pranks and cracking jokes the entire session. Also, there was Daws doing Elroy and Henry Orbit, Penny Singleton playing Jane, Janet Waldo as Judy, Frank Welker voicing the new character: Orbity, and, of course, Don Messick as Astro. The only cast member not present was George O'Hanlon, who was blind by this point and had to have his lines fed to him by Gordon Hunt in a separate session."

"It was tremendous educational experience," admits Bevilacqua. "I have applied what I saw that day in every radio play I have ever recorded. The most important thing I learned was to always record the actors together in one room, if possible, to let them interact and play off of each other. It's a throwback to the days of radio, which was always recorded that way."

Another recording session Bevilacqua attended was for a series of Cap'n Crunch commercials. "I sat next to Jay Ward as he directed Daws, Don Messick, June Foray and Paul Frees. Both Jay and Paul donned handlebar mustaches and Paul pranced around the room almost as if to mock the self-important Orson Welles-like persona he had been cultivating for years. Daws and Don were the most quiet, studiously reading over and marking their scripts. June was the most friendly to me and we have stayed in touch to this day. June is a wonderful person. Again, they recorded live to tape, only stopping for a mistake or quick direction from Jay. In animation today, each actor is recorded separately and rarely sees or hears his fellow actors. I believe this is the main reason cartoon voices today seem so stiff and uninspired. You can't create something exciting alone in a booth. Daws taught me to LISTEN to the other actors and respond accordingly. Even, when I record my Willoughby and the Professor radio cartoons and I am acting all the voices myself, I still perform the entire script straight through, answering myself as I go along. What I gain is the ability to alter (for each take) character two's reaction based on how character one says the previous line. This is one of the most important lessons I learned watching Daws up close."

Among the biggest thrills Bevilacqua got was when he heard Penny Singleton read words he wrote. "Penny was visiting Daws' workshop and I pulled out an Uncle Dunkle script that I wrote in Daws' style called *Bigelow Bee and the Honey Factory* about a bee who needs glasses and flies into Aunt Rapunzel's beehive hairdo by mistake. Penny played Rapunzel, Daws was Donnie (in his Elroy voice), and I played Bigelow. I wish I had recorded it!"

After that, Bevilacqua did begin recording Workshop sessions, including one in which he performed several Daws scripts with his mentor and Nancy Cartwright. "This was years before *The Simpsons*," recalled Bevilacqua. "Nancy wore a green flight jumpsuit and Daws tried unsuccessfully to fix us up, although Nancy and I have stayed good friends. After the workshop, when everyone else left, Daws took Nancy and I into his recording booth and worked with us privately. We performed three of his most subtle character studies: *Two Hamburgers—Hold Everything, Forget Metaphor—Say What You Mean,*

Daws and Joe Bevilacqua

and *Table Talk*. Daws performed the last script with us, playing my dad. It was one of those magical moments when we all really clicked as actors. In *Forget Metaphor*, Nancy and I really sounded like a couple married for seven years intimately talking in bed and learning something new about their relationship as they wake up in the morning. Daws was so impressed with our performances he played the recording for the workshop the next week. He used to play my radio plays for them too, especially the Sherlock Holmes parodies we wrote together. He was proud of his students and felt a lot could be learned from listening to their best work and discussing it."

The 1970s wasn't all workshop related, however. Around 1974 Daws was seriously thinking about collaborating with another writer on a new radio program to expand his masterly satire *All That Jazz* into a 15-minute Monday through Friday series. It was still in the talk stage: the trials of two ad men with one account, Blooper Soap. Daws wanted Jesse White for Mr. Blooper, and Daws would play the bright (older Elroy Jetson-sounding) son of the one of the ad guys, who gave his pop great soap selling notions. They would have to write five 15-minute pilots (one whole episode) and wanted to interest Texaco in it.

A few years later, he considered talking with record companies about putting out "an intellectual comedy record" with 7 to 10 cuts per side of bits like "Margery Dickerson." He also spoke with a local PBS director about filming Daws' workshop for airing as an hour-long show "so I could be teaching not just a handful of people, but thousands or millions maybe. So, who knows, I might get into teaching on a big scale." Not just for actors, but to assist anyone who has to communicate with other people to get the most out of what they're saying. It was aired as part of a five-day exposition on children's TV.

On February 6, 1974, the *News-Chronicle* covered Daws' visit to the St. Paschal Baylon Catholic School in Thousand Oaks, California where the Voice, aided by Yogi Bear and Huckleberry Hound hand puppets, sparked

many a laugh from sixth-, seventh- and eighth-graders. The bear and the dog sang songs and tossed out a stream of one-liners that had the kids ecstatic. Daws was accompanied by studio production manager Art Scott who explained the animation process, including the corner cutting. After the talk Art and Daws teamed up: Art created a chalk character on the blackboard while Daws developed an appropriate voice for it. Show over, Daws was besieged by students wanting autographs and more and more voices.

The following letters from Daws give a first-hand account of his highs and lows of the decade.

> February 15, 1975 [to Keith Scott]
> I did three commercials for a Nestles candy bar for Australia!! Yep, Hanna-Barbera did them. The bar is called—get ready…THE YOGI BAR!! I did Yogi's voice. Poor Don Messick will be impersonated in Australia—maybe you'll get

the nod to do Boo Boo! At any rate, you may be aware of this bar. It would be nice if you sent me one. It's apparently made in the image and likeness of Yogi (sounds Biblical).

March 9, 1975 [to Keith Scott]
Bill Hanna and I are going back East next week to do some promotional TV and radio spots for a new Taft-Hanna-Barbera amusement park which is opening in Richmond, Virginia called *King's Dominion*. I will do several talk shows in Washington, D.C. and radio shows as well. Haven't got the full itinerary; at any rate, it should be stimulating and fun. Don't know if I told you that Hanna-Barbera have bought back the rights to Yogi and Huck and Jinx and Snagglepuss, etc., which belonged pretty much lock, stock and barrel to Screen Gems (Columbia Pictures), so now maybe there'll be some *new* cartoons!!!

May 4, 1975 [to Keith Scott]
I've landed a couple good commercial accounts which should pay the bills for a few years. One is 'Ms. McChicken.' The McDonald's hamburger chain here is going after the chicken market, and Ms. McChicken will be the spokeswoman for the new product, which is being test-marketed now. I am doing Ms. McChicken in a Dame Edith Evans voice without the English accent. Could be a funny bit.

September 1, 1975 [to Keith Scott]
I just met George Clayton Johnson, an important TV science-fiction writer. He is also the author of *Logan's Run*, a new major motion picture about to be released, starring Michael York. Should put MGM back in the black.

He has an idea for a new TV show and wants me to work with him on it. Casting for the dramatic parts; acting in it myself; and possibly directing. Nothing definite, but it sounds intriguing.

September 27, 1975 [Keith Scott]
My workshop threw a surprise party for me on Sep-

tember 20th—husbands and wives, wives and husbands, members of the clan. Food aplenty, libations bland.

Corey had t-shirts made up from the 'flyer' [Daw's mouth drawn like the *Jaws* shark] I sent you. You'll recognize it. Everyone in the room was wearing one. The back of mine said 'Coach.' My wife's: 'Mrs. Coach.'

Much of Daws' letters contained advice and feedback to tapes containing "completed homework" that had been sent him.

October 22, 1975 [to Keith Scott]

The monologue, you know, is the toughest of the actor's ploys, because to be done properly, the audience must see the unseen person spoken to; actually form an opinion of that person. Sudden stresses, dynamics and 'throw-aways' are essential to maintain change of pace. Do not read the monologue, however intelligently, on one *tone level*. Don't worry about your voice—let it break, crack, become heavy with the 'thought mucous' on the vocal chords when emotion is being suggested.

[later] When you are terribly afraid or emotional, your diaphragm fails you. It collapses…you feel a mucous in your throat (imaginary) which makes it difficult for you to swallow. You feel a pain (imaginary) in your sinuses. Try to throw your mind to your tear-ducts and feel some activation. Take in only a thimble-full of breath shallowly, then you will sound legitimate. Try to recreate what happens in everyday life. Let the body originate the performance.

October 15, 1975 [to Joe Bevilacqua]

You know what I wish, Joe? I wish I was ten years younger—I have such energy and enthusiasm and time is not on my side. I'm fifty-eight years old—but damnit! I've got the energy of a thirty-year-old! I'll do what I can. I do love to be in contact with talented young guys like you— I am deeply moved that you look to me for guidance.

November 25, 1975 [to Joe Bevilacqua]

I just got what they call a "holding fee" for that 7-UP Commercial I told you about—where I do the voice for a puppet hamburger (man-size). A holding fee means they are probably going to use the spot but it isn't finalized yet.

I'm trying to get back into writing radio commercials mainly—and possibly on-camera ones for TV.

I'm working with a young actress who has been in my workshop for the past year and a half. Excellent. She has good writing vibes and is very versatile as an actress. We wrote five sample spots about name products which are amusing and naturalistic sounding.

We've been sending the tape and a flyer, which explains our purpose, to various advertising agencies in town.

January 17, 1976 [to Joe Bevilacqua]

You see, I love to write and I don't worry about the sale of material. I would rather let people enjoy it—my workshop, you—whoever—people I dig. My agent doesn't feel this way about it—he says "Why do you help the competition?" I don't look at it that way.

After all, I am your mentor and I want you to make it—and to always be "professional."

On February 16, 1976, *The San Diego Union* did a story on Daws' voice workshop for the Pacific Southwest Regional Festival of Puppeteers of America at the Hilton Inn in San Diego. Some of the many voices (and large hand puppets) Daws performed for the occasion were Huck, Yogi, Quick-Draw, Babba Looey, Cap'n Crunch, just about everyone including Beany. Approximately 350 attended the festival, including professional and amateur puppeteers, teachers, librarians and regular puppet fans. Don Ave, San Diego Guild of Puppetry president and professional puppeteer, was the convention chairman. Hand puppets and marionettes were exhibited as well. The sessions ended with a performance by the Riede Marionettes of Los Angeles.

Aside from acting technique, another component Daws was adamant about was teaching his students how to read professional commercial copy. After all, attaining voice and acting work *was* the point. He wrote a number of "mock commercials" for students like Pat Parris and Corey Burton to practice on, and also delved into his storehouse of real scripts he'd collected over the years, giving endless pointers on how to remain fresh yet true to the words and sense of the message.

If anything, Daws' feedback to students erred more on the side of supportive than critical. But it was being *accepted* into his circle that was the main proving ground; he did *not* waste time on those without the talent, however much overt or hidden.

> August 15, 1976 [to Keith Scott]
> Your tape was a revelation! How you have improved over the past few years. You're smooth now. There is a polish, a confidence, a knowing of where you want to go.
> Your impersonations have been vastly improved, and also your own 'characterizations.'
> Try to rein yourself in a bit, though—don't get the great urge (too soon) to tackle Hollywood. You're good enough, God knows! but you're dealing with a mediocre hiring clique. They don't recognize talent as such. Right now, the 'trash' announcer syndrome is very 'in.' Trash announcer means just a 'guy' or a 'gal' who speaks like the guy or gal next door. For instance, Corey [Burton] is an 'announcer.' I would be good as a 'trash' announcer because I don't have the technique which makes an 'announcer' valid. Cosmetic readings (which I despise!) are rampant, and the sad part is that the advertising 'biggies' think this is the way to go!
> I would say—make it in Australia, get a name for yourself, a good agent, and come over as Helen Reddy did: a viable product. It's always easier for a New York actor who comes out here to 'make it' if he has a great track record already.
> You're good. Damn good. Get the best advice you can 'down under' and don't jump the gun. You're very young—you have time.
> I will be teaching an extension course at Beverly Hills High School this September (twelve weeks) and a ten-week course at Loyola University (College, naturally!)... the latter will be for credit, so I'd better know what I'm doing.
> I will be attracting (I hope) teachers, business people,

> minorities (wanting to find themselves, their identity) and retired persons (which I will never be!). It's a different gig from my workshop which is composed of 'acting' hopefuls. My sessions in the halls of learning will be based on 'sensitivity'—'relating' (still using the old Daws Butler scripts, however—eye contact, etc.).
>
> I have about twelve private students now, plus my own workshop. I don't know why I drive myself like this, Keith. I suppose I have become so bored with the crappy material I have to read to make a little bread that, egotistically, I prefer reading my own stuff (and having others read it) because I think it has more content.

Teaching had become a calling. Soon, he was running a course in the Beverly Hills High School Adult Education Program, but unfortunately it was a temporary situation since state law required a teaching credential to instruct in California secondary schools. (Ironically, he was also teaching a popular course in acting at Loyola University of Los Angeles, where his educational background was apparently not an issue.) Having left school two months before graduation to become an entertainer, Daws didn't have the diploma required to become a teacher. But his accomplishments in the intervening 42 years took care of that. Daws called upon friends, co-workers and family to provide a professional but affectionate tribute to this unknown man who needed no introduction. David Butler, Jay Ward, Myrtis, Les Goldman and Bill Hanna were among his champions who wrote to Oak Park River Forest High School at the end of October 1976 to heap praise upon the industrious voice actor. It had its effect.

The only credits Daws lacked, after withdrawing weeks before graduation, were for American History 1 and 2. In view of Daws' supreme accomplishments, the choice was simple. The diploma dated January 26, 1977 in Oak Park, Illinois made Daws proud and he was able to meet the April 22, 1977 deadline for a teaching application. But only just. Unfortunately the Board of Education had to approve a diploma be awarded to him, even though Superintendent John C. Swanson was in favor of the motion. The Board met on April 14, and a letter was sent to Daws on the 18th proclaiming it would be four weeks more before they could forward an official diploma as they had no supply of blank ones on hand.

In 1976, *The Los Angeles Times* ran an article on Daws in its October

10 edition: "Can't Place the Face, but the Voice Is Sure Familiar." It reported that along with his home workshop, he was launching a course at Loyola Marymount University in Westchester, California two days later. "The Spoken Word: Using the Voice in Speech and Action" continued through December 14 on Tuesdays from 7:00 to 9:30 p.m. He was also teaching an acting class every Monday night at Beverly Hills Adult School. "Maybe I can give the younger people on the way up some shortcuts in the business. I know I could have used them when I was starting out."

But as Daws commented later, "I didn't like the academic feeling. It was too restrictive. You had to do three hours every week and many of the people who came had very, very little talent. I would bring scripts I'd written. I'm sure they got something out of it; they learned to relate and talk with others. It served a purpose.

"For my own workshop, I have anywhere from 8 to 15 people. I've written over a hundred different scripts of every type: comedy, drama, satire, adventure. But they're all exercises in how to do different attitudes. Some are funny, some are heavy. Basically, I'm a very serious guy; comedy is just an adjunct. What I'm doing is teaching sensitivity more than anything else. How to create a character by understanding the lines, interpreting them, rhythms, changes, syncopations, very akin to music.

"Because of time and the scarcity of jobs, these days I try to work with people who *have* talent. Those who can just walk in and read a script, and see what they get out of it absolutely cold. Even if I get that kernel out of them, a respect for words, a quickness about them, then I'll work with them. But sometimes people will come in who just want to be in show business and have no talent. Talent is most important, then: the ability to be a student and do your homework. I've had successful students, but they were talented when they came in. I'm a coach, and sometimes I'll direct very heavily and give line readings. I look at it not like a method actor, but as a structural director. They are weights and balances. Some things are shaded, some things are thrown away. It's very exciting, really."

> September 22, 1976 (to Joe Bevilacqua)
> I am very busy now—I started my Beverly Hills High School night class on the 20th ... how many students? 46!!!!! I expected about twenty-five. I'll work it out somehow—but 46!!!!!

The cast of The Misadventures of Sherlock Holmes, *l to r, Henry J. Quinn as Doctor Watson, Jan Meredith as Mrs. Hudson, Joe Bevilacqua, director, Vernon Morris as Sherlock Holmes.*

I've got about sixteen private students—my own workshop. What am I trying to do, Joe? I'm spreading myself so thin. It's worth it, tho, when I hear you doing such exceptional work! Have you seen Pat Parris' JABBERJAW? She's "Shelly." My young twelve-year-old protégé Billy Simpson [Whimsical Will] was young TAD in "THE LAST OF MRS. LINCOLN" on the tube recently—I got a good group. I was telling one of the directors at Leo Burnett at a Rice Crispies session that I was training the young talent in town for commercial "voice-overs." He said "We need you!"

If I don't write as often as you'd like, just be aware that I am working my tail off! I do think of you and do welcome your cassettes.

Your proud mentor,
Daws

In an October 23, 1976 letter to Keith Scott, Daws wrote, "I have been so damn busy with the workshops—three—and about eighteen private students, plus the commercials, the residuals from same which make teaching financially possible." It also made it possible to start thinking about going back to radio which, after its glory days, just did not pay much for the limited dramatic work airing then.

Sean Wright tells the origin of Daws' involvement with a new Sherlock Holmes series for radio: "I believe it was in mid-1976 that an 18-year-old student at the KIIS Radio school of broadcasting in Los Angeles named Michael Anthony approached the radio station with an attempt to bring back old-time radio drama. His idea was to use the character of Sherlock Holmes as the hook to get radio stations to lease the rights for the project. Michael called me up, as the head of 'The Non-Canonical Calabashes,' the Sherlock Holmes Society in Los Angeles. He told me about his plan and invited me to his office at KIIS to discuss it with him.

"I'd become a radio drama junkie. When I was a teenager catching old radio shows broadcast on KABC-Radio after midnight in 1965. In 1973 I'd written a version of the Sherlock Holmes case, *The Adventure of the Devil's Foot* for KPFK-FM radio station. It had been produced by Mike Hodel, the host of the station's *Hour 25* popular science fiction show. Mike and I would later write a novel published in 1979 called *Enter the Lion: A Posthumous Memoir of Mycroft Holmes*. I'm happy to say that it has become a very well-regarded pastiche of the Sherlock Holmes cases, even though his fat, lazy brother, Mycroft is the main character.

"Michael had not yet put together a production team. Feeling that I'd had some experience doing what Michael wanted, I suggested Mike Hodel join me as a writer, and that Daws Butler would be a terrific director. Daws' name struck like lightning with Michael Anthony. 'Do you really think you could get him to consider it?' I silently chuckled. It was something Daws would be perfect for and ached to do.

"Daws was tremendously interested in the project. He brought along Ben Wright, who had played Sherlock Holmes in the 1948 series at the very end of the Golden Age of radio drama. This time, however, Ben would be Dr. Watson.

"Somehow the very fine Irish character actor, Edward Mulhare, was snagged to play Sherlock. Mulhare had been a very successful stage actor, being the first to take over for Rex Harrison as Professor Henry Higgins on Broadway in *My Fair Lady*. He also played Harrison's old movie role of

Captain Daniel Gregg in the TV series *The Ghost and Mrs. Muir* and would later play David Hasselhoff's mentor, Devon Miles, in the popular 1980s series, *Knight Rider*.

"Five one-hour episodes of *The Sherlock Holmes Radio Mystery Theatre*, as I'd titled it, were produced and put on tape. There was a flurry of interest in the industry and it looked as though the show might just fly high. But sales lagged and I have no idea just what exactly happened after. I fell out of favor with Michael Anthony and I think he eventually fell out of favor with KIIS.

"Even though I wrote two episodes I did not really have much input in the actual performances. As a student in Daws' workshops I'd hoped to be asked to perform as one of the characters but I had little experience in front of the mike.

"I watched one episode get made, with Daws in the control booth, doing a job he had been born to do. It was a great experience watching him work with the actors and the sound effects experts. Everyone loved and respected him a great deal. Daws brought so much experience, talent and enthusiasm to this project, it was a shame the show did not click more decisively."

In *Sherlock Holmes, This Here Is Your Life*, broadcast on June 12, 1976, the announcer began: "The program that shamelessly takes some unsuspecting celebrity and holds him up to massive public humiliation." Sherlock does *not* want to be on the program and leaves, but is dragged forcibly back. Daws is "your host Twinkie, Ralph Backwards." Ben Wright also stars. Holmes was told to bring a pot of honey, told the Pillsbury Baking Powder Biscuit Contest was held here. Big party after the show for all his friends will be at the Motel 6, with "your big brother Mycroft footing the bill." Mycroft is fat and is the largest member at Weight Watchers; had his jaw wired shut to keep from eating, but sent a mumbled tape to wish Holmes well.

It was a classic satire with humor that holds up very well in this *Shrek* era. Sherl's dad was Bernie, who said Sherl spent a lot of time around the football team, in the locker room, sniffing shoes, as the game was afoot. The very effeminate Oscar Wilde is brought out for some *very* camp jokes, followed by La Strade who arrives in a howling police car, demanding to be let in, but like Rodney Dangerfield gets no respect. Next up: William Gillete, who first brought Holmes to the stage. "That gay young blade" sounds like Hokey Wolf/Phil Silvers as he pitches new money ideas at him—"If you're the detective's type, smoke the detective's pipe. I love that!" Everyone from Sigmund Freud to Dracula is ultimately brought in. If only Daws had had Freberg's PR guy, it could've been a classic recording.

Written by Daws, Richard Ekhouse, Mike Hayne, Mike Hodel, Doug MacKewon, the episode starred Daws, Corey Burton, Richard Ekhouse, Mike Hodel, Doug MacKewon, Pat Parris, Billy Simpson, and Ben Wright as Sherl. It was recorded "at Mentor Studios in the Paul Harvey Building in beautiful San Fernando Valley," says Corey over "Springtime for Hitler" music.

Daws wanted *Sherlock Holmes* to click so much that he wrote the following article for *The Commercial Actor*, the premiere magazine for voice actors at the time, which was published in its March 1977 issue.

Creating Radio Drama for Today's Listeners

(A 39-week radio series for national syndication is now in production: *Sherlock Holmes Radio Theatre*, produced by The KIIS Workshop Radio Players, in association with Michael Anthony Productions. Directed by Daws; Executive Producer William Baer.)

"What we want to achieve is to do radio by 1977 standards, which calls for more incisive writing and more gut-level acting, where the actors aren't just reciting lines—'lucking out' on the meaning. That was a big fault of radio in the old days. It had good readers, but you heard only their words, not their feelings. The gut-level feelings are what I want to get, and in some of the typical Conan Doyle scenes where something traumatic occurs, beyond stating the situation dramatically, the actor's reaction must be gut-level, the collapse of the diaphragm, the heat in the chest, the lightness in the head—believable *trauma*.

"In the *Sherlock Holmes* series, I would like to see the characterization of Holmes and Watson become more contemporary, to have a great appeal to the more sophisticated audience of today. I'd like to discover little inroads and insights into their personalities and their relationship, to build a strong, beautiful, wholesome relationship between two men who shared an honest love. There is a warmth between them. They enjoy each other's companionship. I want to create little vignettes within the stories that will bring out this relationship. There are so many facets of Holmes that can be developed. He is a dedicated man. He puts himself in dangerous situations. He has a special feeling toward anyone who is in trouble, whether that person has the money to pay for his services or not. He is a constant student. He's always inviting new challenges. And he likes to show off his knowledge sometimes like a little kid. To be, Sherlock Holmes is a Hamlet character. He can be played many ways. He is an actor's gold. What I want to do is to make people really love the characters in this show. I think if we can accomplish that, that's much more important than just the little adventure story that's on the surface.

"The way that I'd like to work in creating these shows is to use the story conference, where I as a director would call in writing teams, talk about what we're going to do, and give assignments. Instead of writing a script as a Bible that everyone has to stick to, I'd like to have the writers come in, having read the story that we're going to work on, and sit down, share their ideas, make suggestions about how something might be done, take notes, and get a sense of the structure of the script. Then somebody who is the head continuity writer will go home and put it all together, using all these little vignettes, these little jewel scenes. These are the things that will give it color and interest. I don't think that the stories themselves are enough to hold an audience of this day and age.

"Conan Doyle didn't write too many parts for women in his stories. I don't think he was chauvinistic because what he did write for women was very good, but for our purposes, I want to see many more parts written for women. I like women—and besides, they need the work. I think that it's very important for us to have women's voices so that it isn't a male-oriented show. For example, I'd like to make Mrs. Hudson a regular character. She'd be like a mother figure to her two boys who live in her boarding house, an Irish mother instead of a Jewish mother. There could be some wonderful little comic vignettes for her.

"I also want to get away from the stilted Conan Doyle dialogue, which is very difficult to read. I mean, you can read it in front of the fireplace with a glass of sherry, and it's keen. But when you try to get a bunch of actors to read that stuff, if they read it cosmetically, it's garbage. It takes an extremely good actor, if he reads it the way it's written, to make it sound believable. There are many, many lines in which Conan Doyle used complex sentences and I am certain that the same thing can be said much more succinctly. There are lines that are written just for continuity, and there's nothing clever or provocative about them no matter how they're said. You want to get them out of the way as fast as possible and get onto the juicy part. On the other hand, where there's a nice little bit of metaphor, then, of course, it's worth saying in the way it was written.

"We've got to have the best actors in town for this series. I don't want just good readers. I don't want elocutionists. I want good sound actors. I want the actors to take the scripts home and come up with concepts for their characters. Many actors are lazy. They really do just read the meaning of the lines. They miss shadings and rhythms. I've had experiences where I was auditioning people and I'd tell them, 'This character is wide open. You can do anything you want with him. Don't be afraid to be lousy. Take chances.' And even with this preamble, in most cases, they would almost all end up with the same cosmetic reading. They all 'run a little scared.' They want to play it safe. Of course, being an actor myself, I write for actors, and my dialogue flows very easily. So it just reads like butter, and actors tend to grab the first on-ramp, as if it were a freeway. But they forget all the little side roads and the landmarks where all the interest is. I say to stay off the freeway. It's a copout. Let's be gutsy.

"I love actors, and I love writers, and I feel that, as a director, I can be a catalyst for them. I love dramatic radio, and I've always done it, even when it stopped. I've done it through commercials, cartoons—it's all radio to me. I don't like to hear people talk about 'voice actors' because I feel that acting is *acting*. When you act, you act with your shoulders, with your jaw, with your tongue, with your resonating chambers—everything. You are a complete acting force. Radio, the magic of sound, is just a way of distilling it down to the essentials.

"I would really like to see this program bring back radio, with an adult 1977 format. And all the young people that I've talked to about it, anyone under 35 or 40—they're really excited about it. They are avid about having something to exercise those little grey cells so their imaginations can grow. They have been fed on the pap of television for so long, and television is full of cosmetic readings because it's physical. You look at the people and *see* what's going on. But in radio you have to make the *words* come to life. You shade a word here and there. A pause can be dynamite. Radio is really a theatre of the mind and makes all these things come to life.

"I would like to be involved in radio mystery, comedy shows, children's shows like the old *Let's Pretend*. I feel that the market is there and waiting, but I wouldn't want to see it fall into the doldrums of just taking tired properties and redoing them in the old style. But I'm very excited about what we're doing here. It's something that I've looked forward to doing for so long that I feel like Christmas is here—and it's not even December."

At least with fewer cartoons and a *little* more time on his hands, Daws had the opportunity to note his current activities. All of the following letters are to Joe Bevilacqua unless otherwise stated.

April 9, 1977

I have been busy. Two academic workshops—my own—private students—a new radio show—SHERLOCK HOLMES. I will be writing and acting in it—it'll be done in stereo—English actors, mostly. I'm trying to re-create Watson and Holmes in my own image—to get away from the Nigel Bruce, fuddy-duddy Watson that all you young punks see on TV. Watson was an intellectual—I am writing him so.

Then, I am in four Hanna-Barbera productions for the coming season...I also was called on to cast several NBC cartoon shows. I have been b-u-s-y.

I got a kick (pardon the possible pun) out of your sprained ankle...when I was playing at a nightclub in Chicago, in my early days as an entertainer—I broke my ankle and had to go out on the nightclub floor with CRUTCHES!!—The audience thought it was a gag—why, God knows! But they accepted it—and the act was none the worse for it.

May 15, 1977

I have been remiss in my role as mentor—and friend.

But, Joe, I have been busy. I am in four new series at HB. Funny premises—not too funny lines in the shows themselves—but I'll try to funny 'em up.

I spent about four weeks out at HB—casting. Lot of Network interference, of course—but in spite of that, I managed to get some people I liked—into series...and not the same old 'tired' regulars.

I am also working on my 'book'—which will consist of about thirty or more exercises—comedy—serious, bittersweet...

There's a need for such a book—actors...now...have to dig sketches out of plays.

I want to put a book together—consisting of sketches I've written over the past few years, which will enable actors to get together with friends and read together.

I'm doing one series—LAFF-O-LYMPICS for ABC in which I will be doing about fifteen of my old 'tired and true' characters. For NBC, a couple series of UNDER-COVER ELEPHANT—in which I do a sort of Frankie Fontaine (SIVONY) character, but understandable—he's an undercover elephant and wears a mask, (so nobody knows who he is)—another series POSSE IMPOSSIBLE—I do a character called DUKE who sounds like (guess who) John Wayne...one more series, THE CB BEARS. I do a Bilko type character named HUSTLE—he is a prime mover.

Other characters are BUMP—big dumb (typical) scared bear—and a little bear named BOOGIE. BOOGIE is enamored of CHARLIE—a sexy dispatcher who is only heard over the intercom (SOUNDS REMINISCENT OF CHARLIE'S ANGELS, RIGHT? And well it should!!)

 I still have about fifteen private students—and a workshop with about fifteen plus students.

 I been a busy guy, Joe...

Your mentor,
Daws

December 11, 1977

 I'm writing a new science fiction piece—and will send you a copy when it's finished. My stuff seems to be getting heavier. I shouldn't be going through 'phases' at my age.

 Sorry for not getting back to you sooner. I know you were anxious. This is about the heaviest piece you've got from me.

 Be well—have a nice holiday (I decry the commercialism and feel a bit Scroogey, but what're you gonna do?)

 I have been very busy—just did the voice for five SEARS spots—animation—should be on around March. Slightly gravel-voiced exuberant guy—selling the idea of SEARS big Spring sale.

 They didn't want anything [incomplete] or regional—or anti-blue collar—so I [incomplete] a laundered Jackie Gleason. The character [incomplete] and will be a stop-action puppet. He has [incomplete] "*Hold* everything!" "Are you ready? Get a...*grip* on yourself for the big news!" "How's this...for...openers?" (in re: garage door openers) etc.

 I think I'll try to get 16mm prints of these. They won't be great—but interesting. What I'm hoping is that the character pleases the client and he makes it a 'logo' for SEARS tool and lawn department.

 Think good thoughts, Joe—the world has got a chance.

Your busy but devoted Mentor,
Daws

December 22, 1977

I am sending you the script of THIS HERE IS YOUR LIFE, SHERLOCK HOLMES—you will have to listen to the tape—if you want to do that version—or do the full version which runs the show about double in time. Anyway, you can make the cuts if you so desire.

I am also sending you another HEAVY script—'Space Out.'—good and evil. It's an example of how one part, even tho smaller, has depth and weight.

Pat Parris is doing much better—a couple weeks ago she was on three 'on camera' commercials—one for a shoe company—and two for ERA, a detergent monologue.

I was on a local talk show last week—I will send you a tape of it, when I get mine. Corey Burton, whom you may remember, took it off the air reel to reel and is to send me a cassette—I'll have to ride him a bit to get it.

August 30, 1978

I'm finally getting around to knocking out a missive.

I haven't gotten too active, because my right hip (the old one) is acting up. It was in just about as bad shape as the 'new' one used to be—and I get some pain from it—when I'm lying down as well as when I'm standing. So I haven't got the old workshop together—or the private lessons, except for a few.

I'm going to go into surgery the end of September. By the first of the year, if all goes well, I should be in good shape. I don't look forward to it, but it's something that has to be done. I will have a strong leg to support the other this time...and that's something.

I've completed the HB cartoons I was concerned with for this season. I'll be interested to see how my W.C. Fields voice goes over on WIMPY. It was nothing before—and the Network brass decided they wanted a WIMPY voice. (They hate anything original!) Sorry, I *meant* "W.C. Fields" voice—not WIMPY.

I just voiced a GREEN GIANT (MUSHROOMS) commercial—did a little bird, talking to Sprout—also a

RICE CRISPIES COMMERCIAL—with Don Messick and Paul Winchell. I do the voice of POP. Should be coming up in a few months. The Green Giant stuff doesn't get much airplay out here—not too great on residuals.

I am sending you a monologue—written in what I believe to be a truly conversational style. Try your hand at it—maybe put your rendition on a cassette for me.

Good luck in all of your endeavors, Joe. Your mail-order Mentor is proud of you.

I almost forgot—your plant arrived and has become a part of the green-ness in our living room—Thanks, Joe!!
Love,
Daws

The Popeye Show, also known as *Popeye Catches Disco Fever*, was an H-B prime time special that combined elements from the Saturday morning series, *The All-New Popeye Hour* which ran on CBS from 1978 to 1981. Daws was again Wimpy, as he was on another special, *The Popeye Valentine Special* (A.K.A. *Popeye in Sweethearts at Sea*), broadcast on CBS the following February 14. In this, Wimpy was captain of a Valentine's Day Sweetheart Cruise which pitted Bluto and Popeye against each other to win the heart of Olive Oyl amidst the clutches of the Sea Hag, swordfish, dangerous storms and inevitable great disco dance.

September 18, 1978
Dear Joe...
Your reading of A BABE IN THE HOLLYWOODS was a gas! You picked up most of the inflections I did! I put my reading of fame on the cassette, so you can hear them back to back.

I also recorded another monologue—much longer, called SOMEWHERE ALONG THE LINE—or VERBOSITY SELF-TAUGHT. Do your own version first—then listen to mine—I have mentioned this on the cassette, after my reading of A.B.I.HW.

You've got great instincts about interpretation, Joe. Naturally, it pleases the ole mentor when you get on the same wavelength.

I haven't been doing any writing during my recovery. I don't know why—I just haven't. After my full recovery, I plan to hit a lot of publishers—to see about getting all of my 'exercises' published as a handbook for actors. I think it would satisfy a need.

I have to go out to HB now to do a 'bridge' for one of the series, LAFFOLYMPICS, I think.

Sorry you didn't like the new WIMPY. I felt I was on virgin territory, as I considered the old WIMPY quite bland and uninteresting. Here is a case, Joe, where writing instincts could have saved the day—By making Wimpy verbose, using big, colorful words—taking a little time away from the typical Popeye action stuff—a memorable sub-character could have been born. I consider the old Wimpy still-born. But it's not a subject worth pursuing.

Huck and Yogi are wasted, but what're you gonna do?

Keep well—I'm going in the Hospital September 24th—and the operation will be September 26. Think about me.

So long for now.

A mentor or a 'mensch'
(chose one or both),
Daws

March 28, 1979

I'm to do the voice of a robot next week for SALVAGE 1. One voice is gentle and emotional—very humanistic—the other part of the robot is war-like—and I am doing it as George C. Scott!!

As far as you're coming out here—I'd try to make it big back there and have them send for you. The competition out here is unbelievable—I get so depressed when my students are trying to get agents—photos—resumes—gimmicks...but there is not that much work and there is so L I T T L E talent—in my workshop in the past five years, with over a hundred people going through, I have finally come to the realization that a tiny fraction had any talent—that is, taking me and my expertise and sensitivity as a criterion.

Don't just come out here and expect to be discovered! Believe me, Joe—I love you—and want your success—but it is an insensitive morass. Talent is not appreciated—things are thrown together. I worked another SEARS radio show today—I have submitted three scripts which have all been turned down—the director ELLIOTT LEWIS thinks I am a brilliant writer but the material I am giving him is too esoteric and is directed at too small an audience—an audience of intellectuals. He admires me but says I would have to pull back—which I won't do—I won't 'slant.' The hell with it—I have to write to get it out of my system—and if I can sell it, great—otherwise I'll use the material in my workshop. I'm a stubborn cuss.

April 11, 1979

I finished my robot characterizations—the good robot and the George C. Scott—also John Wayne, A Japanese kamikaze...A German lunkhead...Jimmy Cagney...Charles Laughton...A Southern rabble-rouser...Walter Brennan (which I don't even do)...in the manic-pattern of the 'bad' robot...it will either be a tour de force success—or a nothing. I have no idea until the whole thing is put together and I see it on the tube. I know this...I will make a pot full of money. My agent had contracted for me to do it in four hours—that's what they figured it would take—it took almost three times that long—a lot of looped lines for me to do. But by figuring it on the four-hour basis—I stand to make some good loot. Many actors get sucked in to doing the job—in an eight-hour period for the money!! (the *same* money, I should have said). Anyway, they try to screw you whenever they can—they were trying to make out that the robot was one character and that the fact of his having two split characters made no difference. My agent straightened them out on that—I do things by the 'voice.'

Anyway, even if it's a bomb...I get good money...although, I am depressed when something I do doesn't come off. My agent is strictly humorless and strictly business—but the artist in me screams out for artistic satisfaction!!

> I just did three 'audience' shows with Henry Morgan (*Here's Morgan!*)...a stock company of comedic actors, Shep Menken, Frank Nelson, Elvia Allman, Virginia Gregg, Elliott Lewis (himself)—we did a table reading—set music cues with Nelson Riddle...but we had no 'dress rehearsal!!!'—didn't even know what mikes would be available on the show—we had an invited studio audience—about a hundred people—and did the shows by the seat of our pants. Got great laughs...but the professionalism of the stock company made it come off. Very funny material—Henry Morgan kids...immercifully...the medical profession, the legal...Television...you name it. Funny stuff—we'll see what you think when you hear them...should be on about the end of May. It was the most fun I've had in several years—good material gets to me...Henry did accuse me of ad-libbing after the first show...I said 'Henry, your stuff is high voltage—it turned me on...and besides the adlibs got laughs!' We worked out a mutual respect by the time we had recorded all three shows—quite a gifted guy.

The April 24, 1979 Sears' Radio Theatre production of *Here's Morgan!* contained a very funny satire of laugh tracks in current TV shows. "Most of the people laughing on these tapes are now dead," said Morgan, who promised real life people would be laughing or silencing. It was an admirable showcase for Daws, using the essence of Huck and Yogi's voices. Produced and directed by Fletcher Markle, its host was Andy Griffith, and starred Henry Morgan, with Elliott Lewis, Mary Jane Croft, Shep Menken, and Frank Nelson.

> May 19, 1979
> I suppose you've heard the HENRY MORGAN shows. I was on all three of them—and the last one will be on out here on this coming Tuesday night.
> I had a meeting with a guy named Jim Brown, a young guy —about thirty—who is the radio editor for *The Los Angeles Times*...the only real voice of radio here...I read him a few of my 'pieces'—things I write for the workshop and which you have read...My idea being that I wanted

him to see the efficacy of putting such material into a potpourri form for a more esoteric radio form.

He was impressed and felt, as I did, that radio should grow up—and he liked the density and depth of my characters—and their inter-relationships. He knows Norman Corwin—and perhaps he'll hear some things on the grapevine which might lead to my being involved in writing the type of material I excel at—which isn't the trivial crap we're acquainted with. I refuse to 'slant'—but I would break my ass to write stuff I believed in.

My writing gets better all the time—I have a couple new UNCLE DUNKLES which will send along to you when I get them Xeroxed. I am also going to send you (now) a page of Japanese HAIKUs—short poetic forms which call concise discipline—break down big ideas into a minuscule form.

Daws showed off his incredible unscripted comic skills on various radio talk shows in the mid- and late '70s, most notably with the erudite Michael Jackson and the equally swift Carole Hemingway. On Charlie Tuna's show in 1975 callers were allowed the rare privilege of calling up whatever character they wanted to speak with, while others suggested inanimate objects (garbonza beans, blackboards, "a dumb ol' history book") for Daws to animate with original voices.

As his enjoyment in new projects dwindled, Daws became more nostalgic for the memories of old radio. He attended several SPERDVAC (The Society to Preserve and Encourage Radio Drama, Variety and Comedy) conventions in the mid-70s, and began a new radio series sponsored by Sears called *Heartbeat Theater*. It reunited him with many of his old radio buddies from the '40s and '50s, people he could utterly relate to and talk with.

Old friend Marty Halperin remarked: "I was at a Pacific Pioneers Broadcasters luncheon. I was sitting at a table talking to a lot of people when someone asked me, what's your favorite radio program? And I said *Vic and Sade*. And at that point, I suddenly felt a hand on my shoulder. And I turned around and it was Daws! He said that's my favorite too! So our friendship started up all over again. We would trade shows back and forth."

When Marty later asked Daws to be a guest at the class he taught on microphone technique at City College, he accepted enthusiastically. "And it was an incredible talk. I recorded it. It told how he did all of this stuff, how he

Myrtis and Daws Butler.

came up with the voices. And he said, when I do a voice, I am that character. When he does the French, he's a Frenchman. He was such a sweet guy."

Otherwise, Daws still didn't seek out the limelight, even where old busy friends were concerned. Sometimes in the early 1970s Daws would function as usher at his church, The Good Shepherd, and would see Jim Jordan (Fibber McGee on radio) at mass. As Daws would stand by the door with the church bulletins, Jim Jordan would frequently ask him, "Are you working?" But Daws couldn't usher anymore after his hip operation.

Before his hip operation at St. Agnes in 1978, Daws was asked by Bill Hanna to do some appearances for the Boy Scouts of America. His hip replacements were performed at Cedars Sinai Medicate Center, just a mile away from the Butler residence. It would be the first of several maladies to plague his last decade.

"He had a tendency to over drink at times," recalled Myrtis, "but not very much, just used it to get kind of sleepy and not 'with it.' By the time he was having his heart problems and so on, he gave up drinking altogether because with all the medication he was taking, it just did not have the appeal to him. He smoked cigars, but finally his doctor told him, if you want to keep doing voice-over work, you better stop smoking or else you'll be driving a truck. So he gave it up almost cold turkey. And I didn't notice that he gave it up until he told me he had!"

July 10, 1979

I worked on the last SEARS SHOW last week—the 130th—had an interesting fag hotel clerk—two good scenes—one funny—and one a bit frenetic. I'm not too pleased with the series—I only did a few things I can be proud of. One of the things which I found hard to accept was in the actors with which I performed—I've known many of them for twenty-five years or more—and to me, they hadn't developed beyond what they were doing that long ago. I keep digging into the 'words'—my beloved words—trying to find more answers…you, at your early age, are experiencing what I have always felt—show business is a dedication—a way of life.

I was disappointed, in that I couldn't get Pat Parris a job on the show occasionally—I dropped her name about five times and then I gave up—after that they might have resented 'her.' And I didn't want that. She is soooo good. I'm having lunch with her this Friday (the 13th) and then we are going to listen to a new SUSPENSE type pilot (radio show)—which, if sold, could lead to some classy radio production—and one in which both Pat and I would be regulars.

In September, I think, Joe Barbera, Frank Welker and I will do about a ten- or fifteen-minute stint on KIDS ARE PEOPLE TOO—one section includes Dom DeLuise—a nice guy and a talent, right? Look for it in the TV Guide.

I'm doing nothing at Hanna-Barbera this year, other than the WIMPY on POPEYE—which ain't much you must admit.

You do write effective letters—I have saved some—altho I am not as much of a pack rat as I have been in the past…I have all of your cassettes, however—I have heard you 'grow'…

There really isn't a hell of a lot of opportunity out here—I wouldn't advise anybody coming out to tap the meager market that exists for a few.

I'm going to send you a cassette of an album which was put out by OHIO UNIVERSITY—THE BEGINNING AND THE END—funny stuff—your type of stuff—they are a swinging group. My friend, Nancy Cartwright, who went to the University and is now at UCLA —received a copy of the album through the mail—and I made a tape dub of it. Listen to this stuff—you might like to investigate the Ohio facility—you might find it more to your liking and needs than you would at UCLA—they really don't have a Communications Arts center—Nancy has been rather disappointed with their offerings. Anyway, I think you'll enjoy the stuff from Ohio University.

I mailed outa few of the GAS CHAIN LETTERS—I don't think those letters do much good—but we'll see.

I'll get that cassette recorded for you now.

Thanks for keeping me up to date on your doings, Joe. I'm trying to figure out a way to get my stuff (the writing—the sketches—the exercises) recorded in album-form—or in book form for aspiring actors to read—something—I've got all this material and I don't know what to do with it. I've just got to hit publisher after publisher until I find a live one who digs my stuff.

July 22, 1979

I am sending you the HOLY COW routine, done quite simply—not played for caricature-effect...but with a possible sense of reality—believability. If you put on a dhoti and a turban—and took off your shoes and socks, I think you could garner some laughs with this one—

[...]

I'm out in my studio (my womb) early Sunday morning—coffee but no breakfast as yet...just enjoying the quietude, listening to THE BIRDS by Ottorino Respighi. An Italian of note. Altho this was written in 1927, it is remindful of music of the seventeenth century—ancient airs and dances. He was preoccupied by the Baroque...and yet his use of improved instruments, makes his work quite modern—with the overtones of the old. His orchestral colorations are superb. I was just in the mood for him this morning—I luxuriate in my musical collection—and always feel more fortunate to have it around me.

September 22, 1979

Dear Joe (if that is your name)

I've been busy since my return. I went to NEW ENGLAND (with my wife—I am very old-fashioned).

We did some Island hopping—on a flat-bottomed boat—which carried fifty passengers—food on board—lay-over every night—visits to the points of interest every day. Nantucket, Block Island, New Port, etc.

I'm back—it was just Sunday to Sunday.

Two days ago I had to do an impersonation of HOWARD HUGHES—a symposium for HUGHS AIRCRAFT. They dug up a tape of his voice—I read a few paragraphs he had apparently written—did it very low-key. He had a high, nasal Texas twang. Good loot for something like that—

I saw the screening for RAGGEDY ANN AND ANDY—coming up around Halloween—prime-time. Good relationship between June Foray and me...much better than the Christmas mess. By this time, you have seen KIDS ARE PEOPLE, TOO—I was on that with Joe Barbera and Frank Welker.

I contacted Larry Sloan of PRICE-PIERCE-SLOAN—they publish a lot of humor-related paperbacks. I sent him a cassette with me reading my stuff—different type of material. He called me, on my return, seemed to be quite impressed. What I had asked him was—would he sit down with me—I knew I wrote very esoteric stuff, but I wanted to lean on somebody who could possibly suggest places to go—he seemed to think I might work on some of their projects—anyway, it's a start on getting with the writing. I'm so disgusted with the caliber of stuff in animation that I want to get on with what I feel more intellectually compatible with.

Writer/producer/director Chuck Jones scored a hit with the half-hour CBS special *Raggedy Ann and Andy in The Great Santa Claus Caper*, the first of many broadcasts on November 30, 1979. It was an effective adventure in which Raggedy Ann (June Foray) and Andy (Daws) had to battle Alexander Graham Wolf (Les Tremayne) who had invented a new kind of plastic, Gloopstik, which could encase anything within an unbreakable plastic cube, thus keeping it new forever. With such a device, Wolf could ruin Christmas forever. But when he mistakenly uses the Gloopstik machine on himself, the rag dolls tell Wolf they love him, and he is freed by the power of love. June, Daws and Chuck followed their successful collaboration up with *Raggedy Ann and Andy in The Pumpkin Who Couldn't Smile*, broadcast on October 31, 1979. The dolls play matchmaker for a sad, lonely pumpkin (Les Tremayne) and a sad, lonely boy (Steven Rosenberg) who is not allowed to trick-or-treat.

Daws ended the decade with the broadcast of *Casper's First Christmas*, a half-hour special for NBC, shown on December 18, 1979. It again gave Daws title to his old H-B characters, who find themselves lost on the way to their mountain lodge where they'd planned to celebrate Christmas. Luckily they meet the friendliest ghost (voiced by Julie McWhirter) in the (other)world who manages to elicit a visit from Santa and make it a merry, singing Christmas for all. It was a fair piece of work, but as usual, Daws was seeking a challenge.

Chapter 8
Mentor Remembered

The following chapter contains memories of Daws Butler's many students. Rather than divvy them up into other chapters, they are included here in their entireties, as tribute to a most beloved teacher.

Nancy Cartwright (Voice of Bart Simpson)
I was in high school in Kettering, Ohio, just south of Dayton, and I competed on the speech team. I would get critiques from the judges saying, 'You have an unusual voice, you should do cartoons.' But being Dayton, Ohio, they don't exactly do animation there. But I worked at a radio station, that was my first job, and my boss introduced me to a woman from Warner Brothers who represented their music department. To me, Warner Brothers meant Mel Blanc. I thought that was so cool, maybe I could write to him, maybe he could be a friend. I met the woman who said that if I wrote to her she could get my letter to the right person. She kept her word. I wrote to her and told her I wanted to do cartoons, and she passed it on to the right person. The next thing I know, I got a letter from her, at the bottom of which was a P.S. 'Give this guy a call. His name is Daws Butler. He's the voice of Road Runner.'

I called him in my basement (I didn't want to do this in front of my family) and on the other end of the line was this message, 'Yes, this is Percival Pickles. I am Mr. Butler's butler. Mr. Butler's not here right now. You're going to have to leave your name and a message. Wait for the beep. (Pause. Voice) Beep.' This was the late '70s when there were not many answering machines around. So I left a message in an English accent and he called me back that night! And that was it. Long distance phone conversations started that student-mentor relationship that continued. He wanted to know what my dreams were, what I wanted, and I said, 'I'd just like to do cartoon voices.' So he said he'd send me some things. He put a little tape in the mail on how to mark your copy, along with a published interview done with him, and a script. He said in a letter, 'Put this down on tape and send it back to me.' That was our relationship. I would record my voice on cassette and mail it to him, then he'd listen to it and take another cassette and critique me right on there and mail it back to me. I might as well have lived just down the street. It carried on for a while, but shortly, I realized I had to get there. I just have to move to California.

Daws did not teach me how to do voices. Above all, he had the most respect for the writer. It was all in the writing. He taught me to take the words that were presented to me and through the way that they were written and the way that I interpreted them, I would communicate this message. So it was how to make that written word my own. The skill of communication from the artist to the recipient of whatever that message was.

In the workshop, we would do the same script several times, mixing up the parts. He would have men reading women's parts. It was such a great ensemble, and a different one every week too.

Letter from Daws to Nancy:
> *I had lunch with one of the Johnny Carson show writers with the idea of perhaps going on that show. I know that Carson digs the kind of stuff I do, it's just that it's impossible to get to him personally. You have to go through channels, and what they would want, if anything, would be the voice of Yogi Bear, Huckleberry Hound, old hat stuff. I want to go on with my philosophy of not merely acting, but relating. I want to show how to get the words off the page. Ego or not, I feel that I could be entertaining, doing Marjorie Dickerson and such, acting out both parts as a sort of tour de force.*

(About above)
This was the thing that meant the most to him. What his philosophy was as a writer to communicate that.

Greg Burson (Current voice of Yogi Bear)

I first met Daws at a Sherlock Holmes convention of some sort around 1972 and I was producing the Sherlock Holmes radio program at the time. I'd heard about Daws' workshop and asked him if I could get into it. I was surprised he charged just ten dollars a session. And if you didn't have the ten dollars he put you on scholarship. It was a sensitivity workshop rather than a Voice-Overs 101. He taught you how to act without using body parts or gestures. Just your voice, to tell the story. Whether you're [demonstrates] shrugging your shoulders or a little tired, we all saw what he was doing without seeing what he was doing. He was a master at it, if not *the* master. It was quite a unique way of acting, which is vanishing rather quickly, because it's too damn hard to do.

Basically what he first told me is what I learned the most: the words will tell you what to do. And they do. It may not be the way the director wanted you to say it, but it shows that you're treating each word as it should be treated. It's a very delicate way of acting.

It's hard to describe the guy in a way that doesn't sound sentimental or hokey. The greatest joys he had during the workshops were when his students would win auditions. Even if he had been up for the same role himself. I guess the old term 'salt of the earth' would be fitting for him. He was so giving and such a master of his craft and so down to earth, it was hard to believe.

The best compliment I ever received, the one that just thrilled me inside was when Daws took me aside and said, 'Listen, you've learned all I can teach you. From this point on, it's just a friendship relationship.' He was a very dear friend. He'd do everything above and beyond the call.

He gave me my career, for Christ's sake. 10 bucks? Everyone else—if you could find them—charged $50. Now they're $300 to $800.

Joe Bevilacqua (radio producer, actor, host: NPR, XM Satellite Radio's The Comedy-O-Rama Hour)

My father bought me a tape recorder when I was twelve and instead of recording music off the radio, I started making up funny voices and I came up with these characters of Willoughby and the Professor. I started adlibbing these full stories with sound effects and music from 78 records. I started drawing pictures of them, Hanna-Barbera-esque with a ring around the mouth. When I was fifteen, I wrote a letter to Daws Butler in care of Hanna-Barbera, and somehow it got all the way to him. In the letter I just said I wanted to do cartoon voices and he wrote me back and said, 'Forget it, it's too difficult. There's no work out here, the industry is sort of moribund. The most talented voice actors aren't working. Stay in New Jersey and open up a sign painting shop. Sorry to be so discouraging. To be anything else would be cruel.' I wrote him back and said yes, I know all that, but this is what I want to do. He wrote back and said, 'You bounce back well. Usually nobody responds to my discouraging letters. Okay, let's see what you've got.' I sent him a tape of 120 minutes of Willoughby and the Professor stories. And waited patiently. Actually, I bugged the hell out of him for about three months, saying did you listen yet? Did you listen yet? He would send back these little postcards with his caricature on it, saying things like, 'I'm still listening, piecemeal.' One card said, 'You show me no mercy!' And finally, about four months into it, I got a cassette in the mail from Daws. It was an entire half hour of Daws ad-libbing, actually running out in mid-sentence, of him demonstrating his characters, explaining the art of voice acting and how it's real acting. Everything you could possibly want to know about voice acting is on that tape. I still listen to it to this day.

I went into radio and have been in it ever since.

What I learned from Daws was that it's not just the voice, it's the body. The facial structures. He started out as a visual impressionist. He found that if he looked like the person, he could sound like them.

Marjorie Dickerson was the first script he ever sent me. In the workshop, and even doing tapes for his students, he would hand out a script to everyone, everyone would get a chance to read eventually, and then he might pick up the script himself and say, 'Okay, now I'm going to show you how I might do it,' so now we've got the Master running straight through it, doing a particular interpretation. Then, he would go back and do it again and stop and explain to you what his thought processes were and why he chose those particular line readings. And then, of course, give it back to us and ask us to do it again. He was always extremely positive, he wasn't negative in his critiquing. He would encourage you.

Toni Silveri (Voice Actor/Founder
Voice Actor Workshop of Western New York)

There were so many great times, during the four years that I attended Daws' Cold Reading Workshop every Wednesday night, in his garage studio, behind his modest home, in Beverly Hills. The first thing which always amazed me was the cost of these sessions. Five dollars, dropped into a kitty, using the Honor System. There was always coffee and cookies and candy. Being a perpetual student of Workshops in those days, from Voice-Over to Improv to Acting for Film and Situation Comedy and for whatever else we could do as Actors, to profit from the gifts God gave us and the training, which consumed time and money; I sincerely appreciated the five-dollar system. I was in Daws' Workshop from '84 -87 or '88.

Daws was a supportive and generous trainer. His warmth and nurturing talent as a teacher was always there. He always found something good to say about my performance, before he went on to the actual critique. I remember phone messages, which he would leave me, if he especially liked my performance of one of his original works. I CHERISHED THOSE MESSAGES and it kept me going during those times when it seemed that my career would forever remain a hobby. We read his original scripts, copies of which I have also saved and cherished. Later on, when I too created my Voice Actor Workshop, I used his stellar technique to share with my students. I will always remember his voice, forever ageless and full of honesty.

Daws' studio was laden with mementos. Stuffed animals and cells from the many characters he created, awards, photos of himself and special people in the Industry. There was another room where he stored countless copies of performances for radio, television, and films. They were lined up on shelves, mirroring the kudos from a very special and gifted career and life.

We belonged to the same Catholic Church, which on that final day, housed Daws for the last time. Daws was a lectern for that church for many years. On the day of his Memorial Service, it stood as a Who's Who in the Animation and Broadcasting Industry. People kept getting up and telling wonderful stories about Daws. There were tears, and laughter, and Stars mingled with yet to Become Stars. Everyone was equal. Everyone would miss that man, more than spoken words would say.

I keep a picture of Daws and myself on the mantle in my studio, as well as one where he is cuddling my two-year-old daughter.

I have also taught her what Daws instilled in his students…that impossible is only a word!

Tony Pope (Voice actor)

I must mention Daws' name every day. Corey and I were the first two to show up at Daws' workshop, and we've been friends ever since. I started around the fall of 1974 and I continued for four years, religiously, every Thursday night. I was going to night school college and working during the days. Monday, Tuesday, Wednesday and Friday I went to classes, and Thursdays was for Daws. I learned more from Daws than I did from any of my college classes. He gave me a real advantage over other students, and I still feel studying with Daws gives me an advantage over other actors.

When I first went to Daws, I was an impressionist who couldn't act, and I learned how to act. Daws taught me how to read all over again. There was a time when he thought I might not do it, and he said I want you to come to me individually for a while, and I did for about two months. It was wonderful. I learned so much and grew so fast in those two months that when I went back to the workshop everybody was just blown away. That's the way Daws was. I wouldn't be where I am today without Daws Butler. That's why I stopped going, I was working too much. I did lots of radio spots, and did a lot for Disney. I was the voice of Goofy from 1977 to 1987.

I got friendships out of it that still exist, 25 years later. As I look toward retirement in the next decade, if I were to start a workshop, it would be a Daws Butler-style workshop. It wasn't a 6-week course for $300 and you graduate. But with Daws it was very casual. If you couldn't make it, you called him up and said so, I'll be there next week.

At the time it was $10 every Thursday. To be touched by a genius like Daws for ten dollars was *incredible*. I was out of work for a while and he said, you come anyway. When you can start paying me again, you start paying me again. That's the type of person Daws was. I looked at him through such rose-colored glasses at this stage of my life. I was in my 20s at the time. Corey Burton and I were always the last to leave the workshop. Daws would go in the house and down a little schnapps or whatever. The workshop usually went from 7:30 or 8 to 11, something like that. And there were nights when I stood outside and talked to Daws in his driveway until 1:00 in the morning. And then we had to leave because at 1 o'clock you're not allowed to be parked on the street in Beverly Hills. Daws would just stand there and just gab, gab, gab. My biggest thrill was when I got to do the Jetsons, and I got to sit next to Daws. It was wonderful, exciting. Around '83, '84.

The scripts he wrote for the workshop were wonderful. He really tailor-made them so we could get a lot of work in. He would think of characters strictly for the people in the workshop, and nobody else is going to do that. He knew who he was writing for. The scripts were very clever and very funny. I still have them. If the time comes and I do a workshop, I would use the same scripts.

I was the voice of Furby, a toy that was big in Christmas of '98. I based him on Elroy. The ad people in Chicago wanted something young and cuddly. The only thing I could think of was Daws, and Elroy. I went to Elroy, but made him a little bit younger.

Whimsical Will (as heard on Dr. Demento)

1976 Disneyland Records re-released all of the Little Golden Book records. Bob Holt narrated a few of them. Lucille Bliss did some. Prior to that there was a series of filmstrips for Walt Disney Educational Media. Winnie the Pooh on the Way to School. It had the original cast: Sterling Holloway. Daws was doing Owl on most of those. We did about six. Winnie the Pooh for President, which is a rarity, as Disney printed the cast on the label of the record, but there was no Owl in that one. Larry Croce did a lot of the music.

I joined the class in 1975, and was the first kid in the room. I think I felt intimidated by all the adults in the room at first, but they were so receptive and so generous with their comments that I felt at ease after a while.

There was a big thank you party for Daws around 1980. They went through Daws' Rolodex and tried to invite everyone who had ever worked with Daws in any way. It was supposed to be a surprise—I don't know if it was, but they were all invited to his house. It was a huge turn out, with Dr. Demento and Stan Freberg.

He was really the most sincere and the most generous with his time and with his caring. He didn't have to do all this - workshops and private lessons and all, because he wasn't making money off of it. He really truly enjoyed it and looked forward to it, and we certainly did the same.

Corey Burton (Voice actor of many Disney projects)

The workshop was incredible. Even "name talent" came to observe and "work out" with us. We had such guests as Helen Kleeb, William Woodson, Ben Wright (who visited several times, and even recorded scenes with us), among others. They all deferred to Daws when it came to giving advice—telling us that we couldn't be in better hands.

My first professional job was a school slide film for Walt Disney Educational Media called *Chef Omelette's Health Diet* [with Sterling Holloway, Don Messick, Daws, and Hal Smith]. Due to the fact that I had kept in touch with Daws Butler after we met, he knew I did this impression of Hans Conried. And this project came up. Daws said they wanted a Hans voice and Hans was in New York at the time. So I went into Hollywood or wherever and went in with Daws Butler and Don Messick. And I got the gig. I was about 17, I'd turned 18 when the actual session came about. Don, Daws, Janet Waldo and Hal Smith were there. I remember Hal Smith telling me it was an honor to be with me at my first recording session. I had a terrible cold at the time of course. It was made much better by the presence of those people. It was at Bell Sound, the studio's still there.

More work didn't follow immediately. I still use it as a rule of thumb: when you first enter the voice-over world you may get one job your first year, maybe none the second year and maybe another one or two the third year. Things don't really start building until your third or fourth year in the business. Usually by the fifth year you really get a career going. But after that first job with WEDMCO I'd kept in touch with Daws and he called me at Radio Shack (around '73 or '74) where I was working and said he was getting a workshop together. So I did indeed become a part of it. There, among others, I met Jack Ross, who was program director for a local radio station, KVFM stereo 94. He asked me to do a few things. The first was an impression of Rod Serling for a car wash, and various character voices for very local radio commercials. Bits and pieces like that was how I got into it. But the next job with Disney wasn't for another year or two after that. When I was 22 was when I really began a career.

Aside from the connection with Jack Ross, Daws really trained us in a classical way that hadn't really been done before, I guess: to be genuine old time radio actors, and it's invaluable. The great radio actors really were the essence of character voices in cartoons. And having those skills is I think the best training for voice-overs. To be a good radio actor automatically makes you a good voice-over person.

You can do a hundred different characters with the same voice. Peter Sellers, one of the great voice actors of all time, never changed his voice. He did all his characters in one voice, and they were all distinct.

I didn't really do many jobs With Daws, though I was 4.5 years in his workshop. I did a couple of shows with him for Sears, Heartbeat Theatre. The last job with Daws was with June Foray, Bill Scott and Joe Alaskey, which was called *Return to Mocoa* (for an insurance or oil company or union carbide), which Bill Scott wrote and directed. It was an industrial, about business etiquette. An animated piece on how to handle clients, etc. It was an independent project, after Jay Ward.

Myself, Brian Cummings and Tony Pope many times after the workshop we would hang out in front of the house, chat with Daws until 2 or 3 in the morning, going on and on about whatever, not just the voice business. Philosophizing about life in general. Sometimes our paths cross today for an event or work.

Keith Scott
(Jay Ward biographer & the modern voice of Bullwinkle)

I well remember the giddy thrill when Daws Butler, one of the top five voice artists of his generation, responded to my first letter back in 1970. I was just seventeen, a native of Sydney, Australia, and though Daws didn't verify it, mine may well have been the first serious fan letter he received.

I had been a huge admirer of his unique voices since we first started seeing *Huckleberry Hound* in 1959. When I later heard the "Best of the Stan Freberg Show" LPs (wherein Daws received liner note credit) I was able to finally figure out which voices he did for all those Hanna-Barbera cartoons, as well as Jay Ward's *Fractured Fairy Tales*, and even some late 50s Warner Bros. cartoons. I was enamored of his uniquely resonant voice and subtle comedic delivery—I had to meet this man.

Daws Butler was still highly active in 1970, the year I determined to write him; I remember my mother telling me, "Don't be disappointed if he doesn't respond. People like this man would just be far too busy."

But happily, such was not the case: I was soon the recipient of an airmail package from "Yogi Bear" himself, containing color photos, character drawings, and a long, detailed letter that not only answered my many questions about accents and character voices, and his co-workers, but which flattered me by speaking in an intelligent, non-condescending manner. It was as if I was an old pal of his, and his letter went miles beyond the answer I had expected.

Two years later, I had occasion to win a trip to LA. I phoned Daws from the Hollywood Holiday Inn. He and his agent Miles Auer both spoke to me, and Daws invited me and my American friend Corey Burton (who shared my youthful passion for cartoons and great voice acting) to a lecture he was giving for a drama group at Valley State College in Northridge. (The drama class was taught by Chris Allen - the voice of Jay Ward's *Hoppity Hooper!*—who had invited her old friend Daws as guest speaker.) To Corey and me, Daws in person was quicksilver personified—he gave an electrifying and funny address that totally rounded out someone who, until now, had mainly been an intriguing name in television cartoon credits.

Later in the car park, Daws requested we do a little vocal schtick: here was the teacher in him two years before the workshop. And so he heard my early, self-conscious attempts at various voices, like Jack Benny, his own Mr. Jinks character, and a Paul Frees imitation that cracked him up (I think back now, and cringe knowing my teenage mimicry must have sounded rather terrible). But he enthusiastically told us, "Gee, you two definitely have 'an ear,'" and he urged us to call him the following week, to get together at his home recording studio. "You know, we can just toss some stuff around—maybe I can do some characters with you guys, and you know, give ya a coupla tips."

Well, can you imagine the heady high this gave we cartoon-striplings—indeed Corey and I were quite possibly the very first of the baby-boomer "voice buffs"—we admired and seriously analyzed the masters, and desired to do exactly what Daws, Mel Blanc, Paul Frees and the other greats from the radio era did. Trouble is, we had no idea how to get into the business. Daws Butler was to be our unwitting key (indeed Corey relates his own story in this chapter).

Anyway, after that incredible weekend get-together, Daws continued to write me once I was back home in Australia (or as he put it, "long gone back to platypus land"). He also began sending tape letters: rambling yet highly pointed lessons in character voice, dialect construction, and acting techniques. I treasure these tapes to this day. Very early in my career I was already able to apply various pointers the master had shown me, and I discovered exactly what he had predicted: "Keith, you'll start finding little plateaus of ability, acting 'stepping stones' that you didn't even know you had within you."

Some eighteen months later, in October 1974, Daws sent me a tape in which he described his new workshop, which had just started that month. He added that he considered me "a team member in spirit," and how I gave his class a credible kick-off because he could brag that it was already an "international" workshop. I thought he was kidding, but, no, he was serious. Soon he began sending me scripts, and selected tapes of his American students' readings. This went on for several more years until I could afford annual trips from Sydney to Los Angeles, where I could visit him at his home and do in-person readings. This mentor-like, sincere friendship continued until his untimely death. I now look back and marvel at this sweet, unassuming, ferociously talented man.

Can you imagine anyone else—with his level of success, from a sometimes-spiteful town like Hollywood yet—doing what he did for all those hopefuls, let alone for someone who lived 7,000 miles away? (And which he continued doing, for over ten years.) Yes, I miss Daws Butler, particularly his fey humor and nasal chuckle, more than I can relate.

As I inexorably approach the age that Daws was at when he began his teaching, I realize that I now find him even more astounding than I originally perceived. Quite simply, there was never a kinder, more giving, and less egotistical man on this planet, let alone in this profession. And, heavens to Murgatroyd, how we could do with a few more Daws Butlers in this so-far tawdry new Millennium!

Bob Bergen
(Current voice of Porky Pig and many others)

I first started studying with Daws when I was about 16 and continued 'til I was 23. The only reason I stopped was because I started teaching my own animation voice-over workshop that happened to fall on the same night as Daws'.

As you can read on my website (bobbergen.com), I met him at 14 at a mall performance for ASIFA. Daws taught out of a guesthouse in back of his home in Beverly Hills. He had this big ol' table where we'd all sit surrounded by hundreds of stuffed animals and cells from the various cartoons Daws worked on. He always served coffee and butter cookies.

My first Wednesday night workout I arrived a bit early. Daws and I watched some tapes of old cartoons in his living room. He shared anecdotes about what had happened on the day of the recordings. I was amazed he could remember such intricate details. One little tidbit I learned that day was that he voiced both the Jackie Gleason and Art Carney characters in Warner Bros. short *The Honeymousers*. Since Mel Blanc got sole screen credit for the Looney Tunes, I assumed it was he voicing Ralph and Morton.

The most important thing I learned from Daws is that it really isn't about the voice. It's all about the acting. Daws taught that with a good script and a good actor you'll get a good performance. He stressed timing, and the rhythm of the joke or line. Daws wasn't really an acting teacher. He never said this to me, but I think he believed that you were either an actor or you weren't. I believe this myself. A class can give you the opportunity to work with the tools you need to discover your acting talents and range. But you are either born an actor or you aren't. By the way, his class was $10 or a handshake, whatever you had that week.

His scripts rocked!! It was like doing live radio. Using his original scripts is what made Daws' class so unique. Most VO classes used existing commercial or cartoon copy. Because Daws wrote everything we couldn't have a preconceived idea of how to perform the material.

I never did any private classes with Daws, but we chatted on the phone a lot. I remember one of the last things he did was some Huckleberry Hound TV movie. He was kinda down that the recording process had become such an "assembly line," to quote Daws. He said that the days of taking time with a script to find the proper beats and rhythms were gone. Time is money, so they wanted it fast not good. But I know that whatever he did was good. Toward the end, Daws had lots of health issues. He walked with a cane at times. But when he was in front of the mike he came to life as if he was 30!! He really was at home at the mike. He knew my goal was to voice Porky Pig. Sadly, he died before I got that gig. But I always called him when I got a job. I miss that opportunity.

Sean Wright

Daws and I spent an evening listening to a tape I'd made of Harold Peary as "The Great Gildersleeve" reading stories for children—Puss in Boots, Jack and the Beanstalk and Rumpelstiltskin from a Capitol record album released in 1946. I'd wondered if they had had any influence on Stan Freberg's irreverence in his satiric albums of the 1950s-60s. Daws had not heard these stories before and enjoyed them a great deal. Although these tales are given something of a contemporary spin by Peary playing Gildersleeve, Daws did not think that they had any influence on Stan's work.

Daws spoke about glowingly about Peary's wonderful vocal presence, however and how he was by turns hilarious, frightening, serious and jovial without losing his character in the least. And the great thing, Daws pointed out, Peary obviously loved what he was doing. There is no way that kids would not be drawn to his rendition, even when Peary would pause in the story to tell the kids to "turn the record over…I'll wait."

I recall that Daws would occasionally become annoyed because well-heeled film stars like Frank Sinatra and Burgess Meredith would make voice-over commercials. "As if they didn't have enough money," he'd say somewhat exasperatedly. He was never meanspirited about it, but he thought that there was no need for them to take jobs away from him or Walter Tetley, Ben Wright or June Foray when they weren't hurting.

Nancy Senter

Daws was just always so much fun, so bright and self-effacing at the same time. Always a delight to be with.

My major memory of Daws was a night at his house, when he was telling a bunch of us about writing and performing *Time for Beany* with Stan Freberg. He said the two of them rented a room in a Hollywood hotel, so they'd have no excuse not to write…and then they'd get into the elevator filled with people, one of them carrying a bag or suitcase. "Do you think he's okay in there?" "Oh, yeah. Pythons and boas can go for days without eating anything." "Did you bring the rats?" "I thought you brought the rats" "So what are we gonna feed him?"…and on and on, improv heaven. They were each other's perfect foil. We never stopped laughing. What a treasure those two are/were.

Chapter 9
The Great Comeback

The disillusionment of the previous decade was still lingering. Nostalgia would make its great comeback later, but health and a sense of arduous regret at canceled radio series and few "original" characters to delve into were still weighing heavily on the voice actor, as this series of letters written to Joe Bevilacqua reveals.

> January 6, 1980
> *I hope you had a happy one—I'm not a traditionalist myself—I am aware of holidays and what they portend or pretend to portend but I see so much sham also—as Freberg did in Green Christmas—that I can take them or leave them. I'm getting very tired of cliches. Christmas is for people who are genuinely fond of each other and with such lucky people it continues, or should, all through the year—we shouldn't give on cue.*
>
> *I didn't mean to get into all of this philosophy but what the hey!*
>
> *I have a few publisher meetings coming up in the near future—nothing I can talk about now—but a few important people…hopefully, this will be the year for the ACTOR'S HANDBOOK—the collection of 'pieces' which should run the gamut of human emotion—and serve a purpose in college, high schools and dramatic schools all over the country…we'll hope!*
>
> *I'm writing more and more all the time—and it's get-*

ting better—that is, to me, it's getting better—I'm plumbing more psychological and emotional depths.

July 9, 1980

I talked to the editor at McGraw-Hill in San Francisco a few days ago—he was all apologies for not getting back to me—not with a final opinion or decision, but for the failure of someone on his staff in not letting me know the scripts were there—and he was getting around to them. His tone was positive—so I feel good about it—and am awaiting his judgement.

Things are slow, business-wise—nothing for me (so far) at Hanna-Barbera.

Still doing Wimpy—with no funny lines which is a waste for what I consider to be a good W.C. Fields. Oh well.

But in 1980 there was a reprieve from the slowness.

Someone went through his Rolodex and invited everyone who had ever worked with Daws to a surprise party given by his students. It was a huge turnout at the Butler home. Stan Freberg was there in one of his rare meetings with Daws, and it was there that Whimsical Will met Dr. Demento, a relationship that resulted in Will's appearances on the good Dr.'s show to this day. The students all chipped in to give Daws probably the best present he could have asked for: a video recorder, an early VCR. When business was slow and the writing muse sluggish, Daws would record *everything* off TV that took his fancy.

September 29, 1980

The [animators'] strike hasn't affected me much—I do a few of the radio shows—and keep busy with the workshop and promoting my book. The editor from Boston who dug it from the beginning will be in town next week and is coming by. He should be impressed with the workshop and all the pictures and artifacts. Maybe this will be it!

The two-hour TV movie *Yogi's First Christmas* was broadcast before Thanksgiving on November 22, 1980 and starred Daws as Yogi, Huck, Augie Doggie and Snagglepuss who try to save Jellystone Lodge from being sold by its manager due to poor turnout. Lack of significant cartoon work wasn't helping Daws' health issues, either.

Daws, in an audio letter to Joe, told of his ailments: "I told you this heart attack hit me in church on New Year's Day, and it was really spooky to me, you know, I said something to Myrtis about my head felt light, and I was trying to get out of the pew with my cane. I guess I must have blacked out completely, and she looked around and got the eye of a couple of the ushers, and they came down and helped me out of the pew and off my back, and this visiting a heart specialist somewhere in the church had a little nitroglycerin capsule, and he broke that under my nose, and I came around. The paramedics were there by then, and they got me over to the hospital. And I spent two weeks in the hospital with an IV in one side of the bed. I couldn't go to the bathroom; I had a commode by the side of the bed, and, oh God, always checking my vital signs every half hour or so, and yet I didn't feel terribly bad. And my legs didn't bother me, or my leg. It was almost as if this took precedence over that pain I had been putting up with and also this terrible itching which I blamed on the Keflex and the antibiotics and also the tension of licking each one of my little problems one at a time. And I think the tension built up, and it may have had something to do with the heart attack because my weight had been kept within a couple pounds over the last six to eight months, I'd say, so I don't know what made me accumulate water, but it did, and it got in my lungs and the heart wouldn't pump hard enough.

"So, now I've got a regimen of pills. One pill is a nitro-type. And I have another one which controls the beat of the heart. I have to go in the day after tomorrow, and he'll run an EKG and see how I'm doing. And I have to force myself to take it easy and really stay off the phone. I've got a message on the phone that the doctor advised me to take it easy and to knock off the telephone verbosity. And if anyone does call up and Myrtis, well, she just explains that for the next week or until I really check with the doctor, he really wants me to rest because normally I try to bounce back too fast. And that's the danger, and that's been the fault in the past.

"So, I'm trying to be a good boy. And she fixes me very nice meals, and I'm going to get around to drinking brim instead of coffee, margarine instead of butter, and you know just lay low on some of the more choleric and fatty things and no salt, you know, that's out. No sodium. No Chinese food."

April 13, 1981

Dear Joe…

We haven't been in touch since the phone call.

I had to spend a week or so in the hospital…a Prostate Gland problem. Wasn't solved completely…this sort of thing happens to guys when they get to my age—so whatta ya gonna do?

I have to go back in—week or so—I hate it when something's wrong with me. Physically, I mean…mentally, I don't mind—that I can accept—that's what makes me a genius.

Anyway, I enjoyed the call—and will get back to reviewing the cassettes.

I was uncomfortable there for a while but my energy has returned pretty well.

In an hour or so my wife is driving me in to do a Cap'n Crunch session! I still feel a bit weak.

Write when you can. Right now, I gotta get back up there with the big guys.

Love,
Daws

He would go back into the hospital near the end of the month for a urinary problem. But things were not looking up. Daws would have a stroke in the early 1980s which caused him to lose peripheral vision and lead to his decision to give up driving. It led him to have to give up the one thing that kept him going: his work. In order to combat the depth perception Daws was having as a result of the stroke, his old friends helped graciously during recording sessions.

"I used to go to Daws' workshop a lot and help him," said Lucille Bliss (A.K.A. Crusader Rabbit). "When he had a stroke, he called me and asked me to come down so I could read the script with him. He was getting his voice back, but he didn't want to do it with the students just yet. He was such a genius. Such a wonderful, warm, great artist."

June Foray recalled, "He was so brave. When he had a stroke, he was almost dyslexic and couldn't read. When we did the Cap'n Crunch commercials, I was Brunhilde, Bill Scott was another character and Daws was Cap'n Crunch. We would go to the studio and Daws was incredible. Bill Scott would read his line and Daws would copy them in his intonation and character. He was remarkable."

The few gigs at H-B were done the same way, and in his last few years he used his home studio once or twice for some H-B work, recording his lines solo, which were then "pieced" into the full recording.

In an undated audio letter, Daws explained his reading problem in detail: "I've done a few Cap'n Crunch commercials. I've pulled away from doing readings for new programs, because I just can't read fast enough. It's getting better. I'm reading much quicker than I have been. I've worked out a little trick: when I start a line, in a newspaper for instance, I let my eye flip to the right very quickly to see what's at the end of the line, and, if possible, what's at the beginning of the *next* line, as a singer does. That makes tension and isn't the way one should read, but it's a hell of a lot better than it was. I hope within the next three or four months to get back all of my immediate perception. The thing I can't do now is scan. I can't look at a line on a television screen and see it immediately. Same way with reading. A headline, for instance - I may see five of the seven words, then all of a sudden the last two words will open up. It's something in my right vision, something I have to keep compensating for. My general health is fine and when I speak with people on the phone they say, 'Oh, you sound great.' So thank God it hasn't affected my speech, only my memory with words. I seem to remember most of the big words and forget the little words. I have some Holy Water from Lord's that a friend of mine gave me and I bless myself with it every day.

"I watch my weight and my salt intake. When I came out of the hospital, I weighed 128, which is very low for me. Normally I think my weight should be anywhere from 120 to 125. I try to eat single portions, no matter how good anything is. We've found a few restaurants who cater to those on a special diet. Even a Chinese restaurant where I can get Egg Foo Young and a few things that are made without salt; they use chicken broth to cook the chicken or vegetables in. I have a glass of wine or so every day, and I'm reading the newspaper more.

"Show business-wise I'm at pretty much of a standstill.

"When I was in the Navy I used to salute firemen, policemen, it made no difference to me. I never knew what the hell the insignia meant.

"We got a priest from Belgium and he's probably in his 50s. He speaks French and telescopes words within sentences so that they tumble. He doesn't use equal emphasis; a great American thing. He doesn't talk as flat as an American. He's been here about 10 or 15 years and doesn't speak as well as he should. He's been to me once and I worked with him. He has no 'th,' everything is 'zis,' and when I talk back to him or criticize him, I talk back exactly the way he's talking to me. So I wrote a special piece for him, emphasizing th's. This, that, them, those, thistle. I *think* the Americans and the English are just about the only ones in the world who use the 'th' sound. Many foreigners think it's an ugly sound; the tongue going between the teeth and so forth. I also gave the priest my piece on how to mark copy. I want to get him to slow down his pace and stop all that up and down structure, to use equal emphasis, to end sentences, not just gliss from one sentence to another. To listen to him now it's embarrassing to listen to him deliver a sermon. I haven't the *vaguest* idea what he's talking about. And I don't care. I've gotten to the point where unless the actor or priest or speaker makes it legible, I don't want to bother. You're up there trying to reach *me*. I don't have to go to you. That's an interesting concept.

I hope he'll have the time from his parish duties to get together with me once a week or so. There are a few others I'm getting with, though I can't read *with* people yet, as I said.

"I really miss teaching. I don't miss working. The material stinks to such an extent that I don't really care.

"I really feel Myrtis is taking the brunt of this thing because she has to be on top of pills and what I take, and takes my temperature once in a while. My energy varies. Today it's Saturday. Had breakfast, watched a good Agatha Christie movie on television, and I felt tired. A sense of exhaustion, which is still part of the infection in my leg. So I took a nap for two hours, got up and had a little wine and felt better."

> July 20, 1981
>
> Joe—I've really been out of it—had the [urinary] operation June 10—complications—got an infection, a strain of 'mono' (such as the pope had)—My temperature was inconsistent—finally got it worked out…I'm home—resting a lot—I'll listen to your tape soon—everything is an effort yet—I weigh about 113—so I've got some building up to do—more later.

An audio letter given by Daws around 1981 showed things were getting better.

> "I've been very busy the last 6 months. The Popeye thing at Hanna-Barbera, Yogi's Space Race, Galaxy Goof-Ups. They're doing 8 more Laugh Olympics, why, I don't know. The Captain Crunch commercials are still going, regardless of all the piffle that's going on about the sweetened cereals. And I've done a bunch of spots for Six Flags Over Georgia and Astro World and a lot of parks in the south in which Quaker is associated. I'm doing the Captain Crunch voice on kind of a loop for different attractions, where he gives a big come on, talks about the sharks and the whales and the whole bit. And of course that pays off very good. I've done a bunch with Yogi Bear, commercials for the Hanna-Barbera parks, the Taft parks. They bought out Marineland out here on the West coast, and Yogi walks around with the other mannequins, Fred

Flintstone, Snagglepuss and so on. I'm going to do some more voices for the Ice Capades. They want me to do Fred Flintstone and Barney and Jabberjaw. Jabberjaws I couldn't do at all. My voice isn't heavy enough for Fred Flintstone. And the trouble with Barney Rubble is that it's too close to Yogi because they're both generically based on Art Carney. I did it last year but I wasn't very happy with it. And ethically, it doesn't seem right to me, as long as Mel's around. Of course Alan Reed is dead, but Henry Corden is doing it now and he comes about as close as anyone can. And Frank Welker should do the Jabberjaws because that's his character, and I couldn't do it anyway.

December 11, 1981

I'm feeling much better—the temperature is staying normal—the infection is still there—but getting better. I'm a little stiff when walking—but it's not all that painful—and while the doctor makes noises about re-doing the right hip—I don't plan to do anything for quite a while—when you're sixty-five and feel good otherwise—I don't anticipate giving up another year of my life with an operation or a couple!! The hell with that!

And in another undated letter:

I'll be starting the new show which forefronts YOGI BEAR this week probably—I don't know the name of it—but it will include all of the characters I've done. Hopefully, we'll get JIMMY WELDON to do his YACKIE DOODLE. According to Mark Evanier, the writer of the shows, I'll have some editorial clout so I can 'sweeten' up the dialogue as I see it. Should be fun—and my reading is getting better all the time.

I am sending you a new piece I wrote—sort of 'off the wall.'

When asked about "now vs. then" in the animation business, Daws told Morgan White, Jr. on his December 26, 1981 talk radio show: "In the old days, it's the same as it is now for plumbers. If you want to call a plumber, you ask a neighbor who a good plumber is - who isn't going to cheat you and will do a good job and put in pipes that won't break. You call him, he does the job, and everybody's happy. But you don't call in twenty plumbers and ask them questions like what a Stillson wrench is and how to stop a leak. You call *a plumber*. And it used to be in the old days of animation you called in experts, like Don Messick, Mel Blanc, Paul Frees. There were probably 25 specialists who were very adept in this particular field who could do multi-voices, dialects, different age groups. Now the networks call in 40 or 50 people and have them all read something and they have a preconceived idea about what the sound should be so that originality is kind of throttled. Someone will end up doing the cosmetic rendition they're asking for, where they like the tonal sound, but in many instances the people can't act. Then the director will go crazy trying to get a usable reading out of them. So it's really controlled by the networks, not the professional production people who are the artists and the show business people.

"Today, you have maybe eight people in a room, sitting around in front of microphones, each doing one or two voices. You don't have the rapport that developed between Don and me."

> January 18, 1982
> Dear Joe—
> What a way to start the New Year! In the middle of mass—I felt light-headed—dizzy—and blacked out—Myrtis signaled a couple of ushers—and the next thing I knew I found myself lying on my back in the aisle—inhaling a broken nitro-capsule's fumes—and reviving—There happened to be a visiting heard specialist at that mass—He called the paramedics and I was whisked off to the Hosp. My heart had an irregular beat or something—so I spent the last couple weeks there—I was apparently retaining water in my lungs because my heart wasn't strong enough to pump it all out—
> I'm home now—but must take it easy—do light exercises—and get bed rest. I am doing so. I'm out of the woods.
> I thought I wrote thanking you for the Yogi Bear money clip—I had to leave it home so nobody'd swipe it at the hosp.

Jay Ward gave me a Bullwinkle wrist watch—
My two favorite gifts!

Nancy Cartwright's movie, *Marion Rose White*, is on CBS tomorrow night—Hope you see it—she starred in it!

I'm writing in a reclining position—so it's ragged.

March 1, 1982

I realized that my fingers remember where the words are—and while I still have some trouble reading (especially syllables), I can write pretty good—letting my fingers do the 'programmed' work!!

[...]

I've made great strides with my reading—been a bit over a month—and I can read much faster—in another month, I hope to be 'the best cold-reader in the West!!' again.

I feel pretty good otherwise—I'm going to try and get out for more exercise. Having trouble sleeping—think it's inactivity.

Undated letter

The whole animation business is in bad shape. I just talked to a gal at HANNA-BARBERA—she used to work with Charles when he worked out there—in the camera department. She said all they're doing Domestically is THE SMURFS. Everything is being done out of the country. Stinks!!!!

She's thinking very seriously of getting out of the business entirely and get into some sort of business that is unrelated.

I'm up for a part in an animation special—not Hanna-Barbera...and will do it if my agent can work out the deal. He's a hard-nose—but he's done a good job for me for thirty years—so he pulls the strings. I'd like to do it if it works out.

My reading is getting much better—almost back to normal, scanning-wise. I've been reading with my workshop more and more. The legs are still weak—but no pain...just weak. Going up stairs is not a favorite diversion.

Now...the unpleasant part. I got up early this morning to go to the store and get some water bottles filled—I drink distilled water...and ran a red light on a busy street. The other guy tried to miss me, but I got clipped and was spun around a bit—no one was hurt, thank God!—and the damage to both cars is fixable. He was driving a brand-new Mercedes.

I'm going over to see the doctor this afternoon—Just to make sure everything is O.K. Trauma, mostly, and an awful feeling of stupidity!! Running a red light.

I made the decision today that my driving days were over. This hip thing keeps me in a low-grade pain all the time and I think my concentration for worldly things, such as traffic, is off the mark. It's just as well.

Last week, I picked all of my lines for the YOGI BEAR Christmas special—(get this title) THE GIFT OF THE YOGI. I recorded in what they call a closed session—did all the lines 'wild'...Yogi had about six hundred. There were about twelve or thirteen characters, including ones I hadn't done in a while...Hokey Wolf—Augie Doggie—Super Snooper and Blabbermouse. My reading is getting better, but I wanted to do the lines alone—I did about four or five takes on each line—did them in sequence (for a sense of continuity). Did the whole thing with some pick-ups in about four hours. Then I did the music session the next day—about three characters chiming in with an occasional bit of lyric.

September 23, 1982

My reading seems to be improving bit by bit—I'm able to read dialogue with students now—not great, but better than it was.

We're going back east for a week—going to visit my wife's mother in Albermarle, N.C. I'm not looking forward to the plane ride—but everything should be O.K. once we get there—she hasn't seen her mother in a few years. The weather should be fine at this time of year. We'll be getting a motel with a kitchen so I can stay on the salt-free bit.

Undated

My general health is good—the energy isn't what I would like it to be. I've got three or four other letters to answer. One of my students in the workshop is a vice-president in the Screen Extras Guild and does a lot of extra work himself—he's written a Screen Play and wants me to read it—which I will do—but it takes time and my reading isn't all THAT good! This guy has talked to my son Charles about getting into Screen Extra work. Don't know how it will work out...it's up to Charles. I think it would be a good thing. Charles is a good-looking kid now (30-year-old kid) and who knows?? He's good in the vocal acting department—good sense of timing and a good ear for characters and dialects...just hasn't pushed it.

October 11, 1982

What you say about radio is true ... it was, and is—the most graphic, visual medium ever. It limits none of the physical action because that gives the pauses and proper reactions—but we've been through this many times.

Wouldn't it be great if, through your efforts, radio would make a big comeback?

We just got back from the North Carolina trip and I brought a cold with me. We took it easy and didn't try to do much more than fix it with Myrtis' mother and two of our nieces. The leg bothered me, but not as much as I thought. I slept well and napped a bit when the opportunity arose.

The trip to N.J. would have been rough—I just don't have that sort of stamina at this time—but thanks for asking. I'm trying to conserve my energy so as to get the workshop started again.

I got a nice letter from Bill Melillo—expressing his thanks for the residual assistance he got from working with you and with me as your mentor. Wonderful letter!

Well, Joe...that's about it for now. I'll be glad when I get a re-run on my old energy.

Love,
Daws

Daws returned to H-B for a half-hour Christmas special, *Yogi Bear's All-Star Comedy Christmas Caper*, airing for CBS on December 21, 1982. Huck and the usual gang journeyed to Jellystone Park to spend the holidays with Yogi and Boo Boo, but the bears stowed away in a tour bus in order to join their friends in the city. It was a farcical chase show written by Mark Evanier, with carols and another pristine voice cast including Don Messick, Mel Blanc and Janet Waldo.

> March 28, 1983
>
> This Wednesday night I'm taking a stab at the 'old workshop'…I'm inviting about fifteen or so of the former members over—no charge—more of a party than anything…we'll probably get around to reading some stuff sooner or later, but basically, it's just a get-together. Some coffee and cakes.
>
> I really missed the workshop. I'm frustrated that I can't read faster, but it will be fun just assigning parts to members and having them read—with a bit of directorial comment by the mentor.
>
> We saw a movie recently, TENDER MERCIES with Robert Duvall—a sleeper, if there ever was one—a couple of low-grade four-letter words in the beginning and no more. Simple story and Duvall was superb—study this man and how he makes a part his own—he had the Texan's walk—the way he handled his body when dancing—his mastery of the Texas drawl—concentrating on one word or vowel for authenticity…He says 'Theng' instead of 'thing'…this is a characteristic of the West, anyway.
>
> I am unimpressed by THE THORN BIRDS. I watched "THE DAY CHRIST DIED"—and found it to be expertly done—from the standpoint of politics, with Christ as the 'pasty.'**

In 1980, Daws sent a script to Joe Bevilacqua entitled *Sherlock Holmes in Trouble*, a parody in which Holmes was an idiot and Watson the intellectual. The script soon inspired a ten-part series of half-hour radio plays co-written by Butler and Bevilacqua: "The Misadventures of Sherlock Holmes," which premiered on public radio in October 1983. The series featured Vernon Morris as Holmes, Henry J. Quinn as Watson, Jan

Meredith as Mrs. Hudson, Ed Hyland as Professor Moriarty, William Melillo as Inspector Lestrade, Terry Price and Gwendolyn Lewis as Irene Adler, and Bevilacqua as Arthur Conan Doyle, William Gillette and nearly all the other dozens of supporting roles. Between 1980 and 1988, Bevilacqua starred in and produced a series of radio scripts written by Daws, mostly ones created for the workshop, including "The Ad Game," "Somewhere Along the Line or Verbosity Self-Taught," and "More Poetry Than Truth: A Delicious Fiction." Daws had written "A Halloween Happening" with the idea of selling it to the Sears Radio Theater, but the script was rejected as being "too esoteric" as Daws put it. In 1982, Bevilacqua produced his version for NPR. Today, Bevilacqua continues to present new and old performances of Daws' scripts as part of *What the Butler Wrote: Scenes from the Daws Butler Workshop*, a regular segment on his weekly radio show, *The Comedy-O-Rama Hour*, heard on XM Satellite Radio and public radio stations nationwide.

When Joe Bevilacqua won 1st place in a New Jersey State Children's Literature Contest on May 16, 1983, crediting himself as writer "based on characters created by Daws Butler," it gave him the confidence to suggest writing up Daws' Uncle Dunkle stories in a more popular narrative form. Daws, still trying to interest publishers in his book of scenes, was all for it. Alas, they fared just as well. Pitching it to Prentice Hall, Harcourt-Brace-Govanovich, and Simon and Shuster got nowhere, as did a TV series proposal. Daws, ever the optimistic writer, wrote, "The Uncle Dunkles seem to be developing. Let's hope the current market will accept the simplicity of the whole concept. Just a man and a boy relating and having fun."

By October 21, 1985, Joe had sent Uncle Dunkles out to 50 book publishers, with 37 rejections and no responses from the rest. There had been a bite from Peter Pan Records & Tapes who were "very impressed" with the 30 stories he sent. Peter Pan had been producing records and tapes with only characters that had national recognition, but expected to develop a line for original characters in February or March 1986. But the bite did not hook a fish; nor did a proposal for a National Public Radio series.

Daws stated, "See, the thing we would run into was language criticism, for I put Uncle Dunkle in bad English purposely because it gave it a point of truth. But they might say, well you can't do this, and you can't do that. And that's what has really ruined animation. One of the big things is they're so damned concerned about the fact of saying ain't or having a child do something which might be antagonistic, and when they clean it up and white wash it, there's no story left. It's like there's so-called violence in cartoons. Bologna. The violence is on television with live actors. *Hill Street Blues*. As good as they are, there's a hell of a lot of violence on television. Cartoons are the least of it."

When speaking about the amount of changes a network might want if Uncle Dunkle were accepted, the writer in Daws answered, "It's this idea of being commercial. About doing cartoons about products that are already merchandised or that will be merchandised instead of just getting a good story. This to me is like comfortable, easy story telling. Well, they say the kids won't get it. Well, you say, damn it, let them grow up to get it. Let them restrain their minds a little bit. It's true that nobody reads anymore. I think the publishing business must really be in the doldrums. God, I mean, people just do not read anymore. When I get somebody coming over, a student saying he reads all the time, I'm delighted because it's wonderful, but there are many people who don't. And even in dialogue. For instance, I watched *Bladerunner*. It was a pretty interesting thing just from the standpoint of special effects and so forth, but really it's not my kind of picture. If I had my choice between seeing that and something with dialogue, I'd go see the dialogue, you know."

Punky Possum's Mud Bath by Daws Butler

DUNKLE: Say, Donnie…

DONNIE: Yeh.

DUNKLE: Did I hear your Aunt Rapunzel scoldin' you about somethin'?"

DONNIE: Uh-huh. I was out playin' in the mud . . .

DUNKLE: Well, why doesn't she watch ya, instead of standin' on her head on the flagpole!

DONNIE: Oh, she was not!!

DUNKLE: Well, she was doin' somethin'!!

DONNIE: Well, anyway, I got mud all over my new pants.

DUNKLE: That's not so good—even with all the new ways of gettin' clothes clean nowadays.

DONNIE: I just didn't think about it—and I was playin' and it was muddy—and then I was muddy, an . . .

DUNKLE: Say, did I ever tell you about Punky Possum and the mud bath?

DONNIE: Never did! Not that one—tell me about Punky Possum, Uncle Dunkle!!

DUNKLE: Well, way down south lives Punky Possum. Unlike most possums, Punky's pappy for instance, (who likes to sleep a lot), Punky loves to frolic around the forest and have a high old time for himself. Sometimes, he even goes off on an adventure at the nearby farm—which is full of mud puddles—and his idea of fun is…well, listen!

PUNKY: This li'l possum like the mud—might-i-ly
An' you donno the fun a pud-dle full o' mud-'ll be!
Water's for the ducks—but not for me!
This li'l possum like to be mud-dy!
Play in the mud from morn 'til night,
You should see me, I'm a sight!
And so you'll know it's me all right—
Scrape the mud away!!! O boy! Look at all the li'l ole mud puddles!!! This is most enjoyable! It's like takin' a bath wrong end to—'stead of gittin' clean—I gits dirty!!!

DUNKLE: Punky's mother was very concerned by her son's love of mud puddles—she kept a tidy house like most mothers and Punky disrupted everything!! She said:

MAMMY: My Punky earned my trust when jest a li'l guy.
An' when he gits so dirty, there's a reason why.
Like all the other boys—mud is what he most enjoys,
He's muddy as a big mud-pie!!

	I never really worried where my Punky'd play, 'Til he came in all covered with that mud, one day—In trackin' up the floors—he doubled all my chores! Punky shouldn't do me that way!!
PUNKY:	(COMING ON) Mammy! Hey, mammy! I'm home!
MAMMY:	Well, if I didn't recognize your voice, I do declare I'd a-never knowed who 'twas! You git that mud offen you now, hear?
PUNKY:	I haven't got much mud on me!
MAMMY:	Punky, you're about the muddiest li'l ole possum around hear! Everybody's talkin' 'bout ya!!
PUNKY:	Well, ya gotta admit, mammy—I am makin' a name for m'self!!
DUNKLE:	Punky didn't mean to do wrong, but he loved the mud so much and played in it so often, that finally even his sleepy ole pappy noticed it.
PAPPY:	You in trouble, boy! Li'l Punky and his clothes 're caked with mud but I suppose To him there's more where he got those! (DOWN) But duds aren't buds the oak-tree grows! Li'l Punky, don't you see, Has never paid a laundry fee, He jest assumes they clean for free! To prove they're downright neighborly!! (CALLS) Hey, Punky! You hear me, son? You're in big trouble, boy! You come along over here where I'm sleep...uh...where I'm restin'!!!
PUNKY:	(COMING ON) Howdy, li'l ole pappy! I hear you callin' me?

PAPPY: I shore rightly was—'cause you in trouble, boy! You come along home 'cause we got a li'l...uh...talking to do—out back...in the woodshed!

PUNKY: Man possum to man possum?

PAPPY: Huh-uh. Man possum to *boy* possum!

PUNKY: That's what I was a-feared of! (BEAT) Oh, well—on the way back to the house we kin carry us in some wood!

DUNKLE: So Punky and his pappy went home to the woodshed and in the olden days a woodshed usually meant—a spankin'!! Pappy opened the door—and they went inside!

PUNKY: Well...uh...

PAPPY: Well!

PUNKY: Well (BEAT) Hear we are inside the li'l ole woodshed, li'l ole pappy!

PAPPY: Don' you go givin' me anymore of that *li'l ole pappy* stuff, li'l ole Punky!!

PUNKY: (STALLING) Reason I called you "li'l"—ole pappy - li'l ole pappy, is 'cause you is kinda "li'l"—ole pappy!!

PAPPY: Desist! I is not the subject of this confrontation—you is!!

PUNKY: Lemme jist git one thing straight—you gonna confront me—or spank me?

PAPPY: I is gonna confront ya!

PUNKY: Oh, that's good news! You jist dint have the heart to spank me, did ya?

PAPPY: I got the heart—but my hand has got small bones! Now, you listen at me, Punky—you're in trouble, boy!—this mud puddle playin' has gotta stop!

PUNKY: But I love mud puddles! Cain't I jist sorta...taper off?

PAPPY:	Huh-uh.
PUNKY:	Jist wondered.
PAPPY:	I'm a-gonna be fair with ya, Punky—you go on back over by the mud puddles, and if you kin find a good reason for a possum gittin' all muddied up like you does, I won't say nothin' more about it—(UP) Oh, an' Punky!!
PUNKY:	Yes, li'l ole pappy?
PAPPY:	Talk with a pig about mud! See what *he* says.
DUNKLE:	So Punky went back over to the farm. There were the lovely mud puddles, and right in the middle of the biggest one…was…a pig!
PUNKY:	Howdy, Mr. Pig!
PIG:	(GRUNTS)
PUNKY:	What're you talkin'—French?
PIG:	Of course not! That's just a sound I make when I'm enjoyin' the mud.
PUNKY:	I never make that sound.
PIG:	Why should ya—yer not a pig.
PUNKY:	But I like mud!
PIG:	Possums don't need mud—jist gits 'em dirty.
PUNKY:	Gits you dirty, too!
PIG:	But I'm a certified pig and mud is my friend—I got me a couple good reasons for likin' it! Air-conditioned I am not. When the sun is high and hot, So the mud's my favorite spot, Keeps me cool all day! Tho I lack insecticide. When the flies torment my hide, Mud again is on my side—keeps the flies away!!

	...and those are two good reasons for a pig likin' mud!! Pigs don't just like to be dirty—Mud is a heap of protection from the hot sun and insects.
PUNKY:	I never thought of it that way. Well, so long, Mr. Pig—you taught me a good lesson—it comes down to this: mud is for pigs but not for possums!
PIG:	Well said!!
DUNKLE:	And then Punky went back home—he found his pappy and mammy waitin' for him. Dinner was hot on the table—but before he sat down, Punky said:
PUNKY:	This li'l possum gave up mud—it is true, 'cause now I know the good a pud-dle full o' mud-'ll do! Mud is for the pigs—but not me, too, My mud puddlin' days are really through! Swing in the trees from morn 'til night. I'm so clean—it's outta sight! I'm glad I finally saw the light— No more mud—no way!!!!**

Daws was also disappointed and disillusioned by his current writing projects, as produced by Bevilaqua, not attaining success. One criticism was that the pace was too slow. "When they're talking about pace being too slow or something, the only thing I can think of is Monty Python. And Monty Python to me in many cases is much too fast. For instance, remember the one about the argument clinic? Well anyway, I finally taped that off of television when they were doing some reruns of that stuff. And I was very disappointed in it, didn't even keep it because I had figured we had done better in the workshop. It was so Goddamn fast. To me there wasn't any characterization, it was only spitting out words."

Daws felt himself in a different epoch, a mindset that finally made him give up on his book of scripts. "I guess it's why I didn't lose my enthusiasm particularly, but I reached the point where it wasn't important or necessary to try to get out the book of all the scenes. Because I realized, even if I got somebody that liked it, it would go through so much hassling and changing to do it their way. 'And you haven't done enough things for girls. You got too many things for guys. Write five more things for girls.' Instead of letting me say, 'this is what I've got, can I put it in a package?' To me, I'm not even that interested in making a lot of money out of it. It's just that I think it would be a good tool for a lot of teachers. So, anyway, that's water over the dam. Publishers have to nit-pick like crazy."

> April 17, 1983
>
> I put myself through a bit of therapy this morning. I got a call from Hanna-Barbera to come in for a couple auditions. New Show—I forget the name—but it's a show which will have animal characters with the old idea of characterizations. I talked to the director and told him about my reading problem…but, as he was the same director who had put together all of my lines for the Christmas Yogi Bear special…he said that he'd record my test a line at a time—so I did two readings for two different characters. We'll see—whether I do it or not, it was good for me to do.
>
> The legs are feeling almost 'NORMAL'…and my reading is getting dramatically better. I told you that I had started the work-shop again…my energy is getting better also. I hope to get back to writing soon. I've got a couple ideas perking up in the old think-box.
>
> […]
>
> The other night at the workshop, we were talking about the acceptance of pornography…in media. I have none of it in my sketches—altho, it gets a bit spicy once in a while…and I said that words made such a difference…and also made the material acceptable to general audiences. One little poem I remembered from my youth and never forgot, is still a minor classic to me. Breaking it down to actuality it simply says "A camel screwed the sphinx"—the poem goes:
>
>> Now the sexual needs of the camel
>> Are more than anyone thinks…
>> One night, in a mad fit of passion
>> He tried to 'booger' the sphinx.

Now the sphinxes posterior orifice
Is clogged with the sands of the Nile
Which accounts for the hump on the camel's back
And the sphinxes inscrutable smile!!

May 31, 1983

I actually didn't submit my stories to many sources. Bill Hanna tried to get some interest in them for animation—no takers. I sent them to Caedmon Records in N.Y.—they are now out of business, I think...No interest there either. I never did submit them to regular children's publishers. I told you that SONY was interested for a year or so, and then decided to put out public domain children's stories so they wouldn't have to pay royalties to anyone—creepy group.

So the field is wide open, I'd say. Go ahead, with my blessings. If you should be able to sell them for recording production, I would be much more satisfied if I could do the Uncle Dunkle and Donny characters—and let you and your stock company do the others. I still don't think you have the 'feeling' for the principals. This could be gone into later—

April 11, 1983

Good news! My legs have felt almost normal during the past week—some problems in climbing stairs but much L E S S!!!! The reading is also getting better! I'm coming along.

November 2, 1983

Nancy [Cartwright] made herself up like a CHRISTMAS TREE for a Halloween party—she borrowed our artificial tree and used the branches and managed to get it all back together—I'll send you a snap. Not too good, but it shows the imagination of Nancy. I think we had a real fun evening—and I am sending you the routine you and Nancy recorded.

I'm not up to too much. Workshop activity—and reading. I read better as time times by.

I got a new VIDEO-RECORDER. Snazzy! Visual fast-forward—whole thing can be operated with a remote control gadget. Neat! To be able to swoop right down to a desired selection. I'll be recording CHEERS tonight. **

Daws held the lead role on NBC's *Deck the Halls with Wacky Walls*, another twist on *A Christmas Carol*, which premiered as a half-hour special on December 11, 1983. Daws was the "Wacky" leader of six aliens from the planet Kling Kling sent to Earth to learn the meaning of Christmas. It was another tie-in program, based on an already successful Japanese toy called the Wacky Wallwalker, and included commercials for the suction-cup sellers during the 7:30-8:00 p.m. broadcast.

January 8, 1984

I am sending you a book report on some SHERLOCK HOLMES stuff…might be interesting. These things don't usually come in paperback, unfortunately.

I am going to listen to the first section of a GEORGE ORWELL documentary on public radio—I don't know if you are getting it back there—going to run for five weeks. Each one an hour. I'm not going to record it—just listen to it—

The message on my code-a-phone is a little kid voice, saying: "Hi, I'm the 1984 New Year's baby. I feel pretty good—but it is sort of…disconcerting…when George Orwell, picks me up, sits me on his lap…pats me on the head…sighs…and says 'Oh, you poor little kid!!!!'

I had a test for my swallowing problem today. I'll get the results in a day or so. Hope they can work something out. I think it has something to do with nerves—some sort of a spasm that breaks when it feels like it.

February 16, 1984

I haven't got back to you because I've been having more health problems. The swallowing is a bit better—but I need another probe to clear out the entrance to the stomach. Ho-hum!

Then I had a recurrence of the infection in my right artificial hip. I had been taken off the medication for that and the timing was wrong—so back to the pills. Leg, or rather, thigh was as sore as a charley-horse and it knocked off my energy, too—the infection blow up, I mean.

Then, I'd been coughing so much trying to get my throat cleared out to swallow, that I strained the muscles in my right chest. Painful.

I'm not in great shape at this time, but it's getting better.

[...]

I've lost a lot of pazazz. I'm going to cut down on the workshop activity. Maybe I've been pushing too much, I don't know.

[...]

Well, I better get back to doing not much for a while.

If I sound 'down,' I do feel that way. It seems like one thing after another.

March 30, 1984

I'm having my 'swallow box' stretched next week, so no workshop. We will get around to doing it. I'll let you know how the operation comes out.

May 11, 1984

I hope to have the UNCLE DUNKLE recorded early next week.

I don't feel in great shape ... the swallowing is still not quite right. Myrtis and I did go out for lunch today and I had P A N C A K E S!!!! The third time I have dared to have them. Delicious! I really ask for little. Give me a pancake and I'll slobber all over you with gratitude.

Take care. I'm still fighting the good fight.

      Love from an old soldier,
      Daws

May 19, 1984

Andy Kaufman died. I never thought much of him as a stand-up comic. He was interesting and I marveled that he was given the chance to do such odd things— but only on TAXI did he come off as a 'developed' character. One of the best shows that ever came out of TAXI was the marriage ceremony. He and Sitka. It has never been rerun, to my knowledge. I check the TV Guide every week, because I didn't tape it in the first instance—and I lust after it for its perfection of true comedy. I don't know why it wasn't rerun. Part of it has to do with its religious spoofing, I suppose. It was a classic. Maybe they'll run it now.

What you were saying about actors being cemented into a part, as was Archie and Ted was true. The strange thing is that is doesn't always apply. Take Ed Asner, for instance. He's a pain in the ass politically, but that's what he's set on doing, so you can't fault him as long as he remains good at what he really should be doing. He walked off the Mary Tyler Moore show and left the memory of his great Lou Grant character and parlayed it into a 'serious' Lou Grant and the public bought it. He is that rare being…a classical actor. He puts on a new putty nose and false eyebrows and surprises us with a new entity.

Did you see him in "ANATOMY OF AN ILLNESS" the other night? He didn't look like Norman Cousins and I'm sure that Norman was more subtle…but Ed brought the show to life. I thought he was great. His case was excellent, which helped.

He broke through the barrier of the over-familiar. Not many can do it. Harry Morgan can go from show to show and never seem to change anything and yet we believe him. It's a magical quality that not many actors are blessed with.

June 30, 1984

Now I'm on the prowl for the three Warner-Brothers HONEYMOUSERS. I did Ralph and Norton and June did Alice. I've never seen them and the report is out that they are funny.

[…]

The swallowing problem seems to be better. I call it the swallowing problem because I'm never sure if I'm spelling the technical way to say it, correctly.

I made myself some lyonaisse potatoes this morning for breakfast. I love onions and Myrtis can't stand them. She puts onion-lovers just slightly ahead of lepers. I had a hamburger the other day also. That—from a standpoint of importance, ranks with the first climbing of Mt. Everest.

I don't have those awful gagging sessions trying to get the gunk out of my upper stomach.

Along with my other health goodies, I seem to be developing some arthritis in my hands. It doesn't seem to affect my typing, however. I still type lousy.

July 3, 1984

My swallowing is getting better. I'm apparently more relaxed—the spasms don't occur as often. In fact, we went out and I had *S H O R T R I B S* this evening!! With shoestring potatoes. No problems.

I may have to have that stretching done every six weeks or so—but I don't mind.

I'm starting to gain some weight (because I'm retaining food) and I have to watch that. I want to stay about 125; at least under 130.

August 8, 1984

Next week we should be doing the first JETSONS. I'll be glad to see this thing underway.

[...]

Tuesday night Myrtis and I went to a surprise party for Stan Freberg. Apparently, from what he said—the first surprise party he'd ever experienced. Billy May was there— Shep Menken, Peter Leeds, Naomi Lewis, Ray Bradbury...nice group. I knew everybody and we enjoyed the evening which was not too long and I managed to find some food that I could eat. Stan's about ten years younger than me—so that would make him 57.

When we started working together, I was 30 and he was 20.

I do the Elroy voice O.K.—but the damn air conditioning plays havoc with my voice...lowers it a quarter of a tone, at least—and fogs it up as well.

By September 1984 Daws had more private students seeing him on various nights than students in his Wednesday night workshop. Myrtis had been driving Daws to sessions since he wasn't driving anymore at that point due to his perception problem. Occasionally students would take him if they had time. His reading was getting better, however. "I'm getting to be much quicker and more fluent. In a way I'm sorry I lost that ability, but it also makes you humble, realizing how easy it was before. I hadn't been writing anything for the last two years, but now I'm writing

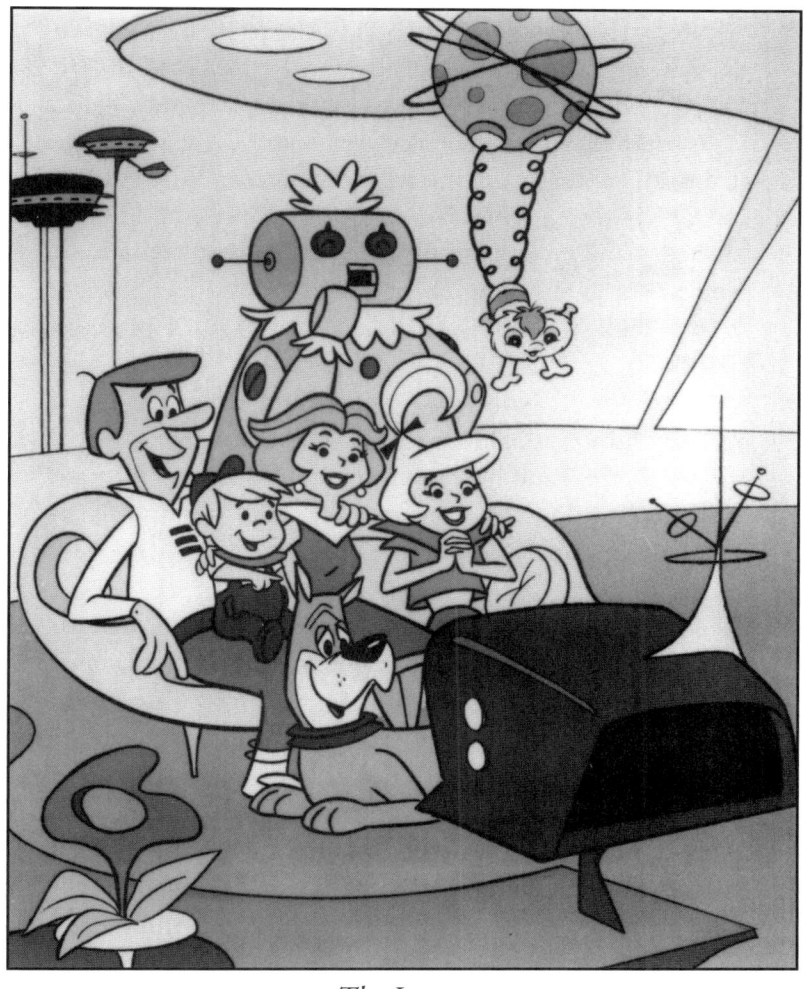

The Jetsons.

more and more non-sequitur-type things. They're fantasies, almost a fairy tale format. Strange people, strange conversations, things that couldn't be true, that could never have happened, yet done with such aplomb and naturalness that you fall in with the characters and believe them." He had his IBM typewriter refurbished after composing six or seven new pieces in the last month, more than he'd written in the last two years.

> October 5, 1984
>
> Sorry I have not gotten back to you sooner—but this JETSONS thing has really taken off—we did two last week and three this week. The one today was starring ELROY—"ELROY IN WONDERLAND." A sort of combination of ALICE IN WONDERLAND and THE WIZARD OF OZ. The director was trying to 'push' Elroy's voice—and it just doesn't work. The voice is so high now that if I give it too much energy, it makes the voice harsh. It worked out O.K.—I just told the director that Elroy could not be pushed—and he went along. We've done about eight now. The scripts are O.K. so far.
>
> On today's show—WILLIAM WINDOM played a part!! and also CLIFF NORTON! I don't know if you know who Cliff Norton is…you would recognize him if you saw him. I asked him if he would come to my workshop sometime and he said he would like that. I didn't ask William Windom…he was friendly…but not approachable enough for that request.
>
> [...]
>
> Penny Singleton is coming to my workshop now. Last week was the first time and she enjoyed it. It looks as if JANET WALDO may want to join the group also. I need some women in the workshop.
>
> I told you that LUCILLE BLISS (THE ORIGINAL "CRUSADER RABBIT") was coming to the workshop, didn't I? She's a terrific actress and has that subtle sense of comedy timing as well as straight acting timing also.
>
> I've been doing a lot of writing lately. I'm sending you a script which is a true non sequitur—"JACK ROBINSON—AT YOUR SERVICE."

Well, I'm going to do a bit of relaxing now—three shows in one week is enough!

On August 15, 1984, Daws became a member of ASIFA (the International Animated Film Society) and was informed the next day that he was to receive the prestigious ANNIE award for his "distinguished contribution to the art of animation." It was to be presented at the 13th annual ANNIE Awards & Banquet on Friday, November 9, 1984 at the Sheraton Premiere at 555 Universal Terrace Parkway in Universal City. Cocktails began at 6:30.

In a letter to Joe, Daws wrote, "I was the only actor to be so honored on the program—the rest were animators. Nice evening—the whole family was there and my agent, Miles. His wife is terminally ill but told him that he should be at the ceremony.

"I'm doing two more JETSONS next week—and I'm 'auditioning' for a new cartoon, the name of which escapes me (if I ever knew)—It's a sort of Charlie Ruggles voice they're looking for and that's a piece of cake—so we'll see. At least my reading has improved to the point where they think me viable."

Yet, Daws was clearly not feeling well. He later wrote, "My problem now, altho it may have something to do with the debilitating effect of the 'heat,' is lack of energy. If I didn't have the workshop to keep my mind truly alert, I might lay around and do nothing. I have to prod myself all the time. I don't have much pep these days. The workshop is a necessity—it keeps me sharp. When one is in effect, my pep seems to return. Last Wednesday night, I had about eighteen or nineteen students—I felt as if I were running a six-ring circus, keeping everybody happy and getting a chance to read—hopefully more than once.

I have some excellent students now. One gal is excellenter than most but she has a bad hazard in that she says, 'Ditn't' instead of 'didn't' and 'wutn't' instead of 'wouldn't.' I'm trying to beat it out of her—she's a Jewish girl from Chicago and this was a neighborhood problem. She'll get rid of it.

I got a black girl last week with a voice like velvet. I don't like to be chauvinistic, but damnit, BLACKS seem to have the edge on smooth musical voices.

I am tired though, Joe—so don't expect me to snap back as fast as you'd like—the springs are a bit spent. I know that you always say 'at my leisure'—but sometimes I realize you want (for which I'm grateful) my reactions."

Daws with his Annie Award and his students Bob Elyea and Earl Kress.

November 6, 1984

I've been at the typewriter quite a bit lately. I've been turning out about two or three new scripts a week. And with my granddaughter, Bernadette, as a member of the workshop, I have to come up with some stuff that a fourteen-year-old gal can do believably.

I did a HOWARD COSELL which you might like.

This Friday night I will be honored by AIFA—the international animation society…I will be awarded an "ANNIE"—(Animation—Annie—get it?)

The whole family will be there, and Art Scott will give me my award. Also at the table will be Earl Kress and Bob Elyea who are two of the good ones. They're gonna wear TUXEDOS yet!! Not me—a good ole black suit is my speed.

We'll be doing another JETSONS tomorrow. We're up to about fourteen. I just turned in a script that Earl Kress and I did—not the script—a treatment—with a few pages of dialogue to show our writing. I shouldn't have to prove anything at this point, but what the hell. It's about Elroy's first girlfriend and George's fortieth birthday, which he finds to be traumatic. We'll see. They're looking at it now.

I saw AMADEUS last week with Myrtis. I think she enjoyed it more than I. It's a fantasy and has little or nothing to do with the real genius, but it was entertaining and the ballet and opera music and performances were fine. A bit overblown (which Mozart doesn't need) but good. They would never do a bio on him which was true—because nobody would go to see (or hear) it. Gotta have some sort of flash these days.

I'm getting tickets to LA CAGUE AU FAUL (a fair spelling)—unless I'm mistaken it should be a blast. Dancing, music, songs and singing and acting—a romp.

Myrtis and I are hanging in there—she's terrific and has seen me through some grim days.

Along with writing for his granddaughter, Daws also recorded something for his sons: Dr. Suess's *The 500 Hats of Bartholomew Cubbins*. "I approached my dad with that," said Chas Butler. "I loved Dr. Seuss and at this particular point, I said, 'Dad, do you think you could take this book and transcribe it into script?' He did a brilliant job. That's my only acting on tape, as Bartholomew. There was no rehearsal. I remember him writing it out, he made copies for all three of us, and he marked the scripts for us, so we would know when to pause, when to do all this stuff, and we went over that before we recorded. But he would work with us as we recorded it. We just did it as we did it. And if we made mistakes, he would go 'Edit 1' so that when he went back to edit, he'd know this was an edit spot. [Joe post-produced it with sound effects and music, which Daws always wanted to do.] *Bartholomew and the Ooblec* was a follow-up that I always wanted Dad to do so we could make it a series. We just never got around to."

November 10, 1984

I still haven't heard if the script Earl Kress and I handed into the producers has been accepted, but I'll—or rather we'll—take our chances.

Last night I was honored by receiving the "ANNIE" award from ASIFA—the animation society. The whole family was there—in a new hotel at Universal City. Art Scott presented me with the award and I gave a nice little speech.

Bill Hanna was going to, but had to go out of town. I had one of my friends, Mark Evanier, who wrote the last Yogi Bear special, select and mount the film to show to the audience. They were all taken from my commercial reel, so the animation was creamier than the actual cartoons, and there was no music or sound effects muddying things up.

December 22, 1984

We did a couple more JETSONS this week. Now we're up to 24—that'll be our next one. My reading gets better all the time, thank goodness. This program seems to be causing a stir in the industry. It's about time—something has to bring animation back.

January 4, 1985

[Wasn't in the Christmas spirit much this year]

We've been knocking out JETSONS. We did the 25th Wednesday of this week. We did one on New Year's Eve and one the day after New Years. We're really turning them out.

I understand they'll be animated out of the country so I hope the quality is passable.

April 20, 1985

We did the last JETSONS Friday—and then there was a cast party, not at the coffee machine, but at a very swank Chinese Restaurant in Universal City. Lots of picture taking—and hugging—and disappointment that the show was over.

I was suffering from a sort of relapse of my cold and couldn't really cut it with Elroy, so I did all of my lines 'wild' today and am going to send the tape to Gordon Hunt Monday so that they can be cut in to the master reel.

April 26, 1985

There's a guy out here in Public Radio who expressed a certain interest in the idea of the kid show [Uncle Dunkle] on radio—he hasn't heard anything yet and I don't know how much it would entail to get it off the ground. Frankly, I just don't want to get that involved with a project.

Now that the JETSONS is finished (to air in September), I have the *other* half-hour show which will feature Huck, Yogi, Snagglepuss, etc.—about ten or more characters. I guess the reason I want to do it is because it looks as if Earl Kress will get to write some of the scripts—and that would be nice.

My energy is good—but I don't want to get too involved in things.

October 15, 1985

I don't really care if they do any more—of either series [Yogi, Jetsons]. I'm tired. I don't know why I'm doing all of these radio interviews—except it gives me a chance to let my mind free. I can't read the way I would like, so the challenge can't be put aside.

I find that I'm taking more naps than before. I probably should have been doing so all along but the energy level dissuaded me.

I haven't been doing any writing lately. Part of the reason is that I don't need any more—and the other is that I don't have the desire.

[...]

I got a new VCR and TV—the TV is a Sony and the VCR is a Magnavox. Everything is there: stereo and HI-FI. Everything controlled cordlessly. I've been recording the JETSONS and the YOGI just to have them.

One of the greatest movies I've recorded is FRANNY AND ALEXANDER—FIVE HOURS!! But what scope!! I think that I told you that one of my students did the voice of Alexander. She's an excellent actress and does a very believable boy. In fact, the whole dubbing job was outstanding. We did some of the JETSONS in the same recording studio where the dubbing was done and the engineer was quite enthusiastic.

I'm recording the record of "CATS!"—but slowing it down so I can hear the words. Myrtis has seen it, but it drives me nuts when they sing so fast and throw away perfectly good words! This way, I can be familiar with what is going on and then I can just sit back and enjoy the physical part of the show.

Well, that's about all for now—I'm going to take it easier than I was—not have too many private work-shop students—and get more rest.

[...]

You're so much farther along than I was at your age. I didn't have your drive, either. I was good and I got work and good comments but I don't think I ever had the ambition to get somewhere. It was thrust upon me ... In the radio days, I got work and enviable parts because I was more versatile than I thought. I was inventive and my interpolations (the things I'm teaching now) made the difference.

All I can say is thank God for Miles and Myrtis—I would have given the stuff away!!

CATS! sounds good—but it is a pleasure to hear it slowed down!!!

Daws Butler's last years were growing more productive. But unfortunately, Hanna-Barbera were merely seeking the same old things. He was simply *hungry* for new challenges. Daws told Dr. Demento during a radio interview, "I take as much interest in doing a new character as doing Hamlet. They're not voices. They're characters. There are only so many voices, like only so many notes in a pattern. [Says musical scale.] That's all you got, you can write a whole symphony with that! By the same token there are only a few voices. I have head tones, I have chest tones, I have a combination of both, which is like a stereo pattern. I have textures where I tighten the jaw. I spread vowels, I use stresses. I get a character out of a lot of little mechanical things, what I call working through a conflict, which establishes the speech pattern of a particular individual. Elroy Jetson is a straightforward thing. Augie Doggie is the same thing, with a tremolo. It's still the same basic voice. [He also does Babba Looey, then Dixie.] It's one voice, but I've done four characters. As far as characters, I probably have done several hundred. But the voices that I use may have broken down to about 30.

"As Elroy, you know, I'm still 9 years old. After being on the air 22 years, I'm still—I'm still 9 years old." Daws had great hope for the 41 Jetsons shows done that year, and praised the powers that be to have all the original cast back. He thought the writing was better: a little more sophisticated than the originals. "Hopefully it'll be like a renaissance." It was to be part of a larger project: *The Funtastic World of Hanna-Barbera*. Three half-hour shows. *Yogi's Treasure Hunt. The Paw Paws. Galtar of the Golden Lance.*

December 6, 1985

I notice on the Jetsons now they're playing quite a few of the old ones. They are better and I suppose they want to get a good rating response.

We're gonna do about six or seven more YOGI'S TREASURE HUNTS. I've got one to do next Monday. This time I'm going to do them at my own tempo and the hell with that 'can you pick it up a little?' If I can just control my own timing, it will help a little. God knows there isn't much timing as it is.

Wasn't that terrible about Bill Scott? [He died of a heart attack on November 29.] It happened so suddenly. Myrtis and I are going to a memorial service at his church this Sunday afternoon. He was an exceptional talent, in every way. I was never close to him as a buddy-buddy friend, but we had a professional regard and affection for each other. I'll miss him—as will many, many others.

The energy is still working for me—but it's keeping me from things I know Myrtis would like to do. I wrote a new piece a few days ago. I hadn't written anything for a couple months—so that's good.

December 17, 1985

Christmas again.

I am sending you sort of a 'spin-off' of a present I got from DR. DEMENTO. He put out a big set of records called: "THE GREATEST NOVELTY RECORDS OF ALL TIME." Six records. He's been doing a bit of barnstorming throughout the country plugging it. I heard him on Larry King's program one night.

Anyway, he gave me a complimentary copy—all six records. 'Personally signed and numbered. Limited edition.' #58—He inscribed on it the following: 'To Daws—

with warmest regards and thanks for your unique talent and great kindness!' (The exclamation mark was his)—and he signed his actual name "Barry."

The thing sells for fifty bucks. In the stores, they are selling the albums individually.

[...]

I'm in LITTLE BLUE RIDING HOOD (slightly) and in GREEN CHRISTMAS (Bob Cratchett—one of my favorite parts with Stan).

He probably sent one of these out to anyone who is in the collection.

[...]

I think I told you that the syndicate picked up about eight new YOGI'S TREASURE HUNTS. I'm doing one this Thursday in which HOKEY and MR. JINKS are featured. I did one last week also—it had ten characters. Earl Kress has written one of these stories.

Cap'n Crunch has been found in the Milky Way—and many kids are going to make some money on the big contest Quaker has. I did a radio spot as the Cap'n, in which he explains what happened to him. I guess they're going to play it all over. I haven't heard it out here yet.

In volume V [of the Dr. Demento set]—the selection "EAT IT" with 'Weird Al' Yankovic CAP'N CRUNCH is mentioned.

December 1985 [to Keith Scott]

Myrtis and I went to the memorial service for Bill [Scott]. There must have been 500 people there—the animation fraternity was well represented.

With Hanna-Barbera and Cap'n Crunch I stay as busy as I want to be.

April 8, 1986

I'm doing a few CAP'N CRUNCH commercials later this week—no activity at HANNA-BARBERA. Did you see Joe Barbera on "60 MINUTES"? Nobody ever mentions the actors. I was surprised to see a few writers given credit—that was good.

We will indeed keep our fingers crossed. It hurts my writer's feelings that we can't find a taker for U.D. and D.

Publishers and radio execs may have passed on Uncle Dunkle, but at least H-B action was beginning to pick up. For *The Flintstones' 25th Anniversary Celebration*, Daws slipped back into Yogi, Huck and Quick-Draw as classroom cutups as a college professor attempts to explain the origin of the phrase "Yabba Dabba Doo." It was an hour-long special combining classic clips with new animation sandwiched between live-action introductions by Tim Conway, Harvey Korman and Vanna White, with songs. It was broadcast over CBS on May 20, 1986.

September 15, 1986
So sorry to hear about your father.
Strokes are like thieves in the night—no warning.
Look at the time it's taking for me to get back my peripheral vision. It's a lot better now—and I read a 30-second spot for CAP'N CRUNCH a few weeks ago—and was very proud of myself—and yet such readings used to be pie. Time.
The UNCLE DUNKLE thing and public radio. It would be a perfect show for them—but they do have these clutches running things.
Did you tell them who I was—and my background. I mean, it was strange, their exclaiming at the prowess (if that's the word I want) of the actor, doing several voices!!
[…]
I'm still writing up a storm. I haven't heard anything from that publisher in Connecticut. That's the one that Gordon Hunt, of Hanna-Barbera, turned me on to.
One of my students had an audition today at one of the few animation companies left—and called me a while ago—and she was so excited. She was cool. She was well prepared. Rehearsal…I tell her she is to be Bravura!!—open all stops.
She's good. Humor. Dramatics. Hard worker.
Myrtis and I are going to take Nancy [Cartwright] out to dinner in a week or so—it's kind of anniversary time—not to the day—but generally.

I got turned on to a great Italian Restaurant—Papa Louis. We'll probably go there—good atmosphere—great food. Tender pasta. I like it cooked a bit more now—to favor my swallowing problem, which isn't as bad as before, but I've still got to watch it—drink with each bite.

Myrtis went back East to be with her mother who is ninety now. Her other sister (Myrtis') had come out here to visit *another* sister who is living in Seattle. Myrtis went back so her Mother wouldn't be alone. She should be back tomorrow or Wednesday. She has been so supportive. I don't think I would have gotten my strength back without her and her care.

I wrote something I'd like you to have. It's verse—but the idea is to not make the rhyme apparent and to recite it as if it were a monologue. Starting out with annoyance—and ending up with a certain AMOUNT of understanding and compassion.

I've been working in verse quite a bit lately. I like the discipline of rhyme and rhythm.

All you can do is keep plugging—you have proved yourself to me.

Even Daws had to keep plugging and proving himself to the next generation. He told an interviewer at the time, "Now the networks have taken over to such an extent I have to go out and audition just like everybody else. And they'll hear 30 people come in and read for a character and I may get it or I may not, but someone in New York at the network has to make the decision. Which I don't agree with. I think that the production people are the artistic people, they should make the decisions. But they don't, and you have to accept that."

The auditioning was wearying as well, in several ways, to the veteran voice. "He knew it was coming in the late '60s, before anyone else did," said Chas. "It got to the point when *he* would have to go in and audition for characters he had been doing for 15 years. In fact, in the years of '86 and '87 he was talking that he would like to retire soon and not do it anymore. Because there was no fun left in it. The networks were taking all the fun out of it, editing and cutting out everything. Getting rid of Babba Looey because he represented a minority. It was all such bullshit. Taking away Quick-Draw's gun because it was showing violence. He really got fed up with it, towards the end there. I would say that if he had survived 1988 he would've retired that year, he would not have done it anymore."

In another letter Daws wrote: "Oh, I'm beat…did several voice-tests in the past few days—a new character at HANNA-BARBERA…SCRAPPY-DOO, a little puppy (a la Augie Doggie) who worships Scooby-Doo…jumps up and down. I have a good chance for it as Joe Barbera loved Augie Doggie and wants a character similar to it." [The role would soon go to old friend Don Messick.]

Yet even up until the time of his death, Daws wrote new scripts and revised his old ones for his workshop and for himself. The muse just would not leave him alone.

He also continued to do interviews, as his popularity was renewed to a new generation of audiences—and directors. On Dr. Demento's radio show, rather than introducing Daws, all of his characters were given an introduction, followed by their voices arriving: Quick-Draw, Babba Looey, Huckleberry, Yogi Bear, Mr. Jinks, Snagglepuss, Cap'n Crunch (who recited a poem), Hokey Wolf, Wally Gator, and Elroy Jetson. Daws remained loyal to his friends, calling Stan Freberg "a great guy, a genius."

The day Daws died, he was set to give a radio interview.

Dr. Demento interviewed him not long before his death, recalling what an ebullient interviewee he was. "The first interview was done at his place; for the second, he came to our studio. I was a little bit in awe, meeting someone whose work I'd listened to and admired for years. He was as gracious as could be. I recall his son Charles was there for the first one, making sure Daws was comfortable, helped set up the equipment. His studio was small but functional. I hadn't heard much about what he looked like. He wasn't very tall, but other than that…He certainly made me feel at home.

"The highlight of the party, where I met Daws, was he and Stan Freberg getting up and trading stories about the old days and Bob Clampett. They talked for about a half-hour, I sure wish I'd had a tape machine! A bunch of people got together and gave him a VCR. They were new on the market at the time. He thanked his friends profusely.

"I play his stuff with Freberg, and stuff from the radio shows. 'Elderly Man River' stands out as one of my favorites. That sounded slightly like his real voice." (Daws' censorious character, decades before today's PC police, was called Mr. Tweedley.)

By 1987, the workshop wasn't as active, but was still going strong for what he called his more advanced students. He was becoming more selective in the talent he thought he could help nurture, due to health reasons.

It was very fortunate that Arnold R. Kunert decided to make his Emmy-nominated documentary *Daws Butler: Voice Magician* when he did. Narrated by longtime Bullwinkle cohort William Conrad and released on November 20, 1987, this hour-long video gave a complete account of Daws' illustrious life, complemented with mostly new interviews with Daws, Myrtis, Don Messick, June Foray and Stan Freberg. Hanna, Barbera and Walter Lantz were also on hand to pay respects to the master.

Freberg: "Before I met Daws Butler I was just a voice man and he taught me a lot about acting. I never really thought that acting has to start in the head and the heart first, then last of all, as a voice."

Foray: "I think if you use the Boy Scout oath, everything in that oath is Daws."

Messick: "Daws is that wonderful combination of talent, respect and courtesy all rolled up into one."

Miles Auer (Daws' agent): "He's concerned with people to a great degree, in any facet of life. He's got a lot of humanity."

Hanna: "Thank God we had him in our early years. If we didn't have him, I don't know if there would've *been* a Hanna-Barbera."

Daws gave his last radio interview in May of 1988 and spoke of the new series of Yogi Bear 40+ cartoons he would be starting in a few weeks. Just when it seemed that things were turning around for more work, Charles Dawson Butler died on May 18, 1988. Six days previous, *The New York Times* ran an article on the 72-year-old legend in their "Word and Image" section. Unfortunately, it was only a few paragraphs in length dealing mainly with the lip techniques necessary in characters and impressions, written (as were other articles at the time) to promote the new HB film, *The Good, the Bad and the Huckleberry Hound*, to be broadcast on May 15, 1988.

Charles Champlin of *The Los Angeles Times* and many other writers paid tribute to a great man and voice that very same month.

Fan letters of condolence flooded into H-B and the Butler household from friends and strangers, all mourning the loss of such a talent. Bill Hanna himself wrote to Myrtis:

"I did not feel quite right about writing any sooner, but I did very much want to know how very much I loved Daws as a very good friend.

A page in Variety *following Daws' death.*

While I did not see him as much in the later years of our long and friendly association, when we did have the opportunity to visit for a short while, it was a most warm and pleasant talk.

"Daws will continue to live and be loved by hundreds of millions of people all over the world as they listen to and watch the hundreds of different characters he gave life and personality to."

"I miss him very much."

The day of Daws' death also created a rush on the H-B PR department which had to rush to supply the huge clamor for Daws bios, pictures and videos of clips that were in demand from around the world.

From LA to China and all places in between, everyone wanted a little knowledge of the man they never really knew. CBS Radio interviewed Bill Hanna, radio's Voice of America interviewed Gordon Hunt, and everyone from NPR to MTV ran the Daws Butler story in the week of May 20. The alphabet soup of television call letters was astounding, from ABC to KTTV to United Press International. *Time, Newsweek, Entertainment Tonight,* and a host of full obituaries paid tribute. KCBS, KNBC, KABC, KHJ-TV, KTLA, KCOP, KROQ Radio, KABC Talk Radio, KFWB, United Press International Radio were just a few of the many.

The Los Angeles County Board of Supervisors issued a "Memoriam" to the Butler family regarding the loss of Charles "Daws" Butler, "in whose memory all members adjourned in tribute and reverence at its meeting of May 24, 1988."

Voice actor Walker Edmiston stated, "When Daws died Hanna-Barbera had to get 10, 15 different people to do what Daws did."

That was probably the superlative tribute of all the tributes, and no doubt would have pleased character actor Daws Butler the most of all.

The next year, Hanna and Barbera celebrated their 50th anniversary in show business with a black-tie event held at the Beverly Hilton Hotel, and *Variety,* in their July 12-18, 1989 issue, ran a special issue with more than 30 pages of articles and congratulatory messages for the groundbreaking animation company. Daws and voices featured heavily in the special section, with an impressive 11 pages devoted to a list of voices for the series throughout the years.

Daws' student Greg Burson took over the hallowed role of Yogi Bear for the new *Yogi Bear Show* that premiered several months after the original Yogi voice passed away.

The Butler children still live within 15 minutes of Myrtis. "I still miss him," says Chas. "There isn't a day that goes by that I don't miss him. I wish he were here now—but then he is. You turn on the TV, and he's there, 24/7."

Marty Halperin: "I took my son over there once when he was four years old, and we're sitting around the house. Two little boys rang the bell and Myrtis went to the door, and I heard one of the little boys say, 'Can Daws come out and play?' That was amazing to me."

Doug Young: "Daws was one of the good ones. One of the very fine persons and actors."

June Foray: "I felt so bad that I couldn't be there to wish him goodbye. I was in London doing appearances, and I read in the *International Tribune* about Daws' passing. Daws was the kind of a person who never said a bad word about anybody. He loved everybody. He was helpful. His hands were always out, ready to guide."

David Butler: "When people learn that Daws Butler was my father, their eyes light up at the thought of all the characters they grew up with and they think how cool it must have been to grow up as I did. A few years before he died, with the help of one of the Hanna-Barbera artists, he had large cards printed up with a caricature of himself and all the cartoon characters whose voices he had done over the years, so he could autograph them for people. My mother saved several that he had signed before he died and we've been reprinting copies ever since. Today, when I give one to someone who has just discovered my relationship to him, they react as if I've given them gold."

Thanks to TBS, The Cartoon Network, their spin-off channel Boomerang!, and ever-expanding cable, no one alive has not heard Daws Butler's voice. Through his teachings and legacy, he continues to be the single best and ultimate characters actor.

Credits

Characters
Aesop, Jr.
Alfie (Cap'n Crunch)
Alfie Gator
Augie Doggie
Baba Looey
Barney Rubble (The Flintstones, four shows only)
Beany (Time for Beany)
Bingo (The Banana Splits)
Blabber Mouse
The Blue Barron (King Vitamin commercials)
Brutus the Lion (The Roman Holidays)
Bumble
Cap'n Crunch
Captain Skyhook
Captain Huffenpuff (Time for Beany)
Chilly Willy
Dixie
Ed Morton & Ralph Krumden (The Honeymousers)
Elroy Jetson
Fibber Fox
The Fish (in The Cat in the Hat)
Fred & Barney (The Flagstones pilot)
Funky Phantom
Hair Bear
Hardy Har Har (Quick-Draw McGraw show: Super Snooper cartoon only)
Henry Orbit

Hokey Wolf
Huckleberry Hound
Joe Rockhead
Lambsy
Lippy the Lion
Loopy DeLoop
Mr. Cogswell
Mr. Jinks
Peter Potamus
Powerful Pierre
Professor Goody (waffle commercials)
Reddy
Quick-Draw McGraw
Quisp
Scooby-Dum
Smedley
Snuffles
Snagglepuss
Snaggletooth
Snap (of Snap, Crackle, Pop Rice Krispies)
The Sun (Raisin Bran commercials)
Super Snooper
Undercover Elephant
Wally Gator
Wimpy (1980s Popeye show)
Yahooey
Yogi Bear

Radio

(unknown)	Dr. Christian
(unknown)	The Phil Harris-Alice Faye Show
(unknown)	The Amazing Mr. Tutt
September 13, 1946	Al Pearce and His Gang (first national show)
July 17, 1947	Family Theater (Song for a Long Road)
August 7, 1947	The Family Theater (No Greater Love)
1948	The Unexpected (Nightmare)
1948	Your Movietown Radio Theatre (Mulligan, The Mighty)

1948	Your Movietown Radio Theatre (The Luck of Adam)
March 19, 1948	Jubilee
April 15, 1948	The Family Theater (Wanted: One Baby)
May 13, 1948	The Family Theater (Song for a Long Road)
July 27, 1948	The Diary of Fate (Stanley Becker)
December 5, 1948	The Whistler (Hired Alibi)
December 7, 1948	Yours Truly, Johnny Dollar (The Milford Brooks, III Matter)
December 23, 1948	Suspense (Christmas Story)
1949	Our American Heritage (Incident Near Harper's Ferry)
1949	Our American Heritage (Top of the World)
February 20, 1949	The Whistler (Ticket to Paris)
December 17, 1949	Yours Truly, Johnny Dollar (Black Magic in Haiti)
1950	The Christmas That Almost Never Was
1950	Magazine of the Air (A Tree in the Meadow) (audition)
1951	The Pendleton Story (The Red Man)
1951	The Pendleton Story (The Rifleman)
June 5, 1951	The Pendleton Story (The Conestogas)
January 6, 1951	The Man Called X (Operation Fifty)
November 21, 1953	That's Rich (Pilot)
December 21, 1953	The Railroad Hour (Snow White and the Seven Dwarfs)
January 8, 1954	That's Rich
January 15, 1954	That's Rich
January 22, 1954	That's Rich
January 29, 1954	That's Rich
February 5, 1954	That's Rich (Dragnet Spoof)
February 12, 1954	That's Rich
February 19, 1954	That's Rich
February 26, 1954	That's Rich
March 5, 1954	That's Rich (Missing Tax Receipts)
March 12, 1954	That's Rich
March 19, 1954	That's Rich (High Noon)

March 26, 1954	That's Rich
April 2, 1954	That's Rich
April 9, 1954	That's Rich
April 16, 1954	That's Rich (The Astronomer)
April 23, 1954	That's Rich (The Pawned Watch)
April 30, 1954	That's Rich (New Job)
May 21, 1954	That's Rich (Almost a Star)
May 29, 1954	That's Rich (New Roommate)
June 5, 1954	That's Rich (Adopting an Orphan)
June 12, 1954	That's Rich (Safecrackers)
June 19, 1954	That's Rich (Name Change)
June 26, 1954	That's Rich (Yacht Race)
July 3, 1954	That's Rich (Getting in Showbiz)
July 8, 1954	That's Rich (Girlfriend's Mother)
July 15, 1954	That's Rich (Slogan Writing Contest)
July 22, 1954	That's Rich (Life Guard)
July 29, 1954	That's Rich (Motion Picture Ball)
August 5, 1954	That's Rich (The Rugged Lover)
August 12, 1954	That's Rich (The Movie Star)
August 19, 1954	That's Rich (The Investment)
August 26, 1954	That's Rich (The Building Inspector)
September 2, 1954	That's Rich (Las Vegas Mish Mash)
September 9, 1954	That's Rich (The Orphanage)
September 16, 1954	That's Rich (Fortune Teller)
September 23, 1954	That's Rich (Rich's Uncle Shows Up - final show)
August 31, 1956	CBS Radio Workshop (An Analysis of Satire)
September 14, 1956	CBS Radio Workshop (A Pride of Carrots)
October 5, 1956	CBS Radio Workshop (Roughing It)
November 4, 1956	CBS Radio Workshop (Joe Miller Joke Book: Colloquy Number 4)
November 11, 1956	CBS Radio Workshop (Report on the Weuns)
1957	Suspense (Back Seat Driver)
January 13, 1957	CBS Radio Workshop (No Time for Heartaches)
February 3, 1957	Suspense (Frankie and Johnny)
February 24, 1957	Suspense (227 Minutes of Hate)

March 3, 1957	CBS Radio Workshop (Ballad of the Iron Horse)
March 3, 1957	Suspense (Present Tense)
May 26, 1957	Suspense (The Big Day)
June 16, 1957	CBS Radio Workshop (Housing Problem)
June 30, 1957	CBS Radio Workshop (Gettysburg)
July 14, 1957	The Stan Freberg Show
July 21, 1957	The Stan Freberg Show
July 28, 1957	CBS Radio Workshop (Never Bet the Devil Your Head)
July 28, 1957	The Stan Freberg Show
August 4, 1957	The Stan Freberg Show
August 4, 1957	Suspense (Flesh Peddler)
August 11, 1957	The Stan Freberg Show
August 18, 1957	The Stan Freberg Show
August 25, 1957	The Stan Freberg Show
September 1, 1957	The Stan Freberg Show
September 8, 1957	The Stan Freberg Show
September 15, 1957	The Stan Freberg Show
September 22, 1957	The Stan Freberg Show
September 29, 1957	The Stan Freberg Show
October 6, 1957	The Stan Freberg Show
October 13, 1957	The Stan Freberg Show
October 20, 1957	The Stan Freberg Show
February 2, 1958	Suspense (The Silver Frame)
May 25, 1958	Suspense (Like Somebody Dig Me)
November 1, 1958	Suspense (The Dealings of Mr. Markham)
1959	NBC's Monitor (Guest)
October 22, 1973	Hollywood Radio Theatre (The Heir Hunters, Part 1)
October 23, 1973	Hollywood Radio Theatre (The Heir Hunters, Part 2)
October 24, 1973	Hollywood Radio Theatre (The Heir Hunters, Part 3)
October 25, 1973	Hollywood Radio Theatre (The Heir Hunters, Part 4)
October 26, 1973	Hollywood Radio Theatre (The Heir Hunters, Part 5)

November 5, 1973	Hollywood Radio Theatre (Someone's Death, Part 1)
November 6, 1973	Hollywood Radio Theatre (Someone's Death, Part 2)
November 7, 1973	Hollywood Radio Theatre (Someone's Death, Part 3)
November 9, 1973	Hollywood Radio Theatre (Someone's Death, Part 5)
November 23, 1973	Hollywood Radio Theatre (The Blessing Way, Part 5)
December 3, 1973	Hollywood Radio Theatre (Queen in Danger, Part 1)
December 4, 1973	Hollywood Radio Theatre (Queen in Danger, Part 2)
December 5, 1973	Hollywood Radio Theatre (Queen in Danger, Part 3)
December 6, 1973	Hollywood Radio Theatre (Queen in Danger, Part 4)
December 7, 1973	Hollywood Radio Theatre (Queen in Danger, Part 5)
February 19, 1979	Sears Radio Theatre (Final Fall)
March 19, 1979	Sears Radio Theatre (The Female of the Species)
March 27, 1979	Sears Radio Theatre (The Terrible Dream of Mr. Glitch)
March 29, 1979	Sears Radio Theatre (First Star Tonight)
April 2, 1979	Sears Radio Theatre (Conspiracy at the Golden Gate)
April 4, 1979	Sears Radio Theatre (Improvisation)
April 6, 1979	Sears Radio Theatre (A Short History of Bakah)
April 10, 1979	Sears Radio Theatre (Fontaine Harris, The Baron De Paris)
April 24, 1979	Sears Radio Theatre (Here's Morgan)
April 30, 1979	Sears Radio Theatre (Henry Boy Brown)
May 8, 1979	Sears Radio Theatre (Here's Morgan Again)
May 11, 1979	Sears Radio Theatre (Milwaukee Deep)
May 15, 1979	Sears Radio Theatre (A Very Nice Couple)

May 21, 1979	Sears Radio Theatre (The Legend)
May 22, 1979	Sears Radio Theatre (Here's Morgan Once Again)
May 24, 1979	Sears Radio Theatre (Munsey's Mob)
June 5, 1979	Sears Radio Theatre (Quartet in Nothing Flat)
June 7, 1979	Sears Radio Theatre (A Sense of Pride)
June 28, 1979	Sears Radio Theatre (The Hamster Caper of Curtis Cleaver)
July 10, 1979	Sears Radio Theatre (Jack and the Energy Crunch)
July 27, 1979	Sears Radio Theatre (The Value of a Hunch)
July 31, 1979	Sears Radio Theatre (Baldy)
August 3, 1979	Sears Radio Theatre (A Short History of Bakah)
October 8, 1983	SPERDVAC Presents (Return of Peggy Webber)
1987	The Tom Snyder Show (Guest)
1987	The Doctor Demento Show (Guest)

Undated

Unexpected	The Nightmare (Little Man, Psychiatrist)
Zero Hour	Someone's Death (Pt. 3) (Tibbett)
Zero Hour	Someone's Death (Pt. 4) (Tibbett, Ortes)
Zero Hour	Someone's Death (Pt. 5) (Tibbett)

Daws Butler Radio Plays Produced by Joe Bevilacqua

1980   "Sherlock Holmes in Trouble"
        The WKNJ Radio Theater
        WKNJ-FM, Union, NJ

        "The Christmas that Almost Never Was"
        The WKNJ Radio Theater
        WKNJ-FM, Union, NJ

1981	"A Study in Lavender" (co-written with Joe Bevilacqua) *The WKNJ Radio Theater* WKNJ-FM, Union, NJ
	"A Halloween Happening" *The WKNJ Radio Theater* WKNJ-FM, Union, NJ
	"The Dying End?" *The WKNJ Radio Theater* WKNJ-FM, Union, NJ
1982	"More Poetry Than Truth: A Delicious Fiction" *The WBAI Radio Theater* WBAI-FM, New York, NY
	"The Care and Feeding of a Poet" *The WBAI Radio Theater* WBAI-FM, New York, NY
	"The Ad Game" *The WBAI Radio Theater* WBAI-FM, New York, NY
	"Uncle Dunkle and Donnie Stories" *The WBAI Radio Theater* WBAI-FM, New York, NY
	"A Halloween Happening" (remake) *The WBAI Radio Theater* WBAI-FM, New York, NY
1983	SERIES: *The Mis-Adventures of Sherlock Holmes* "Sherlock Holmes in Trouble" (remake) "A Study in Lavender" (remake) (co-written with Joe Bevilacqua) "The Death of Mr. Sherlock Holmes" (co-written with Joe Bevilacqua)

"The Giant Rat of Sumatra" (co-written with Joe Bevilacqua)
"Tales from the Vienna Wards" (co-written with Joe Bevilacqua)
"His Second to Last Bow" (co-written with Joe Bevilacqua)
WBAI-FM, New York, NY

1990 "Forget Metaphor (Say What you Mean)"
Spinning on Air with David Garland
WNYC-FM, New York, NY

"Uncle Dunkle and Donnie: Sticky Wicket"
Spinning on Air with David Garland
WNYC-FM, New York, NY

1992 "Somewhere Along the Line…or Verbosity Self-taught"
Evening Muse with David Garland
WNYC-FM, New York, NY

"Don't Ever Knock Punctuality"
Evening Muse with David Garland
WNYC-FM New York, NY

"Table Talk"
Evening Muse with David Garland
WNYC-FM New York, NY

"Two Hamburgers (Hold Everything!)"
Evening Muse with David Garland
WNYC-FM New York, NY

2003-04 SERIES: *What the Butler Wrote: Scenes from the Daws Butler Workshop*
Episode One:
"More Poetry Than Truth: A Delicious Fiction"
"Forget Metaphor (Say What You Mean)"

Episode Two:
: "The Care and Feeding of a Poet"
: "Uncle Dunkle And Donnie: The Cherry Tree Caper"
: "Two Hamburgers (Hold Everything!)"
: "Ear-bending at Nat'n'Als"

Episode Three:
: "Yogi Bear Meets the Celebrities"
: "Uncle Dunkle and Donnie: The Tardy Wedding Guest"
: "Garage Sale (Nice?)"

Episode Four:
: "Silvia Silverman"
: "The Flea"

Episode Five:
: "The Ad Game"

Episode Six:
: "The Treasure of Sarah's Mattress" (re-mastered)

Episode Seven:
: "Margery Dickerson"
: "Huck and Yogi: The Echo"

Episode Eight:
: "Don't Ever Knock Punctuality"

The Comedy-O-Rama Hour
XM Satellite Radio, Sonic Theater Channel 163, Washington, D.C.

Films

unknown	Health and Alcohol Abuse (Disney educational film)
1950	Nice Try, Virgil (Black and white silent short, starring Daws Butler on camera, playing a bumbling hero in gag comedy situations. Narrated by Paul Frees)
1951	Alice in Wonderland (Daws and Freberg recorded "augmented voices in Jabberwocky sequence" but their roles didn't survive the final cut) (Walt Disney)

1959   1001 Arabian Nights (Omar the Rugmaker) (UPA)
1963   As Nature Intended (Commentary) (Crown International Pictures)
1964   Hey There, It's Yogi Bear (Yogi Bear) (Hanna-Barbera/Columbia)
1964   Mary Poppins (Turtle and Penguin) (Disney)
1970   The Phantom Tollbooth (Weather Man) (MGM)
1975   Doc Savage: The Man of Bronze (Loops Spanish voice)

Theatrical cartoons

1948   Short Snorts on Sports (Columbia/Screen Gems)
1949   Counterfeit Cat (MGM)
            Little Rural Riding Hood (City Wolf) (MGM)
            Out Foxed (MGM)
            Speaking of Animals (Apex Productions) (Daws in at least two of this series)
1950   The Chump Champ, (Master of Ceremonies) (MGM)
            The Cuckoo Clock (MGM)
            The Peachy Cobbler (Narrator)
            Punchy DeLeon (UPA)
            The Ventriloquist Cat (MGM)
1951   Droopy's Double Trouble (Mr. Theeves) (MGM)
            Jerry and the Goldfish (Radio Chef Franois) (MGM)
1952   The Dog House (MGM)
            Fit to Be Tied (MGM)
            Gift Wrapped (Warner Bros.)
            Little Johnny Jet (Father Jet)
            Magical Maestro (Mysto the Magician)
            One Cab's Family (MGM)
1953   The Three Little Pups (Guard)
1954   Billy Boy (Farmer)
            Convict Concerto (Walter Lantz)
            The Flea Circus (Pepito) (MGM)
            Hic-Cup Pup (MGM)
            I'm Cold (Chilly, Willy Guard Dog) (Walter Lantz)

1955	Mice Follies (Ed Morton, Ralph Crumden) (Warner Bros.) Pet Peeve (Man) Bedtime Bedlam Crazy Mixed-Up Pup (Walter Lantz) Deputy Droopy (Sheriff, Tall Robber) (MGM) Heir Conditioned (Warner Bros.) Helter Shelter (Walter Lantz) Hot and Cold Penguin (Chilly Willy) (Walter Lantz) Mouse for Sale (Man) Posse Cat (MGM) Pup on a Picnic (MGM) Shhh-h-h-h (Walter Lantz) Smarty Cat (MGM) The Tree Medic (Tree Surgeon)
1956	90 Day Wondering After the Ball (Lumberjack) Barbary-Coast Bunny (Nasty Canasta) Barbecue Brawl Downbeat Bear (2nd Radio Announcer) (MGM) Half-Fare Hare (Warner Bros.) Hold That Rock (Chilly Willy, Smedley) (Walter Lantz) The Honeymousers (Ralph Crumden, Ed Morton)(Warner Bros.) Magoo's Problem Child (UPA) Magoo's Pudde Jumper (UPA) Operation Cold Feet (Chilly Willy) (Walter Lantz) The Ostrich Egg and I (Sam) Raw! Raw! Rooster! (Rhode Island Red) (Warner Bros.) Rocket-bye Baby (Narrator, Joe Wilbur, Captain Schmideo, Lecturer) (Warner Bros.) Room and Wrath (Smedley) (Walter Lantz) Stupor Duck (Narrator, Newspaper Editor) (Warner Bros.) Talking Dog (Walter Lantz) Wideo Wabbit (Bugs Bunny as Groucho, Bugs Bunny as Ed Norton) (Warner Bros.)

1957

Woody Meets Davey Crewcut (Walter Lantz)
Yankee Dood It (Warner Bros.)
The Big Snooze (Chilly Willy) (Walter Lantz)
A Bird in a Bonnet (Warner Bros.)
Blackboard Jumble (Also wrote its story) (MGM)
Boyhood Daze (Warner Bros.)
Cheese It, the Cat! (Ed Morton) (Warner Bros.)
Drafty, Isn't It?
Fodder and Son (Walter Lantz)
Fowled-Up Party (Walter Lantz)
Give and Tyke (Spike, Second Dog, Dogcatcher) (MGM)
Go Fly a Kit (Counter Man) (Warner Bros.)
International Woodpecker (Walter Lantz)
Magoo Goes Overboard (UPA)
Magoo Saves The Bank (UPA)
Magoo's Private War (UPA)
Mucho Mouse (Tom)
Scat Cats (MGM)
Swiss-Mis-Fit (Chilly Willy) (Walter Lantz)
To Catch a Woodpecker (Voice)
Tom's Photo Finish (George) (MGM)
The Unbearable Salesman (Walter Lantz)

1958

A Bird in a Bonnet (Warner Bros.)
A Chilly Reception (Chilly Willy) (Walter Lantz)
Everglade Raid (Walter Lantz)
The Explosive Mr. Magoo (UPA)
Little Televillain (Chilly Willy) (Walter Lantz)
Love Comes to Magoo (UPA)
Magoo's Three-Point Landing (UPA)
Magoo's Young Manhood (UPA)
A Pizza Tweety-Pie (Spaghetti Bird)   (Warner Bros.)
Polar Pest (Chilly Willy) (Walter Lantz)
Salmon Yeggs (Windy)
Scoutmaster Magoo (UPA)
Three-Ring Fling (Windy)
Tree's a Crowd (Colonel Fleabush, Tour Guide, Philbert)

1959	The Vanishing Duck (George) A Waggily Tale (Junior) Watch the Birdie (Walter Lantz) Backwoods Bunny (Pappy Buzzard, Elvis Buzzard) Bee Bopped (Windy) Bwana Magoo (UPA) Little Bo Bopped (Loopy De Loop) (Hanna-Barbera) Log Jammed (Walter Lantz) Magoo's Homecoming (UPA) Merry Minstrel Magoo (UPA) A Mutt in a Rut (Warner Bros.) People Are Bunny (Art Lamplighter) Robinson Gruesome (Chilly Willy) (Walter Lantz) Romp in a Swamp (Walter Lantz) Terror Faces Magoo (UPA) Tom Cat Combat (Walter Lantz) Trick or Tweet (Sam)　(Warner Bros.) Truant Student (Windy, Breezy, Truant Officer Willoughby) Wolf Hounded (Loopy De Loop) (Hanna-Barbera) Yukon Have It (Chilly Willy) (Walter Lantz)
1960	Creepy-Time Pal (Loopy De Loop) (Hanna-Barbera) The Dixie Fryer, The (Pappy Buzzard, Elvis Buzzard) (Warner Bros.) The Do-Good Wolf (Loopy De Loop) (Hanna-Barbera) Fish Hooked (Chilly, Willy, Smedley, Narrator, Dog Catcher) (Walter Lantz) Here, Kiddie, Kiddie (Loopy De Loop) (Hanna-Barbera) Hunger Strife (Walter Lantz) Life with Loopy (Loopy De Loop) (Hanna-Barbera) Mice Follies (Ed Morton) Mouse and Garden (Sam) No Biz Like Shoe Biz (Loopy De Loop) (Hanna-Barbera) Person to Bunny (Elmer Fudd)　(Warner Bros.) Snoopy Loopy (Loopy De Loop) (Hanna-Barbera)

1961	Tale of a Wolf (Loopy De Loop) (Hanna-Barbera)
	Wild, Wild World (Warner Bros.)
	Catch Meow (Loopy De Loop) (Hanna-Barbera)
	Child Sock-Cology (Loopy De Loop) (Hanna-Barbera)
	Clash and Carry (Chilly Willy) (Walter Lantz)
	Count Down Clown (Loopy De Loop) (Hanna-Barbera)
	Fee Fie Foes (Loopy De Loop) (Hanna-Barbera)
	Franken-Stymied (Walter Lantz)
	Gabby's Diner (Seminole Sam) (Walter Lantz)
	Happy Go Loopy (Loopy De Loop) (Hanna-Barbera)
	Kooky Loopy (Loopy De Loop) (Hanna-Barbera)
	Loopy's Hare-do (Loopy De Loop) (Hanna-Barbera)
	Mackerel Moocher (Chilly Willy) (Walter Lantz)
	Papoose on the Loose (Walter Lantz)
	St. Moritz Blitz (Chilly Willy) (Walter Lantz)
	This Is My Ducky Day (Loopy De Loop) (Hanna-Barbera)
	Tricky Trout (Chilly Willy) (Walter Lantz)
	Two Faced Wolf (Loopy De Loop) (Hanna-Barbera)
	Woody's Kook-Out (Walter Lantz)
	Zoo Is Company (Loopy De Loop) (Hanna-Barbera)
1962	Bearly Able (Loopy De Loop) (Hanna-Barbera)
	Beef for and After (Loopy De Loop) (Hanna-Barbera)
	Bungle Uncle (Loopy De Loop) (Hanna-Barbera)
	Bunnies Abundant (Loopy De Loop) (Hanna-Barbera)
	The Careless Caretaker (Walter Lantz)
	Common Scents (Loopy De Loop) (Hanna-Barbera)
	Crowin' Pains (Hanna-Barbera)
	Fish and Chips (Chilly Willy) (Walter Lantz)
	Little Woody Riding Hood (Walter Lantz)
	Rancid Ransom (Loopy De Loop) (Hanna-Barbera)
	Rock-A-Bye Gator (Walter Lantz)
	Rocket Racket (Walter Lantz)
	Slippery Slippers (Loopy De Loop) (Hanna-Barbera)
	Swash Buckled (Loopy De Loop) (Hanna-Barbera)

1963	Voodoo Boo Hoo (Walter Lantz)
Bear Up (Loopy De Loop) (Hanna-Barbera)
Chicken Fracas-See (Loopy De Loop) (Hanna-Barbera)
Chicken Hearted Wolf (Loopy De Loop) (Hanna-Barbera)
Coy Decoy (Walter Lantz)
The Crook Who Cried Wolf (Loopy De Loop) (Hanna-Barbera)
Drum-Sticked (Loopy De Loop) (Hanna-Barbera)
A Fallible Fable (Loopy De Loop) (Hanna-Barbera)
Fish and Chips (Chilly Willy) (Walter Lantz)
Greedy Gabby Gator (Walter Lantz)
Habit Rabbit (Loopy De Loop) (Hanna-Barbera)
Just a Wolf at Heart (Loopy De Loop) (Hanna-Barbera)
Not in Nottingham (Loopy De Loop) (Hanna-Barbera)
Pesky Pelican (Chilly Willy) (Walter Lantz)
Robin Hoody Woody (Walter Lantz)
Salmon Loafer (Chilly Willy) (Walter Lantz)
Sheep Stealers Anonymous (Loopy De Loop) (Hanna-Barbera)
Teepee For Two (Walter Lantz)
The Tenants' Racket (Walter Lantz)
Whatcha Watchin' (Loopy De Loop) (Hanna-Barbera)
Wolf in Sheep Dog's Clothing (Loopy De Loop)
1964	Bear Hug (Loopy De Loop) (Hanna-Barbera)
Bear Knuckles (Loopy De Loop) (Hanna-Barbera)
Deep Freeze Squeeze (Chilly Willy) (Walter Lantz)
Dumb Like a Fox (Walter Lantz)
Elephantastic (Loopy De Loop) (Hanna-Barbera)
Freeway Fracas (Walter Lantz)
Habit Rabbit (Loopy De Loop) (Hanna-Barbera)
Lighthouse Keeping Blues (Chilly Willy) (Walter Lantz)
Raggedy Rug (Loopy De Loop) (Hanna-Barbera)
Ski-Napper (Walter Lantz)

1965	Trouble Bruin (Loopy De Loop) (Hanna-Barbera)
	The Big Mouse-Take (Loopy De Loop) (Hanna-Barbera)
	Crow's Feat (Loopy De Loop) (Hanna-Barbera)
	Fractured Friendship (Chilly Willy) (Walter Lantz)
	Half-Baked Alaska (Chilly Willy) (Walter Lantz)
	Horse Shoo (Loopy De Loop) (Hanna-Barbera)
	Pesty Guest (Chilly Willy) (Walter Lantz)
	Pork Chop Phooey (Loopy De Loop)
	Sioux Me (Walter Lantz)
	Three Little Woodpeckers (Walter Lantz)
1966	Hassle in a Castle (Walter Lantz)
	Operation Shanghai (Chilly Willy) (Walter Lantz)
	Polar Fright (Walter Lantz)
	Practical Yoke (Walter Lantz)
	Rough Riding Hood (Walter Lantz)
	Snow Place Like Home (Chilly Willy) (Walter Lantz)
	South Pole Pals (Chilly Willy) (Walter Lantz)
	Teeny Weeny Meany (Chilly Willy) (Walter Lantz)
	Woody and The Beanstalk (Walter Lantz)
1967	Chilly and the Woodchopper (Chilly Willy) (Walter Lantz)
	Chilly Chums (Chilly Willy) (Walter Lantz)
	Horse Play (Walter Lantz)
	Hot Time on Ice (Chilly Willy) (Walter Lantz)
	Merlin the Magic Mouse
	The Nautical Nut (Walter Lantz)
	Operation Shanghai (Walter Lantz)
	Secret Agent Woody (Walter Lantz)
	Vicious Viking (Chilly Willy) (Walter Lantz)
1968	Chiller Dillers (Chilly Willy) (Walter Lantz)
	Highway Hecklers (Chilly Willy) (Walter Lantz)
	A Lad in Bagdad (Walter Lantz)
	One Horse Town (Walter Lantz)
	Under Sea Dogs (Chilly Willy) (Walter Lantz)
1969	Chilly and the Looney Gooney (Chilly Willy) (Walter Lantz)
	Hook, Line and Stinker (Walter Lantz)

1970	Little Skeeter (Walter Lantz)
	Prehistoric Super Salesman (Walter Lantz)
	Project Reject (Chilly Willy) (Walter Lantz)
	Sleepytime Bear (Walter Lantz)
	Woody's Knightmare (Walter Lantz)
	Buster's Last Stand (Walter Lantz)
	Chilly's Cold War (Chilly Willy) (Walter Lantz)
	Chilly's Ice Folly (Chilly Willy) (Walter Lantz)
	CooCoo Nuts (Walter Lantz)
	Gooney's Goofy Landings (Chilly Willy) (Walter Lantz)
	Seal on the Loose (Walter Lantz)
1971	A Gooney Is Born (Chilly Willy) (Walter Lantz)
	Airlift a la Carte (Chilly Willy) (Walter Lantz)
	Chilly's Hide-a-Way (Chilly Willy) (Walter Lantz)
	How to Trap a Woodpecker (Walter Lantz)
	Kitty from the City (Walter Lantz)
	Reluctant Recruit (Walter Lantz)
	Shanghai Woody (Walter Lantz)
	Sleepytime Chimes (Walter Lantz)
1972	Indian Corn (Walter Lantz)
	Pecking Holes in Poles (Walter Lantz)
	The Rude Intruder (Walter Lantz)
1974	The Dogfather (Mirisch/DFE)
1975	Eagle Beagles (Louis, Pugg)
	Goldilox & the Three Hoods

TV

Series

1949-54	Time for Beany (Beany) (Bob Clampett)
1950s	The Chimps (Crosby Enterprises)
1950s	Yer Ole' Buddy
1956	Crusader Rabbit (Aborted revival - series revived by Shul Bonsall, without Daws) (Jay Ward)
1957	The Ruff & Reddy Show (Reddy, Multiple Characters) (Hanna-Barbera)

	The Woody Woodpecker Show, (Chilly Willy/Gabby Gator/Smedley/Windy)
1958	The Huckleberry Hound Show (Huck, Dixie, Mr. Jinks, Yogi Bear, others) (Hanna-Barbera)
1959	The Alphabet Conspiracy (Voice)
1959-61	Rocky and His Friends (Various Fractured Fairy Tales Voices, Aesop, Jr.) (Jay Ward)
1960	The Bugs Bunny Show (Various Characters)
1960-63	The Flintstones (Additional Voices) (Hanna-Barbera)
1961	The Yogi Bear Show (Yogi Bear, Additional Voices)
	Top Cat (Various Characters) (Hanna-Barbera)
1962	Wally Gator (Wally Gator, Lippy the Lion, Various Characters) (Hanna-Barbera)
	The Jetsons (Elroy Jetson, Henry Orbit, W.C. Cogswell, Various Characters) (Hanna-Barbera)
1963	Quick-Draw McGraw (Quick-Draw McGraw, Baba Looey, Snuffles, Snooper, Blabber, Augie Doggie, Various Characters) (Hanna-Barbera)
1964	Mister Magoo (Various Characters) (UPA)
	The Peter Potamus Show (Peter Potamus, Yahooey, Various Characters) (Hanna-Barbera)
1965-1972	Tom and Jerry (Various Characters)
1966	The Space Kidettes (Captain Skyhook, Static, Various Characters) (Hanna-Barbera)
	The Super 6 (Brother Matzoriley #2, Various Characters) (Hanna-Barbera)
1967	George of the Jungle (Various Characters) (Jay Ward)
	Off to See the Wizard (The Scarecrow)
	Super President (Richard Vance)
1968	The Banana Splits Adventure Hour (Bingo, Various Characters) (Hanna-Barbera)
	The Bugs Bunny/Road Runner Hour (Various Characters)
	Wacky Races (Rock Slag, Red Max, Peter Perfect, Rufus Roughcut, St. Blast, Big Gruesome, Various Characters) (Hanna-Barbera)
1969	The Cattanooga Cats (Lambsy Divey, , Various Characters) (Hanna-Barbera)

1970	The Harlem Globetrotters (Various Characters, Various Characters) (Hanna-Barbera)
	Josie and the Pussycats (Various Characters, Various Characters) (Hanna-Barbera)
1971	Funky Phantom (Jonathan "Mudsy" Muddlemore)
	Help! It's the Hair Bear Bunch (Hair Bear, Various Characters) (Hanna-Barbera)
1972	The Houndcats (Studs)
	The New Scooby-Doo Meets the Harlem Globetrotters (Various Characters) (Hanna-Barbera)
	Roman Holidays (Brutus, Various Characters) (Hanna-Barbera)
1973	Bailey's Comets (Dooter Roo)
	Yogi's Gang (Yogi Bear, Quick-Draw McGraw, Huckleberry Hound, Snagglepuss, Augie Dogie, Wally Gator, Peter Potamus, Various Characters) (Hanna-Barbera))
1976	The Scooby-Doo/Dynomutt Hour (Scooby-Dum, Various Characters) (Hanna-Barbera))
	The Sylvester & Tweety Show (Various Characters) (Warner Bros.)
1977	The C.B. Bears (Various Characters) (Hanna-Barbera)
	Fred Flintstone and Friends (Various Characters) (Hanna-Barbera)
	Scooby's All-Star Laff-A-Lympics (Augie Doggie, Dirty Dalton, Dixie, Huckleberry Hound, Mr. Jinks, Quick-Draw McGraw, Scooby-Dum, Snagglepuss, Wally Gator, Yogi Bear, Various Characters) (Hanna-Barbera)
1978	The All-New Popeye Hour (Wimpy) (Hanna-Barbera)
	The Galaxy Goof-Ups (Yogi Bear, Huckleberry Hound, Various Characters) (Hanna-Barbera)
	Yogi's Treasure Hunt (Yogi, Huck, Snagglepuss, Snooper, Blabber, Various Characters) (Hanna-Barbera)
1979	The Pumpkin Who Couldn't Smile (Raggedy Andy) (Chuck Jones)
	Yogi's Space Race (Yogi Bear Various Characters) (Hanna-Barbera)

1982	Woody Woodpecker and His Friends (Various Characters) (Walter Lantz Prods.)
1983	Deck the Halls with Wacky Walls

Other TV Appearances

1948	Treat for St. Nick (Santa Claus) (KFI-TV)
April 10, 1954	The Spike Jones Show (Beany)
1959	The Alphabet Conspiracy (Wolfgang von Kempelen)
1959	Art Linkletter's House Party (Guest)
1959	KNX, Channel 2, Los Angeles (Guest)
1960	About Faces
1960	Truth or Consequences (Guest)
May 26, 1960	You Bet Your Life (Contestant)
1977	The Mike Douglas Show (Mystery Guest)
1979	Kids Are People, Too (Guest)
1980	The John Davidson Show (Guest)
	That's My Line (Guest)

Specials

1966	Alice in Wonderland/What's a Nice Kid Like You Doing in a Place Like This? (King of Hearts, March Hare) (Hanna-Barbera, ABC)
1971	Dr. Seuss' The Cat in the Hat (Karlos K. Krinklebein/the fish) (Hanna-Barbera, CBS)
1972	A Christmas Story (Gumdrop, Second Dog) (Syndicated)
	Robin Hoodnik (Scrounger, Richard the Iron-Hearted) (Hanna-Barbera, ABC)
	Yogi's Ark Lark (Yogi Bear, Baba Looey, Wally Gator, Huckleberry Hound, Lambsy, Quick-Draw McGraw, Snagglepuss, Various Characters) (ABC, Hanna-Barbera)
1973	B.C.: The First Thanksgiving (Clumsy) (NBC)
1978	The Popeye Show (Wimpy) (Hanna-Barbera, CBS)
1979	Casper's First Christmas (Quick-Draw McGraw, Snagglepuss, Augie Doggie, Huckleberry Hound, Yogi Bear, Various Characters) (Hanna-Barbera, NBC)

	The Flintstones Meet Rockula and Frankenstone (Various Characters) (Hanna-Barbera, NBC)
	The Popeye Valentine Special (Wimpy) (Hanna-Barbera, CBS)
	Raggedy Ann and Andy in The Great Santa Claus Caper (Raggedy Andy) (Chuck Jones, CBS)
	Raggedy Ann and Andy in The Pumpkin Who Couldn't Smile (Raggedy Andy) (Chuck Jones, CBS)
1980	Yogi's First Christmas (Yogi Bear, Snagglepuss, Huckleberry Hound, Augie Doggie, Various Characters) (Hanna-Barbera, Syndicated)
1982	Yogi Bear's All-Star Comedy Christmas Caper (Yogi Bear, Quick-Draw McGraw, Huckleberry Hound, Snagglepuss, Hokey Wolf, Super Snooper, Blabber Mouse, Augie Doggie, Mr. Jinks, Dixie, Wally Gator) (Hanna-Barbera, CBS)
1983	Deck the Halls with Wacky Walls (Wacky) (NBC)
1985	The Fantastic World of Hanna-Barbera (Various Characters) (Hanna-Barbera, Syndicated)
	The Jetsons Christmas Carol (Elroy Jetson) (Hanna-Barbera, Syndicated)
	The Flintstones' 25th Anniversary Celebration (Yogi Bear, Huckleberry Hound, Quick-Draw McGraw, Various Characters) (Hanna-Barbera, Syndicated)
1987	The Jetsons Meet the Flintstones (Elroy Jetson, Cogswell, Henry Orbit, Various Characters) (Hanna-Barbera, Syndicated)
	Yogi Bear and the Magical Flight of the Spruce Goose (Yogi Bear, Quick-Draw McGraw, Snagglepuss, Huckleberry Hound, Augie Doggie, Various Characters) (Hanna-Barbera, Syndicated)
	Yogi's Great Escape (Yogi Bear, Various Characters) (Hanna-Barbera, Syndicated)
1988	Animal Follies (Yahooey, Reddy, Augie Doggie, Snagglepuss, Various Characters) (Hanna-Barbera, Syndicated)

	The Good, the Bad, and Huckleberry Hound (Huckleberry Hound, Various Characters) (Hanna-Barbera, Syndicated)
	Rockin' with Judy Jetson (Elroy Jetson, Various Characters) (Hanna-Barbera, Syndicated)
	Yogi and the Invasion of the Space Bears (Yogi Bear, Various Characters) (Hanna-Barbera, Syndicated)
1989	Dink, the Little Dinosaur (Tiny)

Discography

(unknown)	Belda records
(unknown)	Standard Radio Transcriptions
(unknown)	Talking Komics
(unknown)	Tomcat (for the Teletalkie)
(unknown)	Lucky Pin/I'd Rather Be Anything Than You
(unknown)	Woody Woodpecker Meets Davey Crockett
1962	Magoo in Hi-Fi (Victor #LPM-1362) (RCA)
	Huckleberry Hound and the Ghost Ship (Colpix)
	Quick-Draw McGraw and the Treasure of Sarah's Mattress (Colpix)
1966	Augie Doggie/Pinocchio
1966	The New Alice in Wonderland (HLP-2051) (HBR)
1966	Top Cat as Robin Hood
1967	Ruff and Reddy: Gulliver's Travels

Singles

All That Jazz ("Blooper's Soap Is Real Good!")
Hiawatha/Bongo the Bear (Capitol)
Hey There, It's Yogi Bear
Peppy Possom
Rendezvous Rods (Performed by Pastel Six & Daws Butler)
Ringo (Written by Hal Blair and Donald Robertson, performed by Daws Butler, A. Celentano, Lorne Greene)

Commercials

7-Up – hamburger going to his tailor for something light that won't clash
AC Spark Plugs (with Paul Frees)
A.E. Nugent Chevrolet
American Beer
Aunt Jemima Frozen Waffles – Waffle-Whiffer (bird)
Bardahl Oil
Bell Brand Potato Chips
Cap'n Crunch Cereal - Cap'n Crunch
Cheerios (Aesop and Son)
Chevrolet (First & Sales recurring characters)
Cock o' the Walk (vegetables)
Del Monte Catsup
Der Weinerschnitzel
Desoto Cars
Detroit News
Diamond Walnuts
Dodge Power GiantTrucks
Drewry's Beer
Excedrin
General Telephone
Global Van Lines
Hills Brothers Instant Coffee
Hugh's Groceries
Ice Follies
Kellogg's Corn Flakes (Yogi Bear, Hokey Wolf, Huckleberry Hound)
Kellogg's Raisin Bran – Jinx, Pixie & Dixie (early 1960s)
King Vitamin – The Blue Baron
Kissy Sticks
Larry's Jumbo Combo Sandwich
Los Angeles Times
Marlboro Cigarettes – wrote also; cartoon (1950s)
Max Factor
Morris Cars
National Bohemian Beer

Pete Wilkins' Pontiac
Quisp Cereal – Quisp
Rice Krispies Cereal – Snap
Sears Spring Sale
Seiko Watches
Six Flags (as Cap'n Crunch)
Sugar Pops
Taster's Choice Coffee
Toyota

Documentaries

1979	The Hanna-Barbera Hall of Fame: Yabba Dabba Doo II (Himself, Voices)
1987	60 Minutes ("Bill and Joe and Tom and Jerry" - Daws and Don Messick appeared on-camera)
	Daws Butler: Voice Magician (Himself)

Awards

1950, 1953, 1955	Time for Beany (series)
1961	Cleo (for Los Angeles Times animated TV spot)
1961	Cleo (for Kellogg's Snack-Pack 60-second TV spot)
1984	Annie (ASIFA, Lifetime Achievement)

Index

500 Hats of Bartholomew Cubbins, The, *245*

Aesop and Son, *102, 134*

Al Pearce and His Gang, *35*

Alice in Wonderland, *151*

All That Jazz, *81-82, 171*

Alphabet Conspiracy, The, *134*

Annie Award, 154, 243-245

Armed Forces Radio, 39, 149

Auer, Miles, 35, 49, 118, 129-130, 143, 209, 243, 248, 254

"*Augie Doggie,*" *102, 110, 116-118, 121, 125, 132, 142, 145, 216, 225, 248, 253*

Avery, Tex, 29, 37-41, 47, 98, 106

"*Babba Looey,*" *102, 114-115, 117, 121, 125, 132, 176, 248, 252-253*

Bellem, Robert Leslie, 42-43

Benny, Jack, 20, 34, 42-43, 50, 62, 71, 85-86, 92, 210

Bergen, Bob, 2, 211-212

Bergen, Edgar, 26, 78, 89

Bevilacqua, Joe, 2, 49, 95, 99, 113, 115, 118, 123, 144, 169, 171, 175-176, 179-180, 186, 203-204, 215, 227-228

Blanc, Mel, 1, 36, 41, 50, 73-74, 114, 118, 138, 151, 154, 169, 201, 210-211, 223, 227

Bliss, Lucille, 2, 166, 207, 219, 242

Bullwinkle Show, The, *54, 63, 86, 130, 134, 144, 166, 209, 224, 254*

Burson, Greg, 2, 203, 256

Burton, Corey, 2, 169, 175-177, 183, 189, 206-210

Burton, Johnny, 36-37

Butler, Chas, i, 65-66, 94, 130, 146, 164, 166, 245

Butler, David, i, 31, 147, 178, 257

Butler, Don, i, 12, 64-66, 111, 147-148, 165

Butler, Myrtis, i, 2, 29-32, 48, 64-67, 105, 129, 131, 168-169, 178, 195, 217, 221, 223, 226, 238, 240-241, 245, 247-252, 254, 256

Butler, Paul, i, 65-66, 149

"Cap'n Crunch," 79-80, 91, 102, 124, 144-145, 167, 170, 176, 219, 221, 250-251, 253

Carney, Art, 74, 110-111, 132-133, 139, 211, 222

Cartwright, Nancy, i, 2, 170-171, 197, 201-202, 224, 236, 251

Casper's First Christmas, *199*

CBS Radio Workshop, *83*

"*Chilly Willy,*" 80, 82

"*Christmas Dragnet (Yulenet),*" 71

Christmas That Almost Never Was, The, *133-134*

Clampett, Bob, 2, 47-74, 106, 253

Commercial Actor, The, *183-186*

Conried, Hans, 71, 86, 89, 134, 151, 166, 208

Cummings, Brian, 153-154, 209

Daws Butler: Voice Magician, *254*

Deck the Halls with Wacky Walls, *237*

Dr. Christian, 34-35

Dr. Demento, 2, 132, 207, 216, 248-250, 253

Dr. Seuss' The Cat in the Hat, *151*

Dragnet, *35, 68-71*

"*Droopy,*" 29, 38, 41, 103, 120

Edmiston, Walker, 2, 54, 58, 63, 256

Einstein, Albert, 55-56

"Elroy Jetson," *i, 42, 89, 102, 110, 132, 141, 145, 169, 171, 207, 240, 242, 244, 246, 248, 253*

Evanier, Mark, 2, 113, 152, 222, 227, 246

Flintstones (Flagstones), The, *119, 137-139, 141, 151, 222, 251*

Flintstones' 25th Anniversary Celebration, The, *251*

Foray, June, 2, 41, 69-70, 74, 81, 83, 86, 88-92, 94, 115, 134, 138, 151, 167, 170, 199, 208, 213, 219, 254, 257

Fractured Fairy Tales, *102, 134-135, 209*

Freberg, Stan, 2, 41, 49-54, 56, 60, 63, 68-71, 73-74, 78, 81, 85-95, 106, 108, 183, 207, 209, 212-213, 215-216, 240, 253-254

Frees, Paul, 1, 32, 73, 79, 115, 134, 155, 170, 210, 223

Freleng, Friz, 50, 74, 134

George of the Jungle, *135*

Halperin, Marty, 39, 194, 256

Hanna-Barbera, 2, 37-38, 41-42, 64, 88, 91, 94, 97-135, 137-153, 160-161, 169, 173-174, 187, 196, 198-199, 203, 209, 216, 219, 221, 224, 227, 235, 248-251, 253-257

Hawthorne Thing, The, *43-44*

Here's Morgan, *193*

Hey There, It's Yogi Bear, *146*

"Hokey Wolfe," *111, 123-125, 141, 143, 182, 225, 253*

Honeymousers, The, *74, 90, 138, 211, 239*

"Huckleberry Hound," *i, 29, 38, 73, 80, 102-112, 114-115, 120-121, 123, 129-130, 132-133, 139, 141, 143, 146, 150, 152-153, 172, 174, 176, 191, 193, 202, 209, 212, 216, 227, 247, 251, 253-254*

Huckleberry Hound and the Ghost Ship, *123-125*

Huckleberry Hound—Kellogg's Great TV Show, *120-121*

Jetsons, The, *89, 141-143, 153, 169, 171, 206, 240-244, 246-249*

Jones, Chuck, 50, 151, 198-199

Kress, Earl, 2, 244-247, 250

Lahr, Bert, 112-114

Lantz, Walter, 80, 167, 254

Leeds, Peter, 86, 89-91, 94, 115, 240

Let's Pretend, *39*

"Lippy the Lion," *102, 140-141*

"Little Blue Riding Hood," *69-70, 250*

Marx, Groucho, 56, 107

Marx, Harpo, 56

Mary Poppins, *146*

Messick, Don, 2, 38-40, 72, 76-78, 83, 101-103, 106, 108-112, 115, 119-120, 123-125, 127, 129-130, 133, 141, 145, 169-170, 173, 189, 208, 223, 227, 253-254

Misadventures of Sherlock Holmes, The, *180-186, 227*

Moose That Roared, The, *166*

Morris, Howard, 139, 169

"Mr. Jinks," *102, 104, 108-110, 121-125, 133, 149, 165, 210, 250, 253*

Mr. Jinks "Lend-Lease Meece," *122-123*
Parris, Pat, 169, 176, 180, 183, 189, 196
Peanuts, *131-132*
"Peter Potamus," 102, *141-142*, 144
Phantom Tollbooth, The, *151*
"Pixie and Dixie," *104, 108, 122-123*
"Point of Order," *71*
Pope, Tony, 2, 169, 206-207, 209
"Popeye," 66, 153, 190-191, 196, 221
Pyl, Jean Vander, 115, 121, 138, 141
"Quick Draw McGraw," i, 102, *113-115*, 117-119, 121, 125, 129, 139, 153
Quick-Draw McGraw *(album), 121-122*
"Quisp," 79, 142, 145, 167
"Raggedy Ann and Andy," *198-199*
Reed, Alan, 71, 81, 138, 222
Roman Holidays, *151-152*
Ruff and Reddy, 29, 38, 100-103, 106, 119-120, 127-128
Ruff and Reddy's Adventure in Space, *119-120*
Ruff 'n' Reddy in Gulliver's Travels, *127-128*
Scenes for Actors and Voices, *158-159*, 161
Scott, Bill, 54, 134, 166, 208-209, 219, 249-250
Scott, Keith, 2, 15-16, 165-166, 173-175, 177, 180, 209-211, 250
Sears Radio Theatre, 188, 192-194, 196, 208, 228
Shows, Charlie, 48, 61, 73, 106, 120
Silveri, Toni, 2, 204-205
Smith, Hal, 74, 115, 138, 143, 208
"Snagglepuss," 102, 111-114, 125-127, 139, 143, 151-153, 174, 216, 222, 247, 253
Snagglepuss narrates The Wizard of Oz, *127*
Speaking of Animals, *41*
"St. George and the Dragonet," *68-71*, 89, 154
Stan Freberg Show, The, *85-95*
Super Chicken, *135*
"Super Snooper," 102, 112, 115-117, 121, 123, 125-127, 225
Suspense, *83-85*, 196
That's Rich, *71-73*

Three Short Waves, 16-29

Thompson, Bill, 38, 81, 120, 138

Time for Beany, 42, 45, 47-75, 80, 86, 94, 106-107, 110, 132, 141, 176, 213

"Tom and Jerry," 41, 98-101, 104, 106

Top Cat, *142-143*

Treasure of Sarah's Mattress, The, *125-127*

"Uncle Dunkle," 42, 169-170, 194, 228-234, 236, 238, 246, 251

"Undercover Elephant," 152, 187

Vic and Sade, *33, 50, 145, 194*

"Wally Gator," 102, 140, 253

Warner Bros., 2, 36-37, 41, 47, 49-50, 52, 54, 74, 90, 97, 106, 114, 142, 201, 209, 211, 239

Webb, Jack, 68-70

Welker, Frank, 169, 196, 198, 222

Will, Whimsical, 2, 168, 180, 207, 216

"Wimpy," 153, 189-191, 196, 216

"Winnie the Pooh," 168, 207

Wright, Ben, 166, 181-183, 207, 213

Wright, Sean, 2, 181-182, 212-213

"Yogi Bear," i, 80, 90, 97, 102, 104, 108, 110-115, 120, 123, 130, 132-133, 139-140, 143, 146, 150, 152-153, 172-174, 176, 191, 193, 202-203, 209, 216, 221-223, 225, 227, 235, 246-247, 249-251, 253-254, 256

Yogi Bear's All-Star Comedy Christmas Caper, *227*

Yogi's First Christmas, *216-217*

Yogi's Gang, *153*

Yogi's Space Race, *153, 221*

Yogi's Treasure Hunt, *152, 249-250*

You Bet Your Life, *107*

Young, Doug, 2, 35-36, 102, 111, 115, 117, 122-123, 125, 139, 257

Yours Truly, Johnny Dollar, *44-45*

Zappa, Frank, 56

BearManorMedia

P O Box 750 * Boalsburg, PA 16827

Welcome, Foolish Mortals...
THE LIFE AND VOICES OF PAUL FREES By Ben Ohmart

The official, heavily illustrated biography of the Master of Voice. Read all about the man behind the voices of Disneyland's *Haunted Mansion*, the pirates in the *Pirates of the Caribbean* ride, Boris Badenov from *Rocky & Bullwinkle*, The Pillsbury Doughboy and thousands of radio shows including *Suspense, Escape, The Whistler* and more.

ISBN: 1-59393-0046 $29.95

Every old-time radio and cartoon fan in the world will want this book.

Foreword by June Foray. Afterword by Jay Ward biographer, Keith Scott.

"For the first time in print, the real Paul Frees is revealed. Author Ben Ohmart looks beyond the voices to uncover the man within, coming up with an evenhanded, but honest portrait of a very complicated individual. This is the definitive biography of an amazing artist."
— Laura Wagner, *Classic Images*

PERVERSE, ADVERSE AND ROTTENVERSE
By June Foray

ISBN 1-59393-020-8 $14.95

"I am resolutely determined to explode all the obsolete shibboleths that our parents drove into our adolescent, little minds, and I'm brazen enough to offer my, perhaps outrageous, judgment of the morals and mores of the establishment. It is my critique on society as it stumbled into the last quarter of the 20th Century and the first of our 21st, having lived by the myths given to us in centuries long gone."

— June Foray, from her Foreword

You know the voice actress, now know the essayist!

visit www.bearmanormedia.com or write info@ritzbros.com
Visa & Mastercard accepted. Add $2 postage per book.

BearManorMedia
P O Box 750 * Boalsburg, PA 16827

Walter Tetley: For Corn's Sake
by Ben Ohmart and Charles Stumpf

ISBN: 1-59393-000-3 $24.95

WALTER TETLEY (1915-1975) was the quintessential kid voice of radio. His distinguished voice career began in the early 1930s and lasted until radio's final years in the 1950s. He was also a very private person who never gave interviews, instead choosing to immerse himself in charity and voice work throughout most of his life.

For the FIRST time in print—finally a complete biography on one of radio's most beloved character actors. Including many **RARE PHOTOS** and **THOUSANDS OF CREDITS**, most of which have never been seen or discussed in any article or book. That is because **this biography has been written with the aid of Walter's personal scrapbooks!**

From The Great Gildersleeve to Peabody and Sherman—and beyond. Including a detailed account of Walter's 1930s public appearances.
For fans of old time radio—this is the book to savor!

How Underdog Was Born
by Buck Biggers & Chet Stover
ISBN—0-59595-025-9
$19.95

visit www.bearmanormedia.com or write info@ritzbros.com
Visa & Mastercard accepted. Add $2 postage per book.

What is the **Comedy-O-Rama Hour**?

it's... **CAMP WATERLOGG**

it's... **The MIS-ADVENTURES of Sherlock Holmes**

it's... **The Whithering of Willoughby & the Professor**

it's... **WHAT THE BUTLER WROTE — SCENES FROM THE DAWS BUTLER WORKSHOP**

and so much more!

Tune in on Channel 163  XM Satellite Radio — or check your local NPR station

www.comedyorama.com

BearManor Media

OLD RADIO. OLD MOVIES. NEW BOOKS.

BearManor Media is a small press publishing Big books. Biographies, script collections, you name it. We love old time radio, voice actors and old films.

Current and upcoming projects include:

The Great Gildersleeve *Walter Tetley*
Edgar Kennedy *Don Ameche*
Agnes Moorehead *Guy Williams*
Information Please *Jane Kean*
The Life of Riley *Dolores Fuller*
The Bickersons *Albert Salmi*
The Ritz Brothers *Peggy Ann Garner*
Paul Frees and many more!
Daws Butler

Write for a free catalog, or visit http://bearmanormedia.com today.

BearManor Media
P O Box 750
Boalsburg, PA 16827
814-466-7555
info@ritzbros.com